T0148473

Hope for Alcoholics, Addicts, Inmates (and Those Who Love Them)

Gary L.

Inspiring Voices®
A Service of Guideposts

Inspiring Voices books may be ordered through booksellers or by contacting:

Inspiring Voices
1663 Liberty Drive
Bloomington, IN 47403
www.inspiringvoices.com
1-(866) 697-5313

ISBN: 978-1-4624-0458-2 (e)
ISBN: 978-1-4624-0457-5 (sc)

Library of Congress Control Number: 2012922830

Printed in the United States of America

Inspiring Voices rev. date: 12/05/2012

"Writing to an inmate friend, Gary candidly details his own 'life story,' sharing the spiritual insight gained through surrender and personal responsibility. As you join Gary in this mentoring read, you will better understand your own story. You will see firsthand what a gracious and forgiving God can do when we choose to be real with ourselves and honest with others. This book will come alongside and life you up."

—*Dean Howell*
RETIRED MINISTER/YOUTHCORRECTIONS WORKER

"*Hope for Alcoholics, Addicts, and Inmates* is a wonderful testament to the way God can free anyone from addiction. The book is Gary L.'s story of overcoming his alcohol addiction told through a series of letters to Matt, an inmate in the Oregon Corrections System. Gary shares his own life experiences and uses them to give practical advice to his pen pal using references from Alcoholics Anonymous publications, Scripture, and other writings.

Hope for Alcoholics, Addicts, Inmates is a wonderful read, and I highly recommend it to anyone struggling to overcome drug or alcohol addiction!"

—Mark Hubbell
NORTHWEST EXECUTIVE DIRECTOR, PRISON FELLOWSHIP

"My 'little brother' Gary L. amazes me with the talent he has for helping and inspiring others. When I think of him, I think of adjectives like smart, kind, helpful, courageous, tolerant, grateful, dedicated, and wise. He's a loving brother, husband, father, and grandfather. And one of the best storytellers I know. I am so proud of him and everything he has accomplished in his life and I know he will continue to help and inspire those around him. I am extremely grateful for his recovery."

—*"big sister" Shirley L.*

About the cover: Recovery from alcoholism/addiction is like journeying through a complicated maze. But it's also similar to the process of metamorphosis (change by supernatural means, according to *Webster*). A caterpillar eventually emerges from the darkness of a cocoon into light and freedom, just as alcoholics/addicts move from desolation and darkness to faith, hope, and freedom.

Cover design by Nectar Graphics
www.nectargraphics.com

Inspiring Voices Publishing
Bloomington, IN

Dedication

To my wife, Patsy, who continued to love me through some very difficult years of active alcoholism. I often wondered through those years why she stood by my side when many would have fled. I hated myself at the time, and she refused to. She truly is my angel. Today, because of what God has done in my life, I can return that love.

Foreword

I have known Gary L. for a number of years now. During this time I have grown to respect him both personally and professionally. In his book, *Hope for Alcoholics, Addicts, Inmates*, he has done a masterful job of sharing his story of recovery from alcoholism with Matt. In the sharing of his story, Gary exemplifies some of the core wisdom of Alcoholics Anonymous, which is based on sharing one's experience, strength, and hope with another alcoholic. Gary, like Alcoholics Anonymous, thereby avoids the pitfall of attempting to give advice to another alcoholic, which would simply serve to make them resist recovery.

Another core wisdom of Alcoholics Anonymous, which Gary demonstrates in his book, is that recovery is based on action, not analysis. He ably describes the steps he has taken to put the program of Alcoholics Anonymous into action in his life. The effectiveness of this wisdom in his life is evidenced by his ongoing sobriety.

In addition, Gary shares the scriptures on which his recovery, as well as his Christian life, is based. He thereby helps anyone who reads this book to integrate his Christian faith with the recovery process. They are inextricably intertwined in the origins of Alcoholics Anonymous.

Hope for Alcoholics, Addicts, Inmates, also reflects Gary's considerable professional experience as a Christian minister and spiritual counselor. He has served for years as a spiritual counselor in a number of treatment programs as well as an associate pastor in a church. The breadth of Gary's experience will attract people to this book.

I share these observations with you as a retired professional, who has worked in the fields of spiritual ministry, counseling, and education. My background includes an extensive grounding in ministry and spirituality (the equivalent of a doctorate), a doctorate in counseling and education, and many years of working in these fields. I thoroughly enjoyed reading *Hope for Alcoholics, Addicts, Inmates.*

Gary L. Bowling, PhD

In *Hope for Alcoholics, Addicts, Inmates,* writer Gary L. documents a single personal encounter not unlike hundreds of others he has engaged in the over thirty years I have been privileged to observe his life and ministry.

Gary's unique ability to interpret, translate, and synthesize the pain, disillusion, anger, and rebellion of his own early life into a present-tense testimony of praise and glory to his Lord and Savior Jesus Christ makes *Hope For Alcoholics, Addicts, Inmates,* an inspirational and lovingly confrontational read for anyone serious about practical intimacy with the living Christ.

Carrying the "spiritual awakening message" to others, as stated in Step Twelve, requires the practice of humility through the confession of faults and "sins." One to another. Gary is an example for anyone determined to unashamedly seek the Lord with all his/her heart, soul, mind, and strength.

Hope for Alcoholics, Addicts, Inmates does not chronicle a gospel of personal power and entitlement, nor does it endorse a "form of godliness while denying the Power thereof." It exposes, for its readers, those principles of powerless surrender underlying a genuine confession of unmanageability and lack of control over one's life. It shines light on the path leading toward genuine freedom and victory over every destructive vice known to mankind.

As you read, you will observe the Twelve "Principle" Steps of AA taking on flesh, as Gary candidly becomes a "Living Epistle," known and read by his readers. In becoming an epistle, Gary exposes the substance of his life, the very flesh and bones of his journey, so that his readers may know The Way to an ongoing victory over self.

You will be inspired, encouraged, and exhorted in your reading of *Hope for Alcoholics, Addicts, Inmates.* I challenge you to read with an ear toward the Twelve Steps, but also an ear toward the One who stands ready to pardon and set at liberty those, who, like Gary, have reached the end of themselves and are finally ready to admit it.

Dean Howell, retired minister/ youth corrections worker/ certified alcohol/drug counselor.

Preface

The original title for this work was *Letters to an Inmate*, because that's how it began. But as I continued writing to Matt, I thought that my story might help anyone struggling with substance abuse.

A friend of mine, during a time of alcohol/drug relapse, robbed a bank and subsequently was sentenced to prison. I began writing to him in an attempt to encourage him. In one of his letters to me he mentioned a young fellow inmate who wanted to change his life. He was in prison related to drug offenses. My friend asked if I would write to him and share my experience, strength, and hope. I've been a sober member of Alcoholics Anonymous since March 2, 1971. I responded that I would be happy to write his new friend. While I pondered this new relationship a thought came into my mind, "Write to him every day until you've told him your life story. After writing to Matt every day for over three months, I'd shared with him my entire life. In his letters back to me, he wrote about the changes he was experiencing and how my letters were helping.

Much of my journey has been about a renewed relationship with the God that my grandma introduced me to when I was five. I slammed the door on God when I was ten. My grandma had a stroke, was in a coma for three weeks and died. I heard things in the church like, "God took her to heaven." I needed her with me and became very angry at God for taking her and stayed angry for many years. Instilled in my belief system at that time was an image of a God who took important people from me.

When I entered the rooms of Alcoholics Anonymous at age thirty-one, I was emotionally, mentally, and spiritually bankrupt. I had thought a lot about suicide for a year or so. My best efforts to make life work ended in complete failure. I was so tired of the fight and became convinced that life was never going to work for me. At the time I was married to Patsy, who I now call my angel, and we had two daughters. I had everything to live for but was unable to see it. Sometimes the darkness was overwhelming. Three and a half weeks after my first AA meeting life became darker because I drank again.

The letters to Matt describe the journey out of the darkness into a life I never thought possible. The journey has not been a straight path. It's been more like a journey through a maze. The journey will not be completed until I'm with my creator. In my letters I write about the times when I've missed turns in the maze and traveled down dead-end paths. There have been times of doubt, fear, discouragement, depression, and loss. The constant in the journey has been how God has always been faithful to bring me back to the main path. I am so grateful for that, plus the fact that Patsy has journeyed with me the entire way. Grateful, grateful, grateful, is the word that comes to mind as I write this.

9-15-08

Dear Matt,

I prayed for you this morning.

There is a preamble read at Alcoholics Anonymous (AA) meetings that states in part, "Alcoholics Anonymous is a fellowship of men and women who share their experience, strength, and hope with each other that they may solve their common problem and help others to recover from alcoholism."

In the letters that follow this one, I will attempt to do that. You mentioned in your letter that your dad had abandoned you. I need to let you know that I know what it feels like to be abandoned by a biological father. I was four years old when my parents divorced. My daddy, my hero, decided after a short while that he didn't want to have anything to do with my older sister and me. As a child, I wondered what was so awful about me that my daddy didn't want me around. I know what it's like to feel like a misfit, always on the outside looking in. I know what it's like to rage and destroy things without any fear of consequences. I know what it's like to be locked up at age twenty. I was in a lockdown psychiatric unit at a hospital for three months because of self-mutilation—cutting myself and burning myself with cigarettes. I know what it's like to feel deep shame and guilt. I also know what it's like to wonder, "If there really is a loving God, why is my life such a mess?" I know what it's like to live with a big ball of fear on the inside and then act out in aggressive ways so no one will know I'm afraid. I know what it's like to wonder, "Is life ever going to work for me?" Perhaps you can identify with some of those things.

As I share my experience, strength, and hope with you, I will take you through my experience with the Twelve Steps and how they have influenced my life. I will also share with you discoveries I've made along the way about myself, God, and life. I will quote meditations from various sources, scripture that has been meaningful to me and to the freedom I live in today. I will share with you a Spiritual Journal I wrote when I was a chaplain at an alcohol/drug treatment center in the '80s. Whether you use it or not is up to you.

Here is some personal information. I was born November 8, 1939, have been married since February 9, 1963, and have two married daughters and four grandchildren. My sobriety date is March 2, 1971. I don't mention that in order to say, "Look at me," but in order for you to see what a loving God can do in a person's life in our recovery/spiritual journey. My story is what got me into the rooms of AA. Since then it's been His story. I am just one of many, many stories of lives that God has changed through the recovery journey.

Some years ago, my wife Patsy and I went on an extended road trip. We left Oregon and went through California, Nevada, New Mexico, Texas, Arkansas, Tennessee, Missouri, Iowa, Nebraska, South Dakota, Wyoming, Montana, Idaho, and back to Oregon.

On our journey, we traveled on many different kinds of highways: freeways, country roads, straight roads, curvy roads, bumpy roads, and roads under construction where there would be delays. Sometimes we took a wrong turn and had to backtrack to get back on the right road. Sometimes we got lost and had to ask for directions. There were also dead-end roads. On our journey, we encountered all kinds of weather ranging from hail and freezing rain to temperatures of 110 degrees. We experienced beautiful blue skies and then lightning storms. We also experienced all kinds of terrain: level, uphill, downhill, green meadows, valleys, mountain ranges, and long stretches of desert that seemed to never end.

I say all of that because that is similar to the recovery or life journey. Some want only the nice straight roads without bumps and to be always on the mountaintop. That is not close to reality.

I've learned that I cannot make the journey without a map. Imagine what it would be like to drive from Oregon to New York without a road map or any road signs. I wonder how many dead-end roads we'd take. That tells me I need to be with people who have made the journey. I need to read and follow road signs, the Twelve Steps, Serenity Prayer, and wise counsel. I need to learn from the experiences of others. I need to grow in my understanding and relationship with God, myself, others, and life. Just as our extended road trip was quite a journey, the recovery journey, which I'm still on, has also been exciting. I hope your trip will be as exciting for you as mine has been for me. Remember, recovery is a journey, not a destination.

One of the books I will quote from occasionally is *As Bill Sees It*, written by Bill W., the cofounder of AA.

> At the beginning we sacrificed alcohol. We had to, or it would have killed us. But we couldn't get rid of alcohol unless we made other sacrifices. We had to toss self-justification, self-pity, and anger right out the window. We had to quit the crazy contest for personal prestige and big bank balances. We had to take personal responsibility for our sorry state and quit blaming others for it.

Were these sacrifices? Yes, they were. To gain enough humility and self-respect to stay alive at all, we had to give up what had really been our dearest possessions—our ambition and our illegitimate pride. [1]

Matt, I hope my experience, strength, and hope will be helpful to you!

Blessings to you,
Gary L.

9-16-08

Dear Matt,

I prayed for you this morning.

I need to start at the beginning. I was born November 8, 1939, in Marshfield, Oregon. Some years later, the people voted to change the name to Coos Bay. I had a sister who was nineteen months older. I have several memories from early childhood as if they had happened yesterday.

The first was when I was three. On Sunday mornings Mommy and Daddy, as we called them then, would lie in bed and read the newspaper. My sister Shirley and I would join them when we awoke. We would frolic with them while bouncing on the bed. I still remember the glee and joy I felt. I didn't have a care in the world. I felt loved and was one happy child. After our fun, we would have breakfast that included hot chocolate with marshmallows on top.

I still remember the beautiful home we lived in. It had an elevator that went to the basement, which was used to bring up firewood for the fireplace. It was a real treat to ride the elevator. Another vivid memory is of me standing near our driveway eagerly anticipating Daddy's arrival from work. We had a ritual that was the highlight of my day. After he would pull into the driveway and get out of the car, I would run and jump into his arms, and we would hug. What a great feeling it was as he held me.

I have strong memories of the first day he didn't come home from work. I felt great disappointment that day and the days that followed. Mommy would not tell us why he wouldn't come home. I believe that was the first time I felt real fear. One day Mom came with some boxes and began to pack our belongings. I was terrified. Where was Daddy? Why wouldn't he come home? After packing was completed, we moved from our beautiful home into a one-bedroom cottage. Shirley and I clung to each other during that time as we wondered what was happening.

This was during World War II. Mom had met a US Navy sailor that she fell in love with and divorced Daddy. A new man was in our lives. My daddy had visitation rights, but more often than not when he was supposed to pick us up, he would call and cancel. We would be devastated. I have vivid memories of pacing the floor in my grandma's kitchen waiting for him one day. He never arrived nor did he call. I went to bed that night and cried myself to sleep. Why didn't he come or call? Shirley and I took matters into our own hands several days later.

On a Sunday afternoon, we slipped away from Grandma's and took a city bus from North Bend to Coos Bay. The distance was about three miles, and we had ridden the bus many times. We walked to Daddy's bowling alley from the bus station. I was so excited as I fantasized running and jumping into his arms. He saw us when we entered the bowling alley and a scowl appeared on his face. He immediately went to a phone and called Grandma's home. She and Mom were frantic with worry. A short while later, we were picked up and taken to Grandma's. I believe something was broken on the inside of me that day. I never saw or heard from him again until I found him when I was seventeen and a member of the US Navy. I often wondered as a child, "What is so awful about me that my daddy doesn't want anything to do with me?"

Following is part of a meditation from *Rooted in God's Love*, a series of meditations by Dale and Juanita Ryan.

> If one or both of our parents were some way absent from our lives during our formative years, it will be easy for us to imagine that God will leave us as well. We may experience silence and distance. And we may find ourselves longing for God.
>
> Just as it is good for a child to protest the absence of a parent, it is good for us to protest when we subjectively experience God's absence. It is good to give voice to our longing for God. It is good to write or pray or talk about our deep need for God's presence and love. We can call out to God. We can protest God's absence.
>
> Prayer: O God, do not be silent. Do not be distant. I miss you when you seem so far away. I long for you to be close. I long to know that you care about me. I long for you, God. Nothing can replace you. No one can be God but you. Do not be silent. Do not be distant. Come. Speak. I need you. Amen. [2]

For years, I looked for people to fill a role in my life that only God could fill.

God's blessings to you,
Gary L.

9-17-08

Dear Matt,

I prayed for you this morning.

Here's an afterthought from my previous letter. Although we may experience rejection or abandonment from people we love, there is One who will never reject us.

Not long after the incident at the bowling alley with my dad, Mom and my stepdad left my sister Shirley and me at my grandma's while they went to Washington State to look for a place to live. The Navy had transferred my stepdad to a naval facility there. After a short while Mom came back to pick us up, and we moved. I did not want to leave Grandma's. We moved into a one-room cabin without a bathroom. There was running water to the kitchen sink, but we had to use an outhouse. The stench was horrible. If I needed to go to the bathroom at night, I'd use a bucket, and in the morning Mom would take it outside and dump it. The cabin had a woodstove that was used for heating and cooking. I still remember Mom heating water on the stove for our weekly bath. One week I bathed first, and then Shirley would follow me into the same water. The following week she got to bathe first. She hated being second, but it never bothered me.

While at our new "home," I experienced my first episode of rage. Mom had sent me to a store close by to get some eggs. On the way home I stopped by an old barn, and, in a fit of rage, threw the eggs at the wall of the barn. When I arrived home without the eggs or the money, Mom knew something was wrong. Of course, my responses to her questions were lies. After much prodding, I confessed. Mom had a way with words that could make me feel that I was the worst person on the face of the earth. After the screaming lecture, I was spanked. Looking back I realize that I was not sorry for what I had done, just sorry that I didn't get away with it. We stayed in Washington for several more months until my stepdad received orders to go to the South Pacific. After he left, Mom, Shirley, and I moved back to North Bend and Grandma's house.

Part of a meditation I read this morning from *Rooted in God's Love* says:

> There are days when we feel God's presence. We sense God's love. We see God's power. But we do not always feel or sense or see. There are times of silence, distance and uncertainty. There are the difficult times of waiting for God to appear. [3]

That meditation makes me think of Mount Hood. There are times when the mountain is obscured by clouds; but does that mean the mountain is gone? Of course not. When I don't feel God's presence, does that mean He doesn't exist? No, it just means that something is obscuring my view. That's when I need to exercise faith.

I'm enclosing Day 1 of a thirty-day spiritual journal. Use it if you like.

Yours sincerely,
Gary L

Gary L.

Day 1 date ____________________

Today I will try to remain calm inside. I will try to keep my mind open and not be afraid.

Have you ever put a picture puzzle together without knowing what the completed picture looks like? Sometimes when a person is first in recovery, his/her life seems like that. When all the pieces of a puzzle are poured out on a table, it is impossible to see the completed picture, but we can be assured that every single piece is important to the puzzle. Sometimes, as we pick up certain pieces we will be sure that they must belong in another puzzle, only to learn later that they really do belong in the one that we're working on. Is it possible for God to take all the pieces of our life, even the ones that don't seem to fit, and the ugly ones that we'd like to throw away, and make them all fit into a beautiful picture?

Question for today: Am I willing to believe that all the pieces of my life are necessary to complete the picture?

Write about the most significant thing you experienced or learned yesterday.

Prayer for today

I pray that I may have the courage to begin putting the puzzle of my life together and that I will begin to see the importance of all the pieces.

9-18-08

Dear Matt,

I prayed for you this morning.

After we moved back to my grandma's I started the first grade. I was five years old. I felt like a misfit right from the beginning. I was the smallest kid in class, and that included the girls. As a result, there was a lot of teasing. One day at school, I acted out and was brought to the front of the class and spanked by the teacher. In those days, spanking was an acceptable punishment. I still remember the other students laughing at me and the embarrassment I felt.

A short distance from Grandma's, my teacher was having a new home built. After the workers left that day, I entered the house with revenge in my heart. I was full of rage and had no fear of consequences. A mason had been working on the fireplace that day, and there were courses of bricks that the mortar was not set. I tore down every brick I could. I then found a short piece of rope, put it through a hole in a brick, tied a knot, and, fueled by my rage, I went through the house swinging the brick. I broke all the windows and damaged the plastered walls. I finally exhausted myself and went home. I still remember when a police officer appeared at Grandma's. I knew I was in big trouble but didn't care. An awareness that came to me after I'd been sober awhile is that every time in my life that I got even with someone, it harmed me more than it harmed him or her.

Grace for the Moment, by Max Lucado:

> Anger. It's easy to define: the noise of the soul. Anger. The unseen irritant of the heart. Anger. The relentless invader of silence….
>
> The louder it gets the more desperate we become….
>
> Some of you are thinking … you don't have any idea how hard my life has been. And you're right, I don't. But I have a very clear idea how miserable your future will be unless you deal with your anger.
>
> X-ray the world of the vengeful and behold the tumor of bitterness: black, menacing, malignant carcinoma of the spirit. Its fatal fibers creep around the edge of the heart and ravage it. Yesterday you can't alter, but your reaction to yesterday you can. [4]

Gary L.

Psalm 37:8 Stop your anger! Turn from your rage! Do not envy others—it only leads to harm.

Addiction/alcoholism wants us to live in anger because we're then vulnerable to drink or use. I learned at some point in recovery that the person I was most angry at was myself. Because of that, I not only needed God's forgiveness, but I also needed to forgive myself.

A large part of the recovery journey is allowing God to untangle the snarls in our life.

Matt: Stay open and keep searching.

Gary L.

Day 2 date ____________________

Today I will be diligent in searching for answers for my life. I will leave no stone unturned.

One of the first things that a person does while putting a jigsaw puzzle together is to sort out all the border pieces. But even after the border is put together that in itself does not show what the picture will be. The rest of the pieces are then sorted by color. After all the sorting is completed, a person will begin working on small sections of the puzzle. Eventually, piece by piece, section by section, a picture begins to emerge. That will also happen in recovery. Sometimes when all the pieces of a puzzle are poured out on a table, the task of putting them together looks overwhelming, but one piece at a time the puzzle can be completed.

Question for today: Am I willing to live my life "One day at a time," while it's being put together?

Write about the most significant thing you experienced or learned yesterday.

Prayer for today

I pray that I will not be overwhelmed by all the scattered pieces of my life.

9-19-08

Dear Matt,

I prayed for you this morning.

Romans 12:2: "And do not be conformed to this world, but be transformed by the renewing of your mind, that you may prove what the will of God is, that which is good and acceptable and perfect" (NASB).

The above scripture was written in the Greek language. The word conform gives the idea of something being squeezed or molded. After plastic goes through an extruder, a product comes out. The truth is we are being conformed to this world the moment we are born. All of the influences in our lives begin shaping our belief systems and how we view life. We live according to the beliefs that we have. For example, the abandonment by my dad created the belief in me that I was no good and unworthy of love. That was a false belief, but as long as it was part of my belief system, I lived accordingly. After damaging the home of the teacher that spanked me, another false belief was established, "It's not my fault," and it was because of how Mom responded to what I did. First of all, she was angry at me, but most of her anger was focused towards the teacher. If the teacher hadn't spanked me, I wouldn't have vandalized her home. It was her fault. Mom's response planted the seed in me that if I do something wrong that is a response to something done to me; I'm not responsible. It's their fault. That belief did not serve me well as I tried to navigate through life. That false belief stopped me from taking responsibility for the wrongs I committed.

The word transform comes from the Greek word where we get metamorphosis. As you know, the process that a caterpillar goes through to become a butterfly. So God would say to us, "You have been conformed to this world and because of false beliefs that developed you became someone who I never intended you to be. Now I want to transform you by changing the way you think." To me, that is what real recovery is. Not drinking or using opens the door to what God wants to do in our lives. Think of the perspective that a butterfly has compared to a caterpillar. Webster's dictionary states that metamorphosis is "change by supernatural means." So much of my recovery journey has been about discovering the false beliefs that I lived by, and God giving me new beliefs to replace them. That process will never be over. The book *Alcoholics Anonymous* states on page 58: "Some of us have tried to hold on to our old ideas and the result was nil until we let go absolutely." [5]

I don't know who authored the following poem, but it is so right.

If I continue to think like I've always thought,
I'll continue to do what I've always done.
If I continue to do what I've always done,
I'll continue to get what I've always got.

If my belief systems don't change, the way I live life won't change, and then the results won't change either.

Prayer: God, help me to see the false beliefs that drive me. Replace those beliefs with ones that work.

Blessings
Gary L.

Day 3 date ___________________

Today I will try to keep my mind open. I will not be rigid in my thinking today.

One time a man planted an oak tree in the center of his yard. At the same time, he planted a palm tree in a corner of his yard. As years went by the oak tree grew into a majestic tree. As people walked by, they would comment on how beautiful it was. Meanwhile the lowly palm grew slowly in its obscurity in the corner. One day a tremendous storm hit the town where the trees stood. The following day the mighty oak was laying in the yard, broken by the storm. The lowly palm that had lived in the shadow of the oak was merely bent by the storm and within a few days was standing straight. Which of the trees was really the strongest? Is it possible for us to be so rigid and "strong" that when the storms of life come, we break?

Question for today: Am I willing to be open-minded and flexible, or is it still necessary to show my "strength?"

Write about the most significant thing you experienced or learned yesterday.

Prayer for today

I pray that I will understand that there is more strength in bending with the storms of life, rather than standing rigid against them.

9-20-08

Dear Matt,

I prayed for you this morning.

I need to tell you about my grandma. She was a wonderful person who was short (about four feet ten), stout, and had great hugs. She was a woman of great faith and determination. In 1929, during one of the most difficult times in our country's economic history, she started her own business. It was a clothing alterations business that grew into a women's and children's clothing store. It was a successful business for many years. The first job I had was washing the windows every Saturday. I was eight at the time and got paid a dollar. Grandma and Grandpa were separated because of his alcoholism but never divorced. I suspect that she continued to help him financially after the separation, but they never lived together again. They had one son and four daughters. Mom was the youngest. What a challenge it was for Grandma to raise five children and run a business. But as I said, she was determined. I loved going to her home. It was like a sanctuary to me. I felt loved and safe. We had a ritual when I'd go to her house. The first thing she would do when I arrived was go to the pantry and get the jar of peanut butter. She'd open the jar and give me a big spoon of it to eat. She knew how much I loved it. That was a special time for us.

While my stepdad completed his tour of duty in the South Pacific, Mom, Shirley, and I moved into her home. Grandma was home when the police officer arrived after I'd vandalized my teacher's house. The look of disappointment on her face almost crushed me. She never scolded me, but she withdrew for several days. That was so painful for me. I turned over the proverbial new leaf at that time, and I was determined to be a good boy. I couldn't stand the thought of disappointing her again. In the following years, I turned that leaf over so many times I wore it out. World War II ended, and I dreaded the thought of my stepdad returning home because I knew we'd be moving from Grandma's. The book *Alcoholics Anonymous* talks about "a feeling of impending doom." I certainly had that. When my stepdad returned home, he and Mom bought an old dilapidated house that needed a lot of work. After much cleaning and painting, the house became livable. After the work was finished they sold the house for a profit and bought a large home across the street from the school I attended. I then started the second grade. I was a fairly bright kid and did well academically, but the teacher's comments in the citizenship column of my report cards were less than flattering. I was the class clown, and that did not endear me to my teacher. I would do almost anything to get attention.

Gary L.

The following is a meditation from *Rooted in God's Love*:

The hardest part of recovery is that it requires us to change. We might be intrigued by the idea of recovery. We might be inspired by stories about recovery. We might be convinced of our need for recovery. But the doing of recovery will be hard because we must change. And change is difficult.

We understandably resist change. We are angry that we have to change. We feel shame that we need to change. And we are afraid we will not be able to change. We know that there will be moments when we'll find ourselves saying "I can't do it. It's too difficult." [6]

I'll write the last part of the meditation in my next letter. Here's a prayer from *Rooted in God's Love*:

I am not good at seeing it yet, Lord. Will I bloom and grow? Will my desert wasteland see a harvest? Is there a path for me in this wilderness, Lord? Are there streams of water here? Surprise me, Lord. And change me. Give me the courage, hope and trust to change a little today. Amen. [7]

Matt, remember, this is a "one day at a time" journey.

Take care,
Gary L.

Psalm 46: 1–2: "God is our refuge and strength, always ready to help in times of trouble. So we will not fear, even if earthquakes come and the mountains crumble into the sea."

The *Life Recovery Bible*'s footnote says this about the above scripture:

God is more than able to protect us no matter how strong the pull of temptation might be. If we try to resist temptation in our own strength, we have good reason to fear. But if God is with us, we have no reason to be afraid. God's river of mercy and strength flows just for us when we are weak and thirsty. No power can draw us out of the circle of his protection once we take refuge in him.[8]

Day 4 date ____________________

Today I will be open to the Spiritual side of recovery. I will trust my Higher Power today.

How well do you think a tripod will stand if one of the legs is broken or missing? Many experts agree that the disease of addiction is threefold: physical, mental, and spiritual. Could we use those three as the three legs of a tripod? How many times have people gotten clean and sober and then returned to using? It becomes very obvious that being physically clean and sober is not enough. Some have gotten physically clean and sober and then have searched for ways to get mentally sober. They too have returned to using. This indicates to me that physical and mental sobriety is not enough. Perhaps the leg that's missing is the spiritual. When we begin growing in all three areas, we get three legs of the tripod firmly planted; then when the storms of life come, we have a sobriety that will stand.

Question for today: Am I willing to be open to the spiritual side of recovery?

Write about the most significant thing you experienced or learned yesterday.

Prayer for today

I pray that I will see and understand the importance of spiritual sobriety.

9-21-08

Dear Matt,

I prayed for you this morning.

There will be times that I'll write about recovery "stuff" and take a break from my story. Sometimes I will probably repeat myself. At my age, the short-term memory is not what it used to be.

There's a great story in the book *Alcoholics Anonymous* in the "Chapter to the Agnostics." It's about a man whose use of alcohol had brought him "to the point of self-destruction" (page 56).

> One night, when confined in a hospital, he was approached by an alcoholic who had known a spiritual experience. Our friend's gorge rose as he bitterly cried out: "If there is a God, He certainly hasn't done anything for me!" But later, alone in his room, he asked himself this question: "Is it possible that all the religious people I have known are wrong?" While pondering the answer he felt as though he lived in hell. Then, like a thunderbolt, a great thought came. It crowded out all else.
>
> "Who are you to say there is no God?"
>
> This man recounts that he tumbled out of bed to his knees. In a few seconds he was overwhelmed by a conviction of the Presence of God. It poured over and through him with the certainty and majesty of a great tide at flood. The barriers he had built through the years were swept away. He stood in the Presence of Infinite Power and Love. He had stepped from bridge to shore. For the first time, he lived in conscious companionship with his Creator. [9]

That's a great story. Many of us don't have a dramatic experience like that, but God works with us in the way that is right for us individually. The meditation in the *Twenty-Four Hours a Day* book for today states:

> In improving our personal lives, we have Unseen help. We were not made so that we could see God. That would be too easy for us and there would be no merit in obeying Him. It takes an act

> of faith, a venture of belief, to realize the Unseen Power. Yet we have much evidence of God's existence in the strength that many people have received from the act of faith, the venture of belief. We are in a box of space and time and we can see neither our souls nor God. God and the human spirit are both outside the limitations of space and time. Yet our Unseen help is effective here and now. That has been proved in thousands of changed lives.
>
> **Prayer for the Day**
>
> I pray that I may make the great venture of belief. I pray that my vision may not be blocked by intellectual pride. [10]

Here's the rest of the meditation from *Rooted in God's Love* in my last letter.

> But change is also the most exhilarating part of recovery. We don't have to live in bondage to our addictions. We don't have to run in fear from relationships. We don't have to live as if we were responsible for the world. We can learn serenity. We can find freedom. We can experience love.
>
> Change is the most difficult and the most wonderful part of the recovery process. It engages us in a major internal battle. It is not a comfortable battle. But our capacity to change is the key to our hope. God has given us the ability to change and grow. God calls us to change. God gives us the perspectives and disciplines and encouragements we need. And, as we open ourselves to God's work, God works within us to strengthen us, heal us and make us new.
>
> May God surprise you with your capacity for change. [11]

I think that's a great meditation. During early recovery while pondering the "God stuff," I went to an AA meeting at a church in Coos Bay. During the meeting, I glanced over to a wall that had a wire rack with many free brochures. One title caught my attention, "Act As If."

After the meeting, I pulled it from the rack. This was in 1971. The brochure was a reprint of a Reader's Digest article from either 1950 or 1951. My memory is a little hazy about that, but it was one or the other. It was written by Rev. Sam Shoemaker, who was a spiritual advisor to the cofounders of AA, Dr. Bob and Bill W. The article was so helpful to me.

Rev. Shoemaker's suggestion is to act as if there is a God whether you believe it or not. He also suggested to say what is honest about yourself and your situation to whatever is the Truth behind all creation. Eventually, as one continues to experiment or "act as if," he realizes that "something" is working.

That's a simple concept that you might try.

Your friend in recovery,
Gary L.

Day 5 date ____________________

Today I will be unafraid; I will refuse to be controlled by worry, fear, and anxiety.

Worry—Fear—Anxiety. Those are words that describe how many of us have lived. A man once said, "Worry cuts a channel into which all other thoughts are drained." In other words, when we worry about something, all of our thoughts will continue to return to the worry. Can you recall times when worry about something almost immobilized you? Worry, fear, and anxiety can have a tremendous power over our lives. Usually, when a person first enters recovery, worry, fear, and anxiety are like huge giants; at the same time, his/her faith is very small. As he/she grows in faith, "One day at a time," worry, fear, and anxiety begin to diminish. Wouldn't it be a good feeling to know that faith is increasing and worry is decreasing in your life?

Question for today: Am I willing to believe that increased faith and decreased worry is possible for me?

Write about the most significant thing you experienced or learned yesterday.

Prayer for today

I pray that I will quickly let go of any worry, fear, or anxiety that will come into my mind today.

9-22-08

Dear Matt,

I prayed for you this morning.

When I started the second grade, I still felt like an outsider. My perception was that the other kids didn't want me around. After reflecting on that as an adult, I came to the conclusion that I had become so self-protective as a child that I wouldn't let kids or adults get close to me. I had such a great fear of rejection or abandonment. One thing I've learned about perception is that it's not always based on truth. But if I believe my perception is true, I will live according to that. A lie becomes my reality. So my perception that kids didn't want me around reinforced the false belief that I wasn't worth much. I not only felt lonely as a child, I also felt alone. I could be in a roomful of people and feel alone. I attempted to compensate for my sense of inadequacy, insecurity, and inferiority by doing well academically. Somehow a false belief was born in me that kids who got good grades were better than those who didn't. I was determined to show others that I was better than they were. When I received a report card with good marks, I could look down on others, and my sense of inadequacy and inferiority seemed less.

My motivation for good grades was skewed. I worked hard to get good grades so that I could feel superior to my peers, not because studying hard was the right thing to do. Do you see how self-centered I'd become? There are so many parts of my past that I see differently today because my perception of the past has changed. I was so blind for many years to the part I played in my own life. I was conscious of my perception of what I thought others had done to me but was unable to see my side of the street. Step Four. Alcoholics' Anonymous, page 59: "Made a searching and fearless moral inventory of ourselves." [12] That step was so important in learning to be honest with myself.

Early in my recovery, I heard a man say at a meeting, "My life was like a big ball of string that had been cut through the middle. Recovery has been one knot at a time, putting the ball back together." I really identified with that. There were so many loose ends in my life, and so many perceptions that were not based on truth. Slowly, slowly, one day at a time, the ball is taking shape. There were so many frayed ends, and, in the beginning, the task seemed impossible. Matthew 19:26 says Jesus looked at them intently and said, "Humanly speaking, it is impossible. But with God everything is possible." I began to realize that God would help me and that I didn't have to do it by myself. I believe the last knot will be tied when I see my Creator. Another great promise that we're given is in Philippians 1:6. "And I am sure that God, who began the good work within you, will continue His work until it is finally finished on that day when Christ Jesus comes back again."

I am so grateful that I have help and don't have to figure out how to navigate through life alone.

As Bill Sees It, page 174:

> Mine was exactly the kind of deep-seated block we so often see today in new people who say they are atheistic or agnostic. Their will to disbelieve is so powerful that apparently they prefer a date with the undertaker to an open-minded and experimental quest for God.
>
> Happily for me, and for most of my kind who have since come along in A.A., the constructive forces brought to bear in our fellowship have nearly always overcome this colossal obstinacy. Beaten into complete defeat by alcohol, confronted by the living proof of release, and surrounded by those who can speak to us from the heart, we have finally surrendered.
>
> And then, paradoxically, we have found ourselves in a new dimension, the real world of spirit and faith. Enough willingness, enough open-mindedness—and there it is! [13]

Matt, this is just a suggestion. If there is a Prison Fellowship group that comes in, you might want to check it out. It is a tremendous organization. I prayed for you this morning that God would fill you with hope.

God's blessing to you,
Gary L.

Day 6 date ___________________

Today I will meditate on the phrase: "Rarely have we seen a person fail who has thoroughly followed our path."

If a person was in Portland, Oregon, and decided to go to Portland, Maine, and there were no road signs to guide him, do you think that he'd ever reach his destination? He probably would go down many wrong roads and do a lot of wandering. Chances are, with no road signs to follow or anyone to give directions, he would probably get very discouraged and give up. Many of us have gone through life like that. We know that we're looking for something, but we just can't seem to find it. There is a city named Sobriety. In that city, there is serenity, acceptance, love, hope, faith, and many other things that we've searched for. There is a path from where we're at to that city. Along the path are signs to follow: The Twelve Steps, Serenity Prayer, etc., and people who will help us stay on the path.

Question for today: Am I willing to stay on the path that's been blazed for me, or am I intent on traveling my own?

Write about the most significant thing you experienced or learned yesterday.

Prayer for today

I pray that I will see the pathway to the city called Sobriety and that I will be willing to follow it.

9-23-08

Dear Matt,

I prayed for you this morning.

I hope this letter finds you making progress in your recovery journey. I realize that I've given you a lot to think about. Take the things that I share with you that are helpful to you, and leave the rest. All that I'm sharing is just my experience and how recovery has worked for me.

Back to my story. While Shirley and I lived with Grandma, we began to attend church with her. She really had a close relationship with God. I think she read the Bible every day, and I know she prayed a lot. The thing I enjoyed most about church was when we sang hymns. It was discovered that I had quite a talent for singing and was known as a boy soprano. Something about the words in the hymns touched my soul. The small church had a live remote fifteen-minute radio show every Monday evening, and from age six to eight, I occasionally sang solos on the program. Grandma was so proud of me. One of the hymns I sang that was my favorite was titled "In the Garden" (public domain: C. Austin Miles, 1912). I still remember the words:

> I come to the garden alone. While the dew is still on the roses. And the voice I hear, falling on my ear. The Son of God discloses. And He walks with me, and He talks with me, and He tells me I am His own. And the joy we share, as we tarry there, none other has ever known.
>
> The second verse says "He speaks, and the sound of His voice. Is so sweet, the birds hush their singing. And the melody, that He brings to me. Within my heart is ringing. And He walks with me, and He talks with me. And He tells me I am His own. And the joy we share, as we tarry there. None other has ever known."

It's amazing to me how those words have never left me. While attending church one Sunday, I heard the message that all humans had sinned and fallen short of God's glory. The preacher said that God had sent His son, Jesus, to pay for our sins. He then said that if we would accept what Jesus did for us on the cross, we would be forgiven and would go to heaven when we died. I have to tell you that at that time in my young life, I believed I was the worst sinner in the world, and that was the reason my dad abandoned me. I thought that if I were forgiven, perhaps he would come back. I prayed and asked Jesus into my heart that morning, but when the offering plate went by later, I pretended to put some money in but took some out. I felt so guilty when I went to bed that night and was afraid to go to sleep. My thought was that when I awoke I'd be in hell.

So much of the recovery journey for me has been a process of unlearning "old ideas." *Alcoholics Anonymous* page 58 says: "Some of us have tried to hold onto our old ideas and the result was nil until we let go absolutely." 14

I definitely had some old ideas about God that had not served me well. The *Twenty-Four Hours a Day* book on June 23 has a great meditation.

Meditation for the Day

You need to be constantly recharged by the power of the spirit of God. Commune with God in quiet times until the life from God, the Divine life, by that very contact, flows into your being and revives your fainting spirit. When weary, take time out and rest. Rest and gain power and strength from God, and then you will be ready to meet whatever opportunities come your way. Rest until every care and worry and fear have gone and then the tide of peace and serenity, love and joy, will flow into your consciousness. [15]

Here's another prayer from *Rooted in God's Love*:

Sometimes I get stuck, Lord. When that happens, I desperately want a miracle. I want to change fast, very fast. But that's not what I really need. What I really need is you, Lord. If you haven't given up, then I'm not really stuck. There is hope. Renew my vision of you, Lord. Help me to see again your hopefulness about me. And your love for me. And the joy you take in me. Let this build again in me a capacity for hope. Amen. [16]

I really like the way he words his prayers. Sometimes the only thing I can seem to come up with when I pray is, "Help!" God hears prayers like that also.

Take care,
Gary L.

Psalm 22:24: "For He has not ignored the suffering of the needy. He has not turned and walked away. He has listened to their cries for help."

Day 7 date ____________

Today I will live my life in small segments. I will surrender my past and my future to God.

Did you know that it's possible for one person to eat an entire elephant? The key is to eat it one "bite" at a time. If a person was presented with an entire elephant to eat, the task would seem overwhelming, but one "bite" at a time he could accomplish what at first seemed impossible. Sometimes life seems that overwhelming, but if we live it in small segments, we can accomplish many things. The only problem that we can deal with is the one in front of us. It's impossible to deal with tomorrow's challenges and problems today. Do you really see the importance of living "one day at a time"?

Question for today: Am I willing to live my life in one-day segments, or do I think that principle doesn't apply to me?

Write about the most significant thing you experienced or learned yesterday.

Prayer for today

I pray that I will understand the importance of living "one day at a time."

9-24-08

Dear Matt,

I prayed for you this morning.

When I was young, I believe I was given messages about God that were not true. That skewed my understanding of who God is. I almost saw Him as an ogre when I was young. God was keeping score, and I was falling way behind. So much of my journey in recovery has been about God changing my early beliefs about Him. I did not believe that God was really on my side for sometime in recovery. I knew I could never meet God's expectations. My thinking about all of that has changed dramatically through the years. I continue to ask Him to reveal more about Himself to me. That will go on for the rest of my life. Someone said that if you think you have God all figured out, He'll probably do something to blow all your fuses. I've learned to live in the mystery and the sovereignty of God. I believe that for a long time I wanted to figure God out, so that I could "put Him in a box" and control Him. It was like the prayer, "Let's make a deal." I see the absurdity of that now, but I didn't see it then. Just another example of God's grace, as He helped me have a better understanding.

The book *Alcoholics Anonymous* states on page 60: "We are not saints. The point is, that we are willing to grow along spiritual lines." 17

An interesting thing about something that is growing is that it is also changing. Change is not always easy for many of us. Oftentimes we want things outside of ourselves to change, but real recovery, to me, is about changes that God wants to do in me.

Rooted in God's Love:
Change and Hope

Sometimes it feels like nothing is changing. We feel like we have lost our way—and all hope of finding it again. Ironically we often experience this sense of being stuck during periods that later seem most dynamic in terms of change. Perhaps when change is rapid we are so disoriented that we are unable to see it clearly. In times like this we may not be able to see that anything is changing. It may be hard to believe that all the hard work and effort are worth it. It is during these times that we are most tempted to give up.

> It is a general truth that we want change to take place faster than it does. We think we could more easily tolerate the pain of recovery—if only we could be assured that it would be quick.
>
> But if we insist that change happen so rapidly that we can see it every day, then our capacity for hope will gradually diminish. If we insist that our recovery always have the drama and immediacy of "miracle," then we will not build the deep-down kind of hope that we will need during the really tough times in life. Hope that you can "see," Paul says, is not really hope at all. Real hope is what sustains us when we do not see the change. Hope is the conviction that God has not given up on us. As long as God is committed to us, there is hope for change. [18]

Romans 8:25: "But if we look forward to something we don't have yet, we must wait patiently and confidently." I don't know about you, but waiting patiently has not always been my strong suit. There is a scripture found in Isaiah 40:31: "But those who wait on the Lord will find new strength. They will fly high on wings like eagles. They will run and not grow weary. They will walk and not faint." That is a wonderful promise!

I need strength because sometimes life gets really difficult. I need the kind of strength that comes out of my relationship with God, not some kind of strength I've worked up within myself. I am so grateful that God is in my life and that He gives me the strength to navigate through life.

Blessings to you,

Gary L.

Day 8 date ____________________

Today I will meditate on the word "freedom." I will try to understand what real "freedom" is. There were two families living side by side, and they both had dogs. The only difference between their yards was that one had his fenced, and the other didn't. When the owners let their dogs out, one dog could go anyplace he wanted, while the other dog was confined by a fence. Which dog was the freer? Many would say that the dog that could go anyplace he wanted was the free one, but was he really free? He was "free" to be hit by a car, "free" to be shot by unhappy neighbors, "free" to be caught by a dogcatcher; in contrast, the other dog is safe and secure because of the fence. He is the one that is truly "free." Fences will help us have real "freedom." Would it be possible to fence our yard with the Twelve Steps and living by Spiritual principles?

Question for today: Am I willing to have fences around my life, or do I still want to run loose?

Write about the most significant thing you experienced or learned yesterday.

Prayer for today

I pray that I will understand that "fences" give me security and real "freedom."

9-25-08

Dear Matt,

I prayed for you this morning.

I began the third grade of school with a reputation that was not favorable. I acted out in class and didn't have any friends. Part of the problem was that I didn't trust anyone. In fact, trust has been a difficult thing for much of my life. It's much better today, but that's because I've learned that there are people who can be trusted, and I know that God can be trusted. One of Mom's favorite saying was, "People are no damn good. You can't trust anybody." That belief became part of me. I was one of those kids that parents warned their kids to stay away from. All of that fed a growing core of shame on the inside of me. I wasn't aware of the core of shame until I'd been sober a number of years. So much of my journey since discovering my shame has been about God slowly changing that core. If I live according to the shame, I will make decisions that bring more consequences. Self-sabotage became a way of life for me, and I didn't even know it.

I need to tell you about Hugh. He had been sober about ten years when I first went to AA. He approached me after my first meeting and introduced himself. He then said that I could call him any time of the day or night if I needed to talk, and then he gave me his phone number. That made an impression on me. I drank again three and a half weeks later for a day and a night. After the meeting the following night, Hugh kind of took me under his wing and began to mentor me about recovery. I never asked him to be my sponsor, but that's what he was.

During one of our many conversations, he asked the question, "Would you like someone exactly like you to be your very best friend?" My immediate response was an emphatic, "No!" Why would I want someone with all of my character flaws and shortcomings to be my friend? I would never trust him. Hugh then explained that part of our journey is, with God's help, becoming that person. Again, more evidence that I needed to change and that I could not change without God's help.

My journey of change has been going on since March 2, 1971, and will continue as long as I continue to ask for God's help. It's sometimes difficult for me to comprehend the life that God working through the Twelve Steps has given me. I was so broken down by alcoholism, was convinced that life would never work for me, believed that God didn't want anything to do with me, and was without hope. Because of what God has done in my life, I have a good relationship with myself today and have learned to treat myself as a friend.

Matt, if you had a friend who had been in recovery for a couple of years, and he called and said that he'd decided to get drunk, what would you say to him? I'm sure that you would do everything in your power to talk him out of it. What would it be like to treat yourself that way? We learn to treat ourselves that way on the Twelve Step path.

Matt, treat yourself like a good friend today.

Take care, my friend,
Gary L.

John 12:46: "I have come as a light to shine in this dark world, so that all who put their trust in me will no longer remain in the darkness."

Day 9 date ___________________

Today I will make a list of all the people who I have resentments against.

The word resent means to re-feel something. Oftentimes, a small incident may grow into a giant resentment as a person re-feels it. As a resentment grows, it can sometimes rule our lives. Many chemically dependent people have relapsed as a result of not dealing with a resentment. Resentments are like a poison that will eat us up from the inside out. Is it possible to deal with resentments constructively? The answer is yes. As we learn to accept the things we cannot change, and we learn how to forgive, resentments will lose their power. Acceptance and forgiveness will give us power over resentments. Wouldn't it be a good feeling to be free of resentments?

Question for today: Am I willing to forgive and accept those who have hurt me, or do I still want to carry grudges? Am I also willing to forgive myself for all that I've done?

Write about the most significant thing you experienced or learned yesterday.

Prayer for today

I pray that I will become a person who forgives others easily and that I grow in acceptance of things that I cannot change.

9-26-08

Dear Matt,

I prayed for you this morning.

I got a little off track in my last letter. Sometimes my mind runs in many directions.

Many labels had been placed on me by the time I entered the third grade; troublemaker, rebellious, defiant, self-centered, and incorrigible were some of them. Those are tough things to deal with when you're seven. In spite of the labels, I could go for short periods of time and be a pretty good kid, but when someone crossed me in some way, a monster came out. There was so much conflict internally, and my parents did not know what to do.

In the book of Romans the Apostle Paul says, "The good I want to do, I do not, and the thing I don't want to do, that is the thing I find myself doing." Boy, do I ever relate to that.

After acting out in class one day, I was sent to the principal's office and received a spanking. We lived across the street from the school, and later that evening after everyone had left the school, I returned with Kenny. He was also known as a troublemaker, and I knew that if he was with me, Mom would blame him for what we were about to do. I talked Kenny into helping me put a rock through every window that we could. Some of the windows on the third story avoided our rocks, but not the rest. The windows had small French panes, so it took some time to finish the job. Pushing each rock was a rage on the inside of me. I thought, "I'll show you!"

When a police officer appeared at our home later, Mom's response was exactly as I'd guessed, "He wouldn't have done it if it wasn't for Kenny." I learned how to not take responsibility for my actions, and that kind of thinking (old ideas) followed me into the rooms of AA.

After completing the third grade, my parents decided to move to Empire, Oregon. That would put Dad (I was now calling him Dad), closer to his work, and it would also get me away from the kids "causing me to do bad things."

I'm sure you've heard the term geographic cure. The problem was that when we got to Empire I was there too. The problem was not others; it was me. I saw this as another opportunity to, again, "turn over a new leaf" and started the fourth grade with a determination to do better.

I completed the fourth grade without incident. My parents were so proud of me. It was at this time that I began to use my stepdad's last name. All of the years since the divorce I'd had this fantasy of my dad returning and scooping me up in his arms. Every Christmas and birthday, I hoped that he would appear and shower me with gifts.

By the time I was eight, I finally realized that it wasn't going to happen. Under the realization was a simmering anger at him, and thus was born a hatred toward the man who at one time had been my hero. There was also an inner resolve that some day he was going to pay.

Blessings,
Gary L.

Day 10 date ____________________

Today I will see myself as going through a process of healing.

There is a book that states, "We are transformed by the renewing of our minds." The word transformed is the same as the word metamorphosis, which means, change of physical form, structure, or substance, by supernatural means; a striking alteration in appearance of character. Metamorphosis is the process that a caterpillar goes through to become a butterfly. Is it possible for us to go through a similar process as we grow spiritually? Would you for a moment view yourself as a caterpillar crawling around looking for something? You're not sure what you're looking for, but you keep crawling. A caterpillar crawling around has little defense and is very vulnerable. Do you suppose that it eventually accepts the fact that it's a caterpillar and is powerless to do anything about that?

Question for today: Am I willing to accept my powerlessness, or am I still convinced that I can transform and heal myself?

Write about the most significant thing you experienced or learned yesterday.

Prayer for today

I pray I will see that my Higher Power has me going through metamorphosis and that I am truly being transformed.

9-27-08

Dear Matt,

I prayed for you this morning.

I just received your letter, and I do appreciate your prayers. One rule of thumb I use when needing to make a tough decision is to ask myself the question, "What is best for my recovery?" I believe what is best for my recovery is God's will.

I mentioned in my last letter many of the labels that had been placed on me while growing up. Had I been born in this generation the labels may have been different: ADD, Bipolar, conduct disorder, antisocial, anxiety disorder, sleep disorder, and narcissistic personality disorder. I would be prescribed so many medications that I would probably walk around like a zombie. I've never been professionally treated for any of those things, but God working through the Twelve Steps has removed all of the labels. *Alcoholics Anonymous* states on page 64, "When the spiritual malady is overcome, we straighten out mentally and physically." [19]

One of the meditation books I use is titled *31 Days of Praise*, by Ruth and Warren Myers. On pages 134–35 they write:

> Think of it this way. It's as though in your inner-most being you were previously a caterpillar; you entered the cocoon of Christ's death and through His resurrection emerged as a butterfly. Now, bit by bit as you follow Christ, the ways you think, feel, choose, and live are also being liberated and transformed. And you look forward to the day when your slowly dying body, with its weakness and sinful tendencies, will be changed into a glorious, radiant body just like our risen Lord's.
>
> Thanking and praising God for these facts will help you *see yourself as God sees you. This is vital, for we live as who we see ourselves to be.* (Emphasis mine.) [20]

This tells me that I need to begin seeing myself as God sees me and not see myself according to the labels that I've worn. When I began to see myself as a recovering alcoholic loved by God, rather than a poor, sick, loser alcoholic, the way I lived life began to change. There is not a pill available that will overcome my "spiritual malady," only God can do that. My responsibility is to let Him, "one day at a time."

The *Twenty-Four Hours a Day* book says this on 6–27:

A.A. Thought for the Day

If you can take your troubles as they come, if you can maintain your calm and composure amid pressing duties and unending engagements, if you can rise above the distressing and disturbing circumstances in which you are set down, you have discovered a priceless secret of daily living. Even if you are forced to go through life weighed down by some unescapable (sic) misfortune or handicap and yet live each day as it comes with poise and peace of mind, you have succeeded where most people have failed. You have wrought a greater achievement than a person who rules a nation. *Have I achieved poise and peace of mind?*

Meditation for the Day

Take a blessing with you wherever you go. You have been blessed, so bless others. Such stores of blessings are awaiting you in the months and years that lie ahead. Pass on your blessings. Blessing can and does go around the world, passed on from one person to another. Shed a little blessing in the heart of one person. That person is cheered to pass it on, and so, God's vitalizing, joy-giving message travels on. Be a transmitter of God's blessings.

Prayer for the Day

I pray that I may pass on my blessings. I pray that they may flow into the lives of others.[21]

I hope the above prayer is your prayer also.
This can be a great journey!

Gary L.

Day 11 date ___________________

Today I will view treatment as a cocoon around my life. I will be grateful for the security.

I wonder if a caterpillar has faith. Does it know that someday it will become a butterfly? Perhaps it's the hope of flying someday that enables it to endure the crawling. At just the right time, the caterpillar enters treatment, err ..., I mean the cocoon. Do you see the similarity? In the cocoon, the caterpillar is protected as it begins the process of transformation. Just for a moment, view treatment, the Twelve Steps, counselors, etc., as part of your cocoon. What do you think would happen to a caterpillar if it tried to leave the cocoon before it was time? The process of healing and change cannot be rushed, but we can be sure that as long as we're in the cocoon we will be secure as the process begins, and we can also have the hope that someday we too will fly.

Question for today: Am I willing to be patient as I begin the process of healing and transformation?

Write about the most significant thing you experienced or learned yesterday.

Prayer for today

I pray that I will truly understand and believe that I am in a process of healing and transformation.

9-28-08

Dear Matt,

I prayed for you this morning.

It's Sunday morning and I've been pondering about what to write today. I decided that I would share some scripture that I read this morning from the NLT (New Living Translation) and the footnotes from that, and then end with a prayer.

> I love the Lord because he hears and answers my prayers. Because he bends down and listens, I will pray as long as I have breath! Death had its hands around my throat; the terrors of the grave overtook me. I saw only trouble and sorrow. Then I called on the name of the Lord: "Please, Lord, save me!" How kind the Lord is! How good he is! So merciful, this God of ours! The Lord protects those of childlike faith; I was facing death, and then he saved me. Now I can rest again, for the Lord has been so good to me. He has saved me from death, my eyes from tears, my feet from stumbling. And so I walk in the Lord's presence as I live here on earth! (Psalm 116:1–9)

> Footnotes: How wonderful that God hears and answers the prayers of those who turn to him in distress! When we were in the grip of our dependency or addiction, we may have been blind to the fact that we were in danger of losing our reputation, our friends, or even our life. But then we called out to the Lord, and he saved us. The natural response to this realization should be praise to God. [22]

All of that has been so true in my life. I was suicidal and felt hopeless at the end of my drinking. Depression, despair, and despondency were like clouds over me. And then I cried out to God, and He heard me!

Here's a prayer you might try. God, I need to give to you my shame, guilt, and fear. I also need to stop the self-talk I use that beats me down and tells me I am hopeless. God help me to place my hope in you and to understand that you have a better plan for my life than I do. My plan is what got me on my knees before you. God, help me to trust your plan.

Gary L.

This is just a suggestion. Say this prayer every morning for thirty days and see if it makes a difference. The prayer helps me get out of my own way.

Take care, pal,
Gary L.

Day 12 date ____________________

Today I will meditate on the word "surrender," and try to understand what it really means.

The first time I heard the expression, "You have to surrender to win," it did not make sense to me. In fact, I strongly disagreed. I had always associated surrender with losing. Surrender means the action of yielding one's self into the power of another. If we yield ourselves over to our Higher Power, how can we lose? In any war, the country that surrenders is the one that's restored. There must be surrender, to have restoration. For many of us, our track record proves that as long as we're in the battle, we lose. Wouldn't it be better to surrender and win?

Question for today: Am I willing to look at the benefits of surrender? Am I willing to surrender to win?

Write about the most significant thing you experienced or learned today.

Prayer for today

I pray that I will surrender today and that I will yield myself to my Higher Power.

9-29-08

Dear Matt,

I prayed for you this morning.

After my first disastrous three years in school, I hoped that a new school and a new town would give me a fresh start. The fourth grade was uneventful as far as school went. I did what I was told to do and didn't cause any trouble. I did well academically but still had a sense that I was an outsider or misfit. I tried to develop friendships, but they didn't last long. I always believed that the other kids were the problem, and never saw my part until I had been in recovery for some time. What I discovered was that I was inflexible and that we had to do what I wanted to do. In retrospect, I see how self-centered and selfish I was. I wanted to play with their toys but wouldn't share mine. It's no wonder I couldn't keep friends. I didn't have a clue on how to be a friend.

I only had one episode of rage during that year, and it was at Christmastime. I really wanted a new bike for Christmas and thought that since I had been so good, I would get a nice, new bike. What I got was a used bike without any accessories. I was so angry that later in the day I laid my bike down and, in a fit of rage, took wood from the woodpile and tried to smash the bike. Dad caught me and severely spanked me. I wanted to kill him. Needless to say, that was not a merry Christmas for me. Looking back, I understand why I was punished. Even at that young age, I had a strong sense of entitlement.

While growing up, one of Dad's favorite things to say to me was, "You think this world owes you something." I didn't even know what he meant until many years later, and I have to admit that he hit the nail right on the head.

My rage around the used bike had a payoff the following Christmas when I received one of the nicest bikes of the time. It was a Schwinn Black Beauty. It had chrome fenders, whitewall tires, lights, horn, and a key to lock the handlebars. I was envied by the other kids. The false belief that came from the new bike was, if I rage at my parents for disappointing me, at some point they will try to make it up to me. Unfortunately, that process continued to happen through the growing-up years.

After six months or so, my beautiful bike was just a frame with wheels. All of the accessories had been removed, and I had reversed the handlebars. I threw the bike down after riding and did not put it away at night. It had no more value than the used bike I'd received the previous year. My sister received a girl's Schwinn, and by the time I'd trashed mine, hers was still like new. She was grateful for the gift she received and took care of it, whereas I dishonored the gift.

I think of the gift of sobriety that I've been given and how it's my job to be grateful for the gift and to honor it. I need to share the gift with those who have followed me in recovery. Many out there desperately need this gift, and it's our responsibility to pass it on to them. My sponsor, Hugh, said that if I want to keep the gift, I needed to give it away. What a privilege it is to be on this path. For many of the years before I got sober, I would think, "I wish I could just start my life over." God's answer to that has been placing me on the recovery path. How blessed we are to have another chance at life.

Rooted in God's Love:

Lord, it isn't just me that I am trying to change. I am up against generations of dysfunction. An empty way of life has dominated my family for a long time. It has been passed down to me. No wonder it seems so hard to change. I need your help, Lord. Help me to find hope in your understanding of my struggle. Help me to find hope in your gift of redemption. Amen. [23]

God's grace is bigger than our past!
Gary L.

Philippians 1:9: "I pray that your love for each other will overflow more and more, and that you will keep on growing in your knowledge and understanding."

9-30-08

Dear Matt,

I prayed for you this morning.

One of the things I loved to do starting around the age six was to go to the Liberty Theatre on Saturday afternoon. There was always a cartoon (we called it a comedy back then), followed by what was called a serial. A serial was an ongoing saga of some kind that was continued the following week. If memory serves me correctly, each episode was around fifteen minutes long and always left us with a sense of suspense about the next episode. What might happen next week was often a topic of conversation. We waited impatiently all week to see the next episode. The serials were almost always westerns and in black and white. I still remember heroes like Tom Mix, Roy Rogers, Gene Autry, and Hopalong Cassidy. The heroes always won, and they could get out of the most frightening situations. I always tried to arrive early, because there would be a mad dash to get front-row seats. After the cartoon and serial, we'd watch a full-length movie. The cost for all of that entertainment was fifteen cents. Popcorn was five cents, and a candy bar was five cents, so for a quarter a kid could have a great afternoon.

When I was seven the theatre owner announced that they were going to have a talent contest during the intermission the following week, and there would be prizes. I signed up to compete, and, with great anxiety, I walked onstage and sang, "Popeye the Sailor Man." I still remember the applause as I was awarded second prize. My prize was a leaky fountain pen, but that was not as important to me as the applause. I was intoxicated by the applause but disappointed that I did not win first.

Several years later, when I was in the fifth grade, the local fire department announced that they were sponsoring a talent contest for all ages. I approached Mrs. Wilson, who was the music teacher for grades six through eight, and asked if she would accompany me on the piano. After singing for her, she agreed to play. I was so excited about the contest, and thoughts about it consumed my mind. I remembered the applause from the first talent contest I entered, and that brought even more excitement.

The night of the contest finally arrived, and the anxiety I felt was almost overwhelming. I sang an Irish ballad, "An Irish Lullaby." The audience erupted with applause when I finished, but when the final votes by the judges were counted, I came in second in my age group. Most people would have been excited with second place, but I had a profound sense of failure, disappointment, injustice, and then anger. I felt that the judges were not fair to me. Mrs. Wilson tried to encourage me, but it was of little help.

The following year the contest was held, and I tied for first place and was disappointed with that. By this age I had become so self-centered that anything less than first was not sufficient. When I read Bill W's story in the book *Alcoholics Anonymous* and his drive to be number one, I really identified with that. Anything less than number one fed the core of shame in me that was slowly growing stronger.

Blessings,
Gary L.

John 14:27: "I am leaving you with a gift—peace of mind and heart. And the peace I give isn't like the peace the world gives. So don't be troubled or afraid."

Day 13 date ____________________

Today I will turn over my future to God. I will turn over all feelings of anxiety or fear about the future.

While early in recovery, a man said his life was like a ball of string that had been cut through the middle. There were so many loose ends to deal with, and they seemed overwhelming. He then stated that one of the things that he'd learned in recovery was that he didn't have to put the whole ball back together all at once, but if he would only tie two strands together each day, eventually the ball would be put back together.

Question for today: Am I willing to be patient and see my life going back together one "knot" at a time?

Write about the most significant thing you experienced or learned yesterday.

Prayer for today

I pray that I will be patient with myself and others as I grow in recovery, one "knot" at a time.

10-1-08

Dear Matt,

I prayed for you this morning.

One activity I really enjoyed while growing up was family picnics. Moms, dads, brothers, sisters, cousins, aunts, and uncles would gather at the beach, a lake, or a river for a potluck picnic. It was a carefree day with swimming, games, and great food. Whenever a picnic was planned, I would really get excited. That was often followed by worry that something would happen, and the picnic would be cancelled. Picnics to me were like a time-out from life. I felt carefree and dreaded when it was time to pack up and go home. I didn't realize until many years later that alcohol became my picnic or time-out from life.

On a Sunday morning the day a picnic was planned, the phone rang. Grandma went to church every Sunday, and she would call when she arrived home. The call wasn't from her; it was from the hospital. Grandma had suffered a stroke and was in a coma. A sense of fear and dread came over me. Grandma's home was my place of refuge. She was the most important person in my life. I prayed, "Oh God, don't let her die."

After being in a coma for approximately three weeks, she died. Some people from the church rejoiced, because they said she was in heaven. My response was somewhat different than theirs. I became very angry at God, because in my mind He had taken the most important person in the world to me. To compound my loss, I was not allowed to attend her funeral. I was crushed. Perhaps my parents were trying to shelter me from the pain, but that's just conjecture on my part. No one ever explained to me why I couldn't attend.

That was a dark, dark, time for me. She was such a great person. Rather than truly grieve, I just shut my feelings down. That pattern would continue for many years. I became so hard on the inside. I still have vivid memories about the Sunday the phone rang.

There was a great meditation in the *Twenty-Four Hours a Day* book on July 1.

Meditation for the Day

Learn daily the lesson of trust and calm in the midst of the storms of life. Whatever of sorrow or difficulty the day may bring, God's command to you is the same. Be grateful, humble,

> calm, and loving to all people. Leave each soul the better for having met you or heard you. For all kinds of people, this should be your attitude: a loving desire to help and an infectious spirit of calmness and trust in God. You have the answer to loneliness and fear, which is calm faith in the goodness and purpose in the universe. [24]

I'm so grateful for the things I've learned in recovery. My skewed perception of God for many years was that He took important people from me. After Grandma died, I completely shut off the idea of God. I turned away from Him but discovered many years later that He never turned away from me.

God's grace to you this day,
Gary L.

Hebrews 10:36: "Patient endurance is what you need now, so you will continue to do God's will. Then you will receive all that He has promised."

Day 14 date ___________________

Today I will work on accepting things that I cannot change.

Many years ago in a major college football game, a player picked up a fumble and began running the wrong way. He was eventually tackled by one of his teammates just prior to scoring a touchdown for the opposing team. Do you suppose he was convinced that he was running in the right direction? Probably so. Can we find times in our life when we were convinced that we were running in the right direction, and now, looking back, see that we were not? Is it possible that God intervened in our life just prior to us scoring a touchdown for the opposition?

Question for today: Am I willing to examine my life and be honest enough to admit that sometimes I was running in the wrong direction, but didn't know it?

Write about the most significant thing you experienced or learned yesterday.

Prayer for today

I pray that I will have a clearer perception of myself and my past.

10-2-08

Dear Matt,

I prayed for you this morning.

I attended a meeting last night, and one of my sponsored people was there. He was first incarcerated when he was thirteen and eventually worked his way up to prison as an adult. So, off and on for thirteen years he was locked up. During those thirteen years he tried AA many times, but could never get beyond thirty days of sobriety. He's an alumnus of San Quentin. When he was twenty-six he almost died and hit bottom in a way that he never had in the past. He surrendered his life to God and began a new life.

On July 1 of this year, he celebrated seventeen years of continuous sobriety. He had very little education when he got sober, and reading and writing were difficult for him. In spite of that, with the help of tutors, he became an electrician. He's done some work for me, and he is a great electrician. He's in business for himself and owns his home free and clear. He sponsors many people, especially newcomers. What a remarkable turnaround for a "three-time" loser. Some years after his recovery, He received a full pardon from the state of California.

There are so many inspirational stories like his. Many are in the book *Alcoholics' Anonymous.* My prayer is that you become a great story.

As Bill Sees It, page 104.

Our New Employer

We had a new Employer. Being all powerful, He provided what we needed, if we kept close to Him and performed His work well.

Established on such a footing, we became less and less interested in ourselves, our little plans and designs. More and more we became interested in seeing what we could contribute to life. As we felt new power flow in, as we enjoyed peace of mind, as we discovered we could face life successfully, as we became conscious of His presence, we began to lose our fear of today, tomorrow, or the hereafter. We were reborn. [25]

Matt, I hope that will be your experience.

As Bill Sees It, page 234

Freed Prisoners

Letters to a prison group:

Every A.A. has been, in a sense, a prisoner. Each of us has walled himself out of society; each has known social stigma. The lot of you folks has been even more difficult: in your case, society has also built a wall around you. But there isn't any really essential difference, a fact that practically all A.A.'s know.

Therefore, when you members come into the world of A.A. on the outside, you can be sure that no one will care a fig that you have done time. What you are trying to be—not what you were—is all that counts with us.

Mental and emotional difficulties are sometimes very hard to take while we are trying to maintain sobriety. Yet we do see, in the long run, that transcendence over such problems is the real test of the A.A. way of living. Adversity gives us more opportunity to grow than does comfort or success. [26]

You can't have any good yesterdays until you have some good todays. I hope this is a great one for you.

Gary L.

Joshua 1:9: "I command you—be strong and courageous! Do not be afraid or discouraged. For the Lord your God is with you wherever you go."

Day 15 date ____________________

Today I will believe that my Higher Power will help me find peace and happiness.

Some years ago, some behavioral scientists were doing experiments with fish. In one experiment they placed a large fish in a glass fish tank, and every day the scientists would feed the large fish live minnows, because minnows were its favorite meal. After some time, the scientists placed a glass partition in the center of the tank and then emptied a bucket of minnows into the side opposite of the large fish. It immediately swam toward dinner but would hit the partition. It hit the partition many times and finally gave up. The message had gotten through that every time it went after the minnows it got hurt. The scientists then removed the partition, but the fish would still not go after the minnows. The minnows swam freely because the large fish had been convinced that they weren't available to it. Our Higher Power has removed the partition for our lives, and if the minnows are named Sobriety, Hope, Peace of Mind, Serenity, and Happiness, they are available to us.

Question for today: Am I willing to stop beating my head against the wall and to realize that being clean and sober is available to me?

Write about the most significant thing you experienced or learned yesterday.

Prayer for today

I pray that I will believe that my Higher Power has removed the partition for me.

10-3-08

Dear Matt,

I prayed for you this morning.

By the time I entered junior high (I understand it's now called middle school) there had been two additions to our family. First came my younger sister, and then a brother. Our home oftentimes was like a war zone on the inside, but when we left the house, our family image was great. "What will other people think?" was often said in our home.

Mom was only sixteen when she married Dad. He was twenty-three and was considered the catch of the town. He was a businessman who had a bowling alley and service station, and he played accordion in a band at his family's nightclub. By the time she was twenty-one she was a divorcee with two children and married to my stepdad. Mom was raised with an alcoholic father, and perhaps getting married at sixteen was a way to escape that environment.

My perception today is that Mom had a strong need to be in control, and that was a result from growing up in a home where she had very little control. I believe that was the root of her feelings of insecurity and inadequacy. Perhaps, as an adult, she gained some sense of security by being in control.

By the time I entered junior high, Mom and I had a dance we had created. Oh, it wasn't like the waltz or swing, but a dance we were not aware of. Just as a core of shame was growing in me, I believe Mom had it too. Mom and I had many of the characteristics of people with a "shame based identity" that John Bradshaw writes about in his book *Healing The Shame That Binds You.*

Here's how the dance worked. When I did something wrong, Mom took that as a direct reflection on her. My behavior pushed her shame button, and her response would be anger. I believe that under the anger was fear. From her place of fear and anger the shaming messages would come. She would scream, "Shame on you," or "You should be ashamed of yourself!" followed by carefully chosen words that were meant to wound. She would describe in detail how terrible I was and how I'd hurt or disappointed her. There were times that I'd have rather had a spanking. Many years later, I heard her say to someone that she could get more out of her kids by shaming them than by spanking them.

My next step in our dance was to feel that I was the worst kid in the world and then feel terribly ashamed. The next step was for her to give me the silent treatment. Sometimes several days would go by, and she would completely ignore me. My next step was to do whatever I could to get back into her good graces. I might clean my room without being told, chop wood and stack it, mow the lawn, etc., etc. I longed for her forgiveness, acceptance, and approval. I would grovel. Her next step was to forgive me and speak to me again. When the smile would reappear on her face, I was one happy kid, and so the dance would end until the next time.

We repeated the dance so many times through the years that it became second nature to us, and the core of shame in me was reinforced and continued to grow. It never occurred to me that I got the dance started by my behavior. As I said in an earlier letter, recovery has allowed me to see things in my past that I had been blind to. One way I could avoid the dance was to get someone to help me when I did something wrong, because Mom would blame them. In spite of the dynamics in our relationship, I know today that Mom always wanted the best for her kids,

Blessings,
Gary L.

Matthew 6:31–34:

"So don't worry about having enough food or drink or clothing. Why be like the pagans who are so deeply concerned about these things? Your heavenly Father already knows all your needs, and He will give you all you need from day to day if you live for him and make the Kingdom of God your primary concern. So don't worry about tomorrow, for tomorrow will bring its own worries. Today's trouble is enough for today."

Day 16 date ____________________

Today I will meditate on the Serenity Prayer. I will use the prayer to help me today.

"God, grant me the serenity."

Have you ever wondered why the prayer doesn't say, "God, **give** me the Serenity?" A grant is something that has conditions. It is not a gift. Just as an educational grant has conditions, is it possible that there are conditions for the **grant** of serenity? For example, is it possible for a person to be full of resentments and still have serenity? I think not. Then a condition of the **grant** is that he/she gets rid of resentments. Another condition might be that I forgive myself for things in my past. Will serenity and guilt mix? If serenity is missing, is it possible that some conditions of the **grant** are not being met? What are some of the conditions for your **grant**? Is acceptance of your disease one of them?

Question for today: Am I willing to look for the conditions that need to be met in order to have serenity?

Write about the most significant thing you experienced or learned yesterday.

Prayer for today

I pray that I will start identifying the conditions for the GRANT of serenity.

10-4-08

Dear Matt,

I prayed for you this morning.

While in recovery, I've had to do a lot of work in regards to the relationship I had with my mother. The awareness I have today is that she did the best she could. I know that Mom always wanted the best for her kids; she wanted us to have full and successful lives. She loved us almost to a fault. In fact, one time she defended me about an issue at school in which I was clearly at fault. Our relationship was not all negative, and there were many wonderful times with her. If Mom could have done better, she would have.

Another discovery that came with this new insight is that her core of shame, feelings of insecurity and inadequacy, and need to control were no different than mine. It was inevitable that we would have tremendous conflict. There were many years that all I could see was her side of the street. It became very easy to take the role of victim and blame her.

When I began to get honest with myself and see how I had contributed to the conflict, the door to healing was opened. As I said in an earlier letter, my perception of the growing-up years has changed significantly since I began to get honest with myself.

Rooted in God's Love:

People in the recovery process are people with painful memories. We remember our losses. We remember our sins. We remember the sins which been committed against us. It is part of the hard work of recovery to face these memories, to grieve them and to come to terms with them. But sometimes the painful memories become so powerful that it seems like nothing will be able to compete with them for our attention. The memory of pain consumes us. In times like this we need a powerful new memory that can challenge the dominance of our painful memories.

> Jesus invites us to receive a new and startling memory. "Remember me," Jesus says, "Eat the bread and drink the wine and remember that I gave my life for you. I gave my life because I love you. Take this new memory. Allow it to shape the way you think about yourself and about life and about me."

It is not that the memory of Jesus' sacrificial love erases all of our painful memories. Painful memories still have to be faced and grieved if healing is to come. But God offers us in Jesus a memory powerful enough to compete with the most powerful of painful memories. The death-grip that painful memories have had on our attention can be broken by the powerful memory of God's love.

Prayer

Help me to remember you, Lord. Help me to find a place in my mind and heart for the memory of your love for me. I want the memory of your love, Lord, to be the most powerful of my memories. I want it to be The Memory that shapes me. Help me to remember your love. Help me to remember you. Amen. 27

I really appreciate the prayers that Dale and Juanita Ryan write.

Blessings, brother,
Gary L.

Proverbs 3:21–24: "My child, don't lose sight of good planning and insight. Hang on to them, for they fill you with life and bring you honor and respect. They keep you safe on your way and keep your feet from stumbling. You can lie down without fear and enjoy pleasant dreams."

Day 17 date ___________________

Today I will meditate on the word "acceptance." I will try to understand why "acceptance" is so important to being clean and sober. "To accept the things I cannot change."

The Serenity Prayer gives us the purpose of serenity and that is so we can accept the things we cannot change. Without serenity, we are unable to grow in acceptance; consequently, we will fight the circumstances of life. Acceptance is contingent on serenity, which is contingent on meeting the conditions of the GRANT of serenity. What are some of the things we cannot change? We can't change other people, our past, or our disease, just to name a few. How much time and effort have we spent trying to change the things that can't be changed? It's really a waste of time. As we grow in acceptance, issues of life that previously tore us apart will lose their power. We can then put our efforts into changing the things we can.

Question for today: Am I willing to grow in acceptance of things I cannot change, or do I want to continue to fight life?

Write about the most significant thing you experienced or learned yesterday.

Prayer for today

I pray that I will understand the importance of growing in acceptance of things I cannot change.

10-5-08

Dear Matt,

I prayed for you this morning.

One of the things that excited me about going into junior high was that I would be able to be involved in Mrs. Wilson's music program. She was such a wonderful person. She was the most influential teacher during all of my school years. I doubt that I would have completed junior high if not for her. She affirmed and encouraged me and really cared about me. For one thing, she made me feel that I was her star. I realized many years later that she treated all of the students that way. I sang in the mixed chorus, a barbershop quartet, and a triple trio, and always sang solos at our concerts. I lived for the applause.

Another thing I enjoyed was basketball. We had a B team that was comprised of sixth- and seventh-graders and an A team that was all eighth-graders. I had a lot of natural ability and believed at the time that I was the best player on the team. In other words, I really had a "me-first" attitude. As a result, I rarely played in games because I was a ball hog and a show-off, and the concept of team play never occurred to me. I remember being so angry at the coach for not playing me. I had such a victim mentality by that time, that I was unable to see my part.

As I said in a previous letter, as I began to get honest with myself, my perception of the past changed. My sponsor, Hugh, said to me many times, "Gary, you need to get honest with yourself." Step Four: "Made a searching and fearless moral inventory of ourselves" has been a great tool in that process.

Academically, I didn't do well, because I wouldn't do assignments that I didn't want to do. On some assignments that I did complete, the work was shoddy because I was a procrastinator and threw the assignment together at the last minute. I was also the class clown and would do almost anything for attention. Consequently, I spent a lot of time in the principal's office. There were also many conferences with my teachers and parents.

By this time, I was running with the "wrong" crowd. We were considered troublemakers and punks. We vandalized property and shoplifted. We were the guys that parents told their kids to stay away from. I reveled in the attention. I also started smoking in the seventh grade and really thought I was cool. Those were very difficult years for my parents, and my behaviors caused much conflict between them. Mom wanted to protect me by blaming others for my problems, and Dad thought I should be held accountable. They were never able to get on the same page on how to deal with me.

Gary L.

I hated Dad. In fact, I hated anyone who tried to hold me accountable. As a teenager I would fantasize about killing him but never could come up with a plan that I was 100 percent sure I wouldn't get caught. That's a lot of hate to try to live with. In future letters I will share the healing that happened between us because of recovery.

Take care,
Gary L.

Ecclesiastics 7:9: "Don't be quick tempered, for anger is the friend of fools."

Proverbs 14:17: "Those who are short-tempered do foolish things, and schemers are hated."

Proverbs 16:32: "It is better to be patient than powerful; it is better to have self-control than to conquer a city."

Day 18 date ____________________

Today I will meditate on the word "courage" and try to learn where "courage" comes from. "Courage to change the things I can."

"Courage means to be of a battle-ready mind, to be vigorous. It is an action word. It's to be spiritually vigilant, alert, poised, ready to spring into action. It is the quality that enables a person to face danger and difficulty with firmness, and without fear or depression" (Author unknown). Do you see the importance of courage to our sobriety? It takes courage to accept our enemies. It takes courage to forgive. It takes courage to say, "I'm sorry." It takes courage to not grumble and complain when things don't go our way. It takes courage to stay clean and sober. It takes courage to take responsibility for our lives. God wants to give us courage. He wants us to win. He's on our side.

Question for today: Am I willing to take inventory of the things within me that need to be changed and then ask God to give me the courage to change them?

Write about the most significant thing you experienced or learned today.

Prayer for today

I pray that God will fill me with courage, in order that I might face life without fear of depression.

10-6-08

Dear Matt,

I prayed for you this morning.

At the end of the eighth grade, my parents did another geographic, and we moved to the small community of Hauser, Oregon. They had bought an old farmhouse with approximately four acres of land. Dad was really excited about the move because he had been raised on a farm in Iowa and had a vision of cows, chickens, and a garden. This would also move me away from the guys I ran with. I also saw this as an opportunity for a fresh start, to "turn over a new leaf."

After three tumultuous years of junior high, I entered Marshfield High School when I was thirteen. My eighth-grade graduation class had fewer than thirty students, and Marshfield had a student body of around nine hundred students. I was still a shrimp at four feet ten and weighed less than a hundred pounds. I had a lot of fear when school started, and it wasn't long before I felt like a misfit again.

One of my classes was choir, and I went in with the expectations of being the "guy," as I had been in junior high. What I discovered was that in a choir of around sixty students, there were many good voices. I did not stand out as I had at Empire, and, in addition to that, my voice was beginning to change. I was no longer the boy soprano who could hit the high notes. I was just another voice among many. I began that year with lofty expectations but ended with disappointment, resentment, and anger.

Again, I had the reputation of being the class clown and became more of a detriment to the choir than an asset. Continuing my role as victim, it was easy to blame everyone else for my disappointment.

I tried out for the freshman basketball team, and although I was the smallest student at Marshfield, I made the squad. I was really excited about that. A trap that I fell into many times while growing up is that I would set unrealistic expectations. Although my name was the last name on the list when it was posted, I fantasized myself as a starter and a star.

Another problem arose when we were being fitted for uniforms, because they didn't have a uniform small enough for me. I took the uniform home, and Mom tried to alter it to fit me, but she didn't shorten the jersey enough. At our first game, I tucked the long jersey into my shorts, and with a few minutes left in the game the coach put me in. When I ran onto the court, the tail of my jersey fell through the legs of my shorts, and the crowd began to laugh.

My shame center became inflamed within me. I was red with embarrassment and completely humiliated. I never returned to the team.

That was a really dark time for me. All of my hopes and expectations had been dashed by the end of the school year, and the shame within me grew. A sense of hopelessness was like a dark cloud over me. I wondered, "Will life ever work for me?"

Matt, may God surround you with His presence today. May you feel His great love for you.

Gary L.

Psalm 46:1, 2: "God is our refuge and strength, always ready to help in times of trouble. So we will not fear, even if earthquakes come, and the mountains crumble into the sea."

Day 19 date ____________________

Today I will meditate on the word "wisdom." I will try to understand the importance of "wisdom" for my life and "wisdom to know the difference."

How often do we put time and effort into trying to change the things that cannot be changed and then do nothing about the things that can be changed? I believe the reason that we do that is because we lack "wisdom to know the difference." We need wisdom in order to differentiate between what can and what cannot be changed.

How blessed is the person who finds wisdom and the one who gains understanding. For its profit is better than the profit of silver and its gain than fine gold. Wisdom is more precious than jewels; and nothing you desire compares with her. Keep sound wisdom and discretion, so they will be life to your soul, and adornment to your neck. Then you will walk in your way securely, and your foot will not stumble, when you lie down you will not be afraid; when you lie down, your sleep will be sweet (Proverbs 3:21–24, NASB).

Wouldn't it be great to lie down without fear and to have sweet sleep? As we grow in wisdom, fears will decrease and sweet sleep will increase.

Question for today: Am I willing to ask my God for wisdom, or do I still believe that I can figure things out by myself?

Write about the most significant thing you experienced or learned yesterday.

Prayer for today

I pray that I will become a seeker of wisdom and understanding, knowing that as I seek, I will find.

10-7-08

Dear Matt,

I prayed for you this morning.

Soon after we moved to Hauser after the eighth grade, I met twin brothers who were in the same grade as me but were a year older. We spent a lot of time roaming the sand dunes that were nearby and exploring old logging roads. A small lake nearby was where we fished.

During that summer, their family left for an extended vacation. While they were gone, I broke into homes, a man's workshop, did acts of vandalism, and stole items to sell. Someone saw me break into the shop and reported me to the police. I had taken a lot of hand tools. When the police arrived at our home, I was without excuse because I did the crime alone. There was no one to blame. The man decided not to press charges if I would return his tools. I hadn't sold them yet so I returned them. My parents were so angry, and Dad really worked me over after the police left. That incident left absolutely no impression on me, and I decided that I just needed to be more careful the next time. When my friends returned from vacation, I was able to drag them into acts of vandalism and stealing. Not surprisingly, Mom thought they were a bad influence on me. She was in so much denial about who I really was.

During my freshman year at Marshfield I met a kid named George (not his real name), who was also a misfit of sorts. George was the son of a bank president and had been born with a severe spinal defect. As a child, he had numerous surgeries and had spent long periods in hospitals. Even with all the medical expertise of the time, George had severe curvature of the spine and could not completely straighten up. To compound his problem, George had a poor relationship with his father. George's father had been a great athlete when he was young, was popular, and was considered a big man on campus. George felt alienated from his father and was doted on by his mother. George grew up with an attitude and had difficulty getting friendships, just like me. I'll never forget one example of how his mother spoiled him; George's mother brought him to our home to spend a couple of days with me. After we got up the first morning I began to make my bed. George was stunned that I sleep on the same sheets two days in a row. His mother not only changed his sheets every day, she also ironed them. One of the benefits from being a friend of George was that his parents were generous. They were grateful that George finally had a best friend. That year I was invited to attend the state high school basketball tournament in Eugene with George and his father. His dad not only paid for everything, he also gave me spending money. The summer after our freshman year his parents invited me to attend the state fair for several days with them. Again, all expenses were paid by his parents, and they again gave me spending money. I thought, "This is one sweet deal." By the time we started our sophomore year, his parents began to suspect I was working them. I would ignore George for extended periods of time, but when I was invited to do something fun, and they were paying the bill, I was right there. When it was time for the state basketball tournament that year I was invited. They said that I would have to pay my way. I dropped George like a dirty sock. By this time in my life the only value I saw in people was about what they could do for me. I stayed in relationships as long as something was in it for me. People were merely pawns in the game of life. I had become so hard on the inside that I felt no guilt or shame about that. Early in recovery I began to see how I had gone through life using people and not caring about anyone but myself. When I was younger, Dad would often say, "You are so self-centered." That's a hard way to go through life, and I had to get real honest with myself about that. Something else happened during the spring of my sophomore year: I took my first drink of alcohol.

There was a great meditation in the *Twenty-Four Hours a Day* book yesterday.

Meditation for the Day

The Unseen God can help to make us truly grateful and humble. Since we cannot see God, we must believe in Him without seeing. What we can see clearly is the change in a human being, when we sincerely ask God for the strength to change. We should cling to faith in God and in His power to change our ways. Our faith in an Unseen God will be rewarded by a useful and serviceable life. God will not fail to show us the way we should live, when in real gratitude and true humility we turn to Him.

Prayer for the Day

I pray that I may believe that God can change me. I pray that I may be always willing to be changed for the better. 28

Matt, as you've probably discovered by now, I have many opinions and theories. I don't claim to be an authority on anything but my own spiritual journey. Take the things that are helpful and set the rest aside.

God is so good,

Gary L.

Psalm 23:24: "For he has not ignored the suffering of the needy. He has not turned and walked away. He has listened to their cry for help."

Day 20 date ____________________

Today I will compare myself between now and my first day of treatment and try to see how much growth has happened.

Growth is a funny thing. It's difficult to see, especially on a day-to-day basis. Two men each planted the same size and kind of tree on the same day. Every day for a year, one of the men looked at his tree. After a year, he became very discouraged because his tree didn't seem to be growing. The other man watered and fertilized his tree at the proper times but paid little attention to its growth. After a year, he measured his tree and was amazed and excited at how much his tree had grown. Sometimes it's difficult to see our growth on a daily basis, but we are growing, if we're doing the things we need to do. Perhaps if we just do what we need to do daily and quit trying to see our growth, we will not become discouraged with our progress.

Question for today: Am I willing to believe that I really am growing, or is it necessary that I see evidence on a daily basis?

Write about the most significant thing you experienced or learned today.

Prayer for today

I pray that I will surrender my growth to my God, knowing that His timing is perfect in all things.

10-8-08

Dear Matt,

I prayed for you this morning.

I had two firsts during the spring of my sophomore year in high school. One, I skipped school for the first time. In spite of all my acting out in school, I had never skipped. The second was that I had my first drink of alcohol. I had made a vow when I was twelve or thirteen that I would never drink alcohol. The reason for the vow was that my alcoholic grandpa moved in with us.

After grandma had kicked him out, he was shuffled between the homes of his adult children until he wore his welcome out. Well, it was our turn. I know that Grandma helped him financially, but he also had another source of income that was either some kind of disability or Social Security. One time he got to the mail before Mom and intercepted his check. He disappeared, and the next thing I remember was a call from the police station. He had gotten drunk and involved in a bar fight and had been arrested. Dad went to the jail, bailed him out, and brought him home. Sometime later, he was on the loose again, and this time a bartender called for someone to come and get him. When Dad got there, Grandpa didn't want to leave, and they almost came to blows. Grandpa, after much coaxing, came home with Dad. I remember the screaming match between Mom and Dad. Mom wanted to take care of him, and Dad wanted him gone.

Another thing I remember about that incident was the smell in the house when Grandpa messed the bed and threw up in it. That's when I made the vow, "I will never drink alcohol."

So, on that beautiful spring day some years later, I reneged on the vow. Many students skipped school that day and went to the sand dunes to play. I was with three guys. One of them had an uncle that made wine, so we went by his house and took a case from the back porch. When we got to the dunes, the first bottle was opened and passed around.

At first I declined, but by the time the bottle was passed around again, I took a big swig. I gagged because the taste was horrible. I don't think I'd ever had anything that tasted that vile. It was homemade raisin wine. After the initial gagging, I felt a warmth on the inside that was like nothing I'd ever felt. It was magic to me. "Why doesn't everyone drink?" I wondered.

I did not drink like a normal person that day. One of the things I remember was that all of my fear went away. I was ready to take on the world. I became the life of the party and became extremely drunk. It took the guys several hours to get me sober enough to take me home. Without knowing it, I turned my will and life over to the care of alcohol that day. It became my higher power and my ruler for the next sixteen years. I believe today that I was an alcoholic just waiting for the first drink.

The following morning when I awoke, I had a horrible hangover, went to the bathroom, and violently threw up until there was nothing left. That was followed by the dry heaves. I said to myself, "I will never drink again." That was the first of many times during the following sixteen years that I quit forever.

Within a week, I had "forgotten" how sick I had been and remembered the feeling alcohol gave me, and I got drunk again. This was on beer, and I couldn't stand the taste of it either. I began living for the weekend parties. The biggest challenge for me was to find something with alcohol in it that tasted good. Everything I tried tasted horrible to me, but I was willing to endure the taste in order to get to the feeling.

I was fifteen when I received my first minor in possession charge. Mom and Dad were so disappointed. I would continue to disappoint them for many years.

I liked the meditation in the *Twenty-Four Hours a Day* book this morning.

Meditation for the Day

Pray—and keep praying until it brings peace and serenity and a feeling of communion with One who is near and ready to help. The thought of God is balm for our hates and fears. In praying to God, we find healing for hurt feelings and resentments. In thinking of God, doubts and fears leave us. Instead of those doubts and fears, there will flow into our hearts such faith and love as is beyond the power of material things to give, and such peace as the world can neither give nor take away. And with God, we can have the tolerance to live and let live.

Prayer for the Day

I pray that I may have true tolerance and understanding. I pray that I may keep striving for these difficult things. 29

Forgiving others is a balm for our soul.

God is great!

Gary L.

Psalm 18:1–2 "I love you, Lord; you are my strength. The Lord is my rock, my fortress, and my savior; my God is my rock, in whom I find protection. He is my shield, the strength of my salvation, and my stronghold."

Day 21 date _____________________

Today I will believe that all of life's difficulties are important for my spiritual growth.

A man picked up an agate on a beach one day and decided to polish it in a rock tumbler. After the agate had been in the tumbler for several days, the man removed it, only to discover that it still looked the same. He learned that one agate by itself will not polish. He then placed two agates in the tumbler. After several days he removed the agates, only to discover that although they had beat each other up pretty well, they still were not polished. He then placed the agates in the tumbler, but this time he added a polishing compound. After several days of the agates rubbing against each other with a polishing compound present, he removed two beautiful, shiny, agates. Do you suppose that as we have conflict with people that rub us the wrong way, that if we use spiritual principles as the polishing compound, we too can begin to shine?

Question for today: Am I willing to see the spiritual benefit of people who rub me the wrong way?

Write about the most significant thing you experienced or learned yesterday.

Prayer for today

I pray that as I learn to apply spiritual principles to the conflicts of life that I will begin to shine.

10-9-08

Dear Matt,

I prayed for you this morning.

I received your letter yesterday, and it's always good to hear from you. I'm glad that the spiritual journal has been helpful. My belief is that God wants to save you, heal you, help you, and equip you to pass on a message of hope to others. Wouldn't that be a great purpose for your life?

Toward the end of my sophomore year, I acted out in choir. The choir director had her back to us while she was writing on the blackboard. I had some small exploding devices called cherry bombs that exploded on impact, and I threw one at the blackboard. When it exploded, she screamed, turned toward the class, and looked directly at me. I thought what I did was hilarious, but very few of the students laughed. Well, another trip to the principal's office.

After talking to me, and me not taking what he was saying very seriously, he made a suggestion. He thought it would be a very good idea for me to attend North Bend High School the following year. He intimated that life might be very difficult if I didn't transfer. In other words, if I returned to Marshfield, I was dead meat. My parents were informed of his recommendation and agreed that a fresh start in a different school might help. Turning over a new leaf was becoming routine.

The summer after my sophomore year I tried to get drunk as often as possible. I had an upstairs bedroom, and late at night my friends would raise a ladder to my window, and away we'd go to drink and raise Cain. The ploy worked until the night I threw up on the side of the house. My night wandering was brought to a halt.

Until I got caught, my friends and I had a routine. A tavern several miles away stored beer on the back porch. I still don't remember how we discovered that. One of the twins would go into the tavern and order a beer. He was obviously underage and would be refused. He'd then cause a scene, and while that was going on his brother and I would each grab a case of beer from the back porch and take off running. After getting the beer, it was party time. Mom and Dad wondered why it was difficult to get me up in the morning.

My friends had a 1947 Fraser, and we'd drive to North Bend. There was a parking lot behind the buildings on the main street of town, and many loggers and longshoremen parked there while they were drinking in the bars. During the '50s, few people locked their cars. We'd sneak through the parking lot, opening car doors and looking for bottles stashed under the front seat.

Between the tavern and the cars, we were able to keep a substantial supply of alcohol.

During our nightly adventures, we did acts of vandalism. We lived near Highway 101, and we'd climb a high bank along the highway and throw eggs at passing cars. We thought it was hilarious when we hit our target. When cars stopped, we'd take off running. Another time we found a bag of roofing nails and threw them on the highway. Anger, hate, and vindictiveness drove me. Today, because of what God has done in my life, I look back and wonder, "Who was that kid?"

One of the great promises in scripture is Philippians 1:6. The *New Living Translation* says it this way, "God, who began a good work within you, will continue his work until it is finally finished on that day when Christ Jesus comes back again."

I really enjoy the NLT, not only because it is easy to read, but because it also has great footnotes that tie our recovery to scripture. Here's an example of footnotes regarding Philippians 2:1–11.

> We are never an island unto our self; we are a part of a whole, a member of Christ's body. If we are part of a loving community, when others hurt, we hurt; when we hurt, others hurt. Early in the recovery process we may need to concentrate on our own welfare. But as we grow, we have to move beyond self-centeredness and become interested in others. Part of making amends to people we have harmed is showing them that we have changed. As we love others, we will find that others will love us. As our relationships grow stronger, our addiction will lose its grip on us.
>
> Jesus Christ is our ideal model for humility in obedience and service. Our thoughts, attitudes, and actions are to be patterned after Christ. His willingness to humbly obey his Father is a great example for us. As we take an honest moral inventory of our life, we must humbly admit our faults so we can begin to change our destructive patterns. If we follow Jesus Christ in humility, learning to admit our failures without hesitation, nothing will be able to stop our recovery. 30
>
> I read this in *As Bill Sees It* this morning:
>
> A man who persists in prayer finds himself in possession of great gifts. When he has to deal with hard circumstances, he finds he can

face them. He can accept himself and the world around him.

He can do this because he now accepts a God who is All—and who loves all. When he says, "Our Father who art in heaven, hallowed be Thy name," he deeply and humbly means it. When in good meditation and thus freed from the clamors of the world, he knows that he is in God's hands, that his own ultimate destiny is really secure, here and hereafter, come what may. 31

Blessings,

Gary L.

Psalm 55:22: "Give your burdens to the Lord, and he will take care of you. He will not permit the godly to slip and fall."

Day 22 date ____________________

Today I will not take anybody's inventory but my own. I will practice tolerance and understanding today.

If a person was going to invest in a business, one of the first things he would do would be to take a complete inventory. He would want to know both positive and negative aspects of the business. As we take an honest and fearless moral inventory of ourselves, it is important that we look at both positive and negative aspects. God wants to help us take inventory in a way that does not defeat or discourage us, but so we can identify the giants within. A giant cannot be killed until it's identified. Oftentimes it is easy to take inventory of all the things outside of us that have caused us pain and then blame the condition of our life on those things. God wants to set us free of the "blame game," because that too can be a giant.

Question for today: Am I willing to take an honest, fearless, moral inventory of myself, or am I going to keep playing the "blame game?"

Write about the most significant thing you experienced or learned yesterday.

Prayer for today

I pray that as I take personal inventory, I will not condemn myself with what I discover.

10-10-08

Dear Matt,

I prayed for you this morning.

I began my junior year at North Bend High School, but that was the last place in the world I wanted to be. I continued to cause problems at school and at home. I had become defiant and oppositional and couldn't stand anyone telling me what to do. I failed my subjects because I would not study or do homework. The school authorities did not know what to do with me, nor did my parents. I continued to drink whenever I could. I had another minor in possession charge, and my standard response to threats of consequences was, "I don't care," and I didn't. I thought the school year would never end. Skipping school that year was standard routine for me.

My older sister was going with a guy who was the son of a doctor who hired a student each summer to work at his summer cabin. The doctor hired me, and I was excited about that. On his property was a building that was used to process cranberries from his cranberry bog. A corner of the building was partitioned off into a room for me. I was paid one dollar per hour and had free room and board for the summer. That was a sweet deal for a kid in the '50s. The job included cutting wood, carpentry work, processing cranberries, and clearing brush. I worked hard during the day, but at night I would leave with friends and do the things I had done the previous summer: steal, vandalize, and get drunk. I had a place in the cranberry shed where I hid my stash of alcohol, and I still remember the panic I felt when my supply was low. I had a tremendous fear that I would run out.

After the summer ended I returned to school, but it was obvious to everyone that I probably would not graduate. I was way behind in credits because of all the failed classes, and I had no intention of trying to make them up. I skipped frequently and had many trips to the principal's office.

There was a grove of trees close to school property where many of us would go at noon to smoke. On occasion, someone had some alcohol to share. One day after drinking at noon, we returned to school and were met by the principal. Someone had snitched, and he was waiting for us. He would not allow us onto school property and said that in order to get back into school we'd need to bring a parent. I was so angry because I knew what the repercussions would be at home.

After the conference, I was allowed back in school. On a Friday night I went to the football game. As I was walking through the parking lot, I saw the principal's new car. With vengeance in my heart, I walked the length of his car and raked the paint down to bare metal with a key. I felt completely justified in doing that. After all, he had gotten me into a lot of trouble. Oh, how deceived I was. I could not see my part.

Shortly before I turned seventeen, the authorities who were involved in my life and my parents had a meeting. Out of that meeting came an ultimatum to me—be sent to McLaren School for Boys, a juvenile correction facility, or join the military when I turned seventeen. The military would not take someone like me today. Their standards have changed since the '50s, but back then the military was used to "make men" out of guys like me. The day before I turned seventeen I boarded a bus to Portland and was sworn into the navy the next day.

Once again turning over a new leaf, I was actually excited about joining the navy. By this time, I was sick of my life and saw the navy as an opportunity for a new start.

I am so grateful that God gives us a fresh start.

Psalm 16:11: "You will show me the way of life, granting me the joy of your presence and the pleasures of living with you forever."

Wow! What a promise.

Gary L.

John 16:33: "I have told you all this so that you may have peace in me. Here on earth you will have many trials and sorrows. But take heart, because I have overcome the world."

Day 23 date ___________________

Today I will look at the areas of my life that need pruning.

Two men who lived next to each other in the country decided that they would each plant an orchard. One man diligently plowed and fertilized the ground and then carefully planted the new trees; the other man just planted his. As time went by, the first man was careful to prune, spray, and fertilize his trees at the proper times, while the second man just let his grow. When it came time for the first harvest, the first man's orchard had a bountiful harvest of beautiful, large, and disease-free fruit. The second man also had a crop to harvest, but the fruit was small, withered, and diseased. Just as pruning is necessary in an orchard, it is also necessary in our lives. We need the areas of our life that defeat us to be pruned. Could we say that our Higher Power is like the first man, and the second is like "self-will run riot?"

Question for today: Am I willing to surrender myself to be pruned so that I too can produce a bountiful harvest?

Write about the most significant thing you experienced or learned yesterday.

Prayer for today

I pray I will understand that pruning is vitally necessary for new growth to happen.

10-11-08

Dear Matt,

I prayed for you this morning.

I don't know about you, but trusting others was difficult for much of my life. I'm still not where I'd like to be, but much further ahead from where I was. My trust in God has also grown, whereas in the beginning of sobriety I had zero trust in God. Since those early days, He has proven Himself to me over and over again. During the end of my drinking, I would have been described as angry, self-centered, selfish, bitter, self-pitying, depressed, resentful, and vengeful. That's a hard way to live. Until God began bringing me out of those places, I was very suicidal at times. I could shift from great feelings of hope to thinking, "I wonder what it would be like to be dead?" When I entrusted my life to God is when life began to change.

My part is to take an honest inventory in order to see what needs changing. As long as I'm playing the blame game, justifying, rationalizing, and playing the victim, I won't be able to see the flaws.

Here's another meditation from *Rooted in God's Love*:

> It is easy for us to lose our way. We may start off with confidence. We think we know where we are and where we are headed. And, then, somewhere along the way in life we get lost. We find ourselves alone and we don't know where we are. We get confused and disoriented. We don't know how to find our way back, how to get "on track" again. Fortunately, God pays attention. God notices that we are lost. And, because of the great value God sees in us, God sets out to find us. God searches for us. God pursues us until we are found.
>
> When God finds us, most of us expect God to say: "Where have you been? I've been looking all over for you! Can't you follow directions? What's wrong with you? I don't want to have to come back out here again to find you." But there is not a hint of scolding, shaming, yelling or blaming in this text. When God finds us, God is full of joy. God picks us up and carries us home. God celebrates.

God pays attention, notices when we are lost, searches for us and celebrates when we are found. Recovery is the gift of being found by God.

Prayer

I was lost, Lord. Alone. Disoriented. Confused. Afraid. You found me. I expected blame rejection when you found me. I expected you to be full of rage. I expected you to see me as an inconvenience. But you greeted me with joy. With celebration! Thank you for finding me. Thank you for carrying me home with joy. Amen. 32

I had to stop running from God long enough, so He could find me. Someone said, "God loves me so much that he carries a picture of me in His wallet." Isn't that a great thought?

Blessings,
Gary L.

Nahum 1:7: "The Lord is good. When trouble comes, he is a strong refuge. And he knows everyone who trusts in him."

Day 24 date ____________________

Today I will meditate on the "grace of God," and how that grace affects my life.

We often hear the term, "The grace of God." But do we understand what that means? The word "grace" means unmerited favor. In other words, grace is a gift that can't be earned by our efforts. Most of the gifts we receive are for special occasions, while the gift of grace is for all occasions. Sometimes we think that God's grace is available to us only when we perform well. I like to view the "grace of God" as the part of God's character that covers all the areas of my life that He hasn't changed yet. Is it possible for us as we receive the "grace of God" on our lives, to let it flow through us to the people we come in contact with?

Question for today: Am I willing to let the "grace of God" flow through me, or do I just want to be a receiver of grace and not a giver?

Write about the most significant thing you experienced or learned yesterday.

Prayer for today

I pray that I will be a channel of God's grace today; I pray that grace will dominate my relationships today.

10-12-08

Dear Matt:

I prayed for you this morning.

Today I just want to share with you some great meditation material from three of the books I use. I'll continue my story in the next letter.

Twenty-Four Hours a Day

A.A. Thought for the Day

Today is ours. Let us live today as we believe God wants us to live. Each day will have a new pattern that which we cannot foresee. But we can open each day with a quiet period in which we say a little prayer, asking God to help us through the day. Personal contact with God, as we understand Him, will from day to day bring us nearer to an understanding of His will for us. At the close of the day, we offer Him thanks for another day of sobriety. A full, constructive day has been lived and we are grateful. *Am I asking God each day for strength and thanking Him each night?*

Meditation for the Day

If you believe that God's grace has saved you, then you must believe that He is meaning to save you yet more and to keep you in the way that you should go. Even human rescuers would not save you from drowning only to place you in other deep and dangerous waters. Rather, they would place you on dry land, there to restore you. God, who is your rescuer, would certainly do this and even more. God will complete the task He sets out to do. He will not throw you overboard, if you are depending on Him.

Prayer for the Day

I pray that I may trust God to keep me in the way. I pray that I may rely on Him not to let me go. 33

As Bill Sees It

A New Life

Is sobriety all that we are to expect of a spiritual awakening? No, sobriety is only a bare beginning; it is only the first gift of the first awakening. If more gifts are to be received, our awakening has to go on. As it does go on, we find that bit by bit we can discard the old life—the one that did not work—for a new life that can and does work under any conditions whatever.

Regardless of worldly success or failure, regardless of pain or joy, regardless of sickness or health or even of death itself, a new life of endless possibilities can be lived if we are willing to continue our awakening, through the practice of A.A.'s Twelve Steps. 34

Grace for the Moment, by Max Lucado

Repentance Is a Decision

No one is happier than the one who has sincerely repented of wrong. Repentance is the decision to turn from selfish desires and seek God. It is a genuine, sincere regret that creates sorrow and moves us to admit wrong and desire to do better.

It's an inward conviction that expresses itself in outward actions.

You look at the love of God and you can't believe he's loved you like he has, and this realization motivates you to change your life. That is the nature of repentance. 35

A shorter definition of repentance is "a change of direction." I was headed in a direction that was going to kill me. God's grace changed the direction of my life. I am so grateful! Ponder those writings.

Take care, my friend,
Gary L.

Matthew 11:28–30: "Then Jesus said, 'Come to me, all of you who are weary and carry heavy burdens, and I will give you rest. Take my yoke upon you. Let me teach you, because I am humble and gentle, and you will find rest for your souls. For my yoke fits perfectly, and the burden I give you is light.'"

Day 25 date ___________________

Today I will be attentive to positive thoughts. I will set aside negativism.

For a few moments, view your mind as a radio receiver. Although there are many stations broadcasting, a radio can only tune in clearly one station at a time. There is a station with the call letters, "DISEASE" that is broadcasting. Its messages are like these: "You'll never make it," "What's the use?" "You're different," "You don't need these people," etc. All of its broadcasting is negative. There is another station with the call letters "SOBRIETY." It broadcasts messages such as: "You can make it," "You have value," "There is a purpose for your life," "You are forgiven," etc. If you were listening to your radio and a station was broadcasting something you didn't like, what would you do? You would probably change the station. Our responsibility is to change the station when we're tuned in to the one that wants to destroy us.

Question for today: Am I willing to tune in to the station called "SOBRIETY," or do I still want to listen to negative messages?

Write about the most significant thing you experienced or learned yesterday.

Prayer for today

I pray that I will tune in to the positive station today. If the negative station invades my mind, I pray for the strength to change the dial.

10-13-08

Dear Matt,

I prayed for you this morning.

Well, there I was, just turned seventeen and was a member of the US Navy. I was full of fear and anxiety on one hand but excited and hopeful on the other. I saw this as a new start and was determined to make it work and hoped that I would not mess it up.

After being sworn in at Portland, I boarded a flight for San Diego, where I would go through boot camp at the US Navy Training Facility. Boot camp was very difficult because of my size. I was five feet four and weighed around 120 pounds. I barely made the minimums set by the navy. I was the smallest guy in my company and looked like a child compared to my peers.

In addition to my physical limitations, I had difficulty staying awake in classes and procrastinated on studying. As a result, when we took final exams, I failed. I was the only one in the company that was not allowed to graduate. As a result of my failure, I was placed in a company that would graduate in one week and was given another chance. I was crushed, embarrassed, humiliated by my failure, and angry at the navy. All of my dozing in class and my procrastination had caught up with me, but I didn't want to look at that. I passed the exam the second time around. What a relief!

After boot camp, I was assigned to a ship that home-ported in Seattle. I rode from San Diego to Seattle on a Greyhound bus. That was a long bus ride. I reported to the ship, and after some orientation, I was assigned to work in an engine room. In boot camp, we took aptitude tests, and it was determined that I had some mechanical aptitude, and so I was designated as an engineman.

After being on board for a short while, I was invited by some shipmates to go to the Enlisted Men's Club on base. There was not an age requirement to drink on base, and I thought that was very cool. I could hardly wait. I had not had a drink for several months, and now I could drink legally. Well, before the night was over, I put on quite a show for my buddies. I ended up dancing on a table, and we were asked to leave. That's the last thing I remember before waking up in my bunk the following morning. My shipmates filled me in on the rest of the night. On the way back to the ship, I passed out, and they had to carry me on board. As they carried me down to where my bunk was, I began to vomit. Of course, they ended up cleaning up my mess. After they gave me the details, I couldn't wait to go back to the club and do it again. I saw that as having a really good time.

The ship I was on was the USS *Koiner* DER 331, which was a converted World War II destroyer escort. The "R" in the designation stood for radar. Our duty was to go out in the Pacific Ocean for twenty-one to twenty-five days on what was called picket duty. With the radar turned on, we would patrol a designated area of the West Coast and be on the alert for possible attacks on the United States. There was much fear about the USSR during that time. When we returned to port, we did maintenance on the engines and then we'd go out again. While at sea I had a break from drinking, but as soon as I could, after getting back in port, I headed for the Enlisted Men's Club to drink. In spite of drinking every chance that I had, I worked hard in the engine room and was promoted to engineman third class. I was moving up!

After approximately a year and a half in Seattle, our ship was transferred to Pearl Harbor. I could hardly wait to get there. I desperately wanted to be able to drink in the bars there, but I was underage. I applied for a new ID card, claiming that I had lost mine. I'd figured out a way to change the birth date on the card and altered it as soon as it was issued to me. There were grave consequences for doing that if I was caught, but I was willing to take the chance. By the time we arrived at Pearl Harbor, I was ready to party!

I like the writing in the *Twenty-Four Hours a Day* book this morning.

Meditation for the Day

God's kingdom on earth is growing slowly, like a seed in the ground. In the growth of His kingdom there is always progress among the few who are out ahead of the crowd. Keep striving for something better and there can be no stagnation in your life. Eternal life, abundant life, is yours for the seeking. Do not misspend time over past failures. Count the lessons learned from failures as rungs upon the ladder of progress. Press onward toward the goal.

Prayer for the Day

I pray that I may be willing to grow. I pray that I may keep stepping up on the rungs of the ladder of life. 36

Keep growing,
Gary L.

Gary L.

Proverbs 14:29–30: "Those who control their anger have great understanding; those with hasty temper will make mistakes. A relaxed attitude lengthens life; jealousy rots it away."

Day 26 date ___________________

Today I will try to grow in understanding of my Higher Power. I will think of the ways He has helped me since I've been in treatment.

I heard a man say that he had worked the first three steps of the AA program in relation to alcohol as a Higher Power. He explained that at the age of fifteen he felt powerless over many problems of life. He took his first drink at the age of fifteen and no longer felt powerless. Up to that time in his life, he had never found anything that would do for him what alcohol did. He came to believe in the power of the alcohol. He then turned his will and his life over to it. Do you think that prior to taking the first drink he was searching for a power that would help him in his life, but what he found was a counterfeit?

Question for today: Am I willing to turn my life and will over to the care of God, or am I still convinced that I can run my own life?

Write about the most significant thing you experienced or learned today.

Prayer for today

I pray for the strength and courage to help me turn my life and will over to the care of God.

10-14-08

Dear Matt,

I prayed for you this morning.

For many years, I believed that things outside of me were the cause of my problems. But I began to discover early in recovery that I was my primary problem. I couldn't do anything about the externals except change the way I reacted to them. For example, I can respond with anger, self-pity, or take the victim stance, or I can respond with love, acceptance, forgiveness, compassion, understanding, etc. The second responses are spiritual responses, whereas the first responses come from my self-centeredness. I began to understand that as God began to change the inside of me, He would help me to react to externals in ways that are more appropriate.

By the way, this is a lifelong process. Recovery is not a destination, it is a journey. The Big Book (what we in AA often call *Alcoholics Anonymous*) states on page 60:

> Many of us exclaimed, "What an order! I can't go through with it." Do not be discouraged. No one among us has been able to maintain anything like perfect adherence to these principles. We are not saints. The point is, that we are willing to grow along spiritual lines. The principles we have set down are guides to progress. We claim spiritual progress rather than spiritual perfection. 37

That quote has saved many of us who struggle with perfectionism or have black and white thinking. (It's all or nothing)

Psychiatrists and psychologists use the term narcissistic to describe some people. In AA we use the term "self-centeredness." A narcissist believes they're really important and his or her wants and needs are more important than others. Life really does revolve with them at the center. They're grandiose about their achievements even if they're imaginary. Their specialness causes them to seek out people with status, and they believe that others admire them. They're acutely aware how they believe they should be treated by others, with little awareness of how they should treat others. They may look extremely confident on the outside in order to be admired by others. They are quick to take advantage of others to get what they want. They believe they're entitled to have success without earning it and that others owe them allegiance. They have little empathy for what others go through. Some can be very arrogant but don't think they are. Some will have some sense that who they are on the inside is not what people see, and they live in fear of discovery. Dishonesty and deceit is a way of life for many.

That pretty much describes who I was when I entered the rooms of AA. I didn't have all of the characteristics, but most of them.

God has not removed all of the characteristics that fit me, but He has worked in them. Because of the way He has changed me and is continuing to change me, I am not the same person that I was when I got sober. Philippians 1:6 promises that He will complete the work He began in us. That is a great promise.

The *Twelve and Twelve* states this on page 76:

> The chief activator of our defects has been self-centered fear—primarily fear that we would lose something we already possessed or would fail to get something we demanded. Living upon a basis of unsatisfied demands, we were in a state of continual disturbance and frustration. Therefore, no peace was to be had unless we could find a means of reducing these demands. The difference between a demand and a simple request is plain to anyone. 38

The following is from *Rooted in God's Love*:

> **Change**
>
> The hardest part of recovery is that it requires us to change. We might be intrigued by the idea of recovery. We might be inspired by stories about recovery. We might be convinced of our need for recovery. These and many other cognitive processes are relatively easy for us. But the doing of recovery is will be hard because we must change. And change is difficult.
>
> We understandably resist change. We are angry that we have to change. We feel shame that we need to change. And we are

afraid that we will not be able to change. We know that there will be moments when we'll find ourselves saying "I can't do it. It's too difficult."

But change is also the most exhilarating part of recovery. We don't have to live in bondage to our addictions. We don't have to run in fear from relationships. We don't have to live as if we were responsible for the world. We can learn serenity. We can find freedom. We can experience love. [39]

Well, pal, I gave you a lot to think about today. Don't strain your brain!

Gary L.

Day 27 date ___________________

Today I will try to be as open and honest as possible. I will let people see the real me.

A chameleon is a strange little lizard. It changes color to fit its environment. Because of our need to fit, have we sometimes been like the chameleon? A man said that one day he would wear a suit and drink martinis with businesspeople and the next day wear old jeans and drink cheap wine in a tavern. The interesting thing was that he had the ability to change "colors" in order to fit either place. Were either of the two people the real him, or was he just performing because of his need to fit? Our Higher Power wants to help us discover who the real us is. Many have been so busy changing "colors," that they never discover who they really are. The primary reason the chameleon changes color is to protect itself. Has our performing also been a protection so that people won't discover who we really are?

Question for today: Am I willing to let people discover the real me, or am I still afraid?

Write about the most significant thing you experienced or learned yesterday.

Prayer for today

I pray that as I begin to discover the real me, I will be able to let others see that person.

10-15-08

Dear Matt,

I prayed for you this morning.

I believe that I had alcoholic thinking before I took my first drink. Looking back, I see how my beliefs and values were so skewed. For example, when our ship arrived at Pearl Harbor in 1958, I could hardly wait to check out the bars armed with my new fake ID card. Some of my shipmates bought expensive cameras so that they could explore the island and take pictures of the scenery. That made absolutely no sense to me. Why waste money on a camera when you could use that money to party. I saw what they were doing as total nonsense. One of the things I discovered about my alcoholic mind is that sometimes right things seem wrong and wrong things seem right. My perspective is so different today.

As soon as possible after our arrival at Pearl Harbor, I was told about a street called Hotel Street. My first trip there I was in awe. Both sides of Hotel Street were lined with bars and a number of tattoo shops. To me, it was the most exciting place I'd ever seen. That's some more of that skewed thinking. Two of my many character defects at the time that were linked closely together were grandiosity and "big-shot-ism." It was common for me to buy drinks for my buddies and the many women in the bars. That really made me feel important. The statement, "Get drunk and be somebody." was a way of life for me.

Well, as you probably know, a serviceman's pay is not that great, so in order to carry out my role as a big shot, I began to borrow money from my shipmates, who were more than willing to loan money at a very high rate of interest. One day, the day before payday, I wanted to party, but I was broke. I borrowed ten bucks from a guy and agreed to pay him back twenty the next day. Before long, I was in debt to the loan sharks more than my ability to repay. It's pretty difficult to avoid someone on a small ship, and there were times I would borrow from one person in order to pay someone else back. It became a vicious cycle, and the pressure was really on. It never occurred to me that if I stopped drinking and borrowing, I could get my financial mess straightened out.

Another element that was involved was I liked to gamble but was lousy at it. I remember being so angry at the guys who were charging such a high rate of interest. Duh, I was the one asking for the loan. No one was twisting my arm.

Here's another meditation from the *Twenty-Four Hours a Day* book.

Meditation for the Day

To God, a miracle of change in a person's life is only a natural happening. But it is a natural happening operated by spiritual forces. There is no miracle in personalities too marvelous to be an everyday happening. But miracles happen only to those who are fully guided and strengthened by God. Marvelous changes in people's natures happen so simply, and yet they are free from all other agencies than the grace of God. But these miracles have been prepared for by days and months of longing for something better. They are always accompanied by a real desire to conquer self and to surrender one's life to God.

Prayer for the Day

I pray that I may expect miracles in the lives of people. I pray that I may be used to help people change. [40]

Blessings
Gary L.

Day 28 date ____________________

Today I will meditate on the word "hope," and I will be grateful for the hope that I now have.

Many years ago, a group of people were in bondage to a powerful nation, and they were treated as slaves. The people prayed that God would set them free and give them a new land to live in. God promised them a new land and then raised up a leader to lead them there. The new land was to be a paradise. The leader united the people and began leading them away from the nation they were in captivity to. The leader of that nation did not want them to leave, so he sent his army after them. God performed a miracle and destroyed the army. The people were really excited about what God had done. Amazingly, within a few days after the miracle, some of the people wanted to return to the country where they had been slaves. Why do you think they wanted to return? Tomorrow we'll look at some possible reasons.

Question for today: Am I willing to go forward to the land called "Sobriety," or does the old land of slavery still appeal to me?

Write about the most significant thing you experienced or learned yesterday.

Prayer for today

I pray that I will be grateful for the miracle of recovery that's been started in my life.

10-16-08

Dear Matt,

I prayed for you this morning.

As I was approaching the completion of three years in the navy, my life was a mess. Although I had risen in rank, becoming a second-class petty officer, I still did not make enough money to live the lifestyle I desired. Consequently, I ended up with more debt than I could pay back. Shipmates who I owed money began to threaten me. My reputation about not paying back stopped the money supply.

Compounding my money woes was the fact that I loved to gamble, and lost consistently. I frequently called my parents and conned them out of money until they finally said, "No more." I had purchased a life insurance policy after completing boot camp. It had accumulated some cash value, so I cashed it in. The financial pressure was relieved momentarily, and the avenues of credit were opened again. Before long, I was in a bigger mess, and the pressure was really on.

A guy on the ship reenlisted at about that time, and he bragged about the large reenlistment bonus he'd received. After doing some investigation, I found that a person could reenlist up to a year before his time was up. That seemed like the answer I was looking for. After jumping through some hoops, I reenlisted for six years. My bonus was over a thousand dollars, which was equivalent to five months pay. Remember, this was in 1959 and a thousand dollars was a lot of money. I had forty-two days of leave that had accumulated, so just before I was to receive my bonus I applied for leave to go home to Oregon. I neglected to pay the guys I owed before I left.

Within a few weeks after arriving home, I was broke. Between my "big-shot-it-ism" and friends who let me play that role, all of the money was gone. I stole tools from my uncle's garage and sold them. I sold some of Dad's tools. I was desperate to keep the party going. It's amazing that when the money was gone, so were my "friends."

When I returned to the ship I had pay coming, but it wasn't enough to pay the guys I owed, who, by the way, were really steamed when I went on leave without paying them as I had promised. Life was really getting messy for me. Here I was in debt, I had six more years to do in the navy, and the sharks were circling. Then I got caught making wine in the engine room. For that I was demoted to third-class petty officer. I was relieved of being in charge of an engine room, and my pay was reduced accordingly.

Gary L.

Looking back, it's amazing to me how I could not see my part in the mess my life had become. I blamed bad luck at gambling, my superiors who were picking on me, and shipmates who "badgered" me to pay them. I was in a corner and didn't know what to do. Again, it never occurred to me to stop drinking and gambling. Hopelessness became my companion. I wondered, "What am I going to do?"

Blessings,
Gary L.

Psalm 46:1–2: "God is our refuge and strength, always ready to help in times of trouble. So we will not fear, even if earthquakes come and mountains crumble into the sea."

Day 29 date ____________________

Today I will go forward with faith. I will set aside any thoughts of returning to the old land.

Why did some of the people want to return to the land of slavery? Although they had hated being slaves, is it possible that they had learned survival skills as slaves? As slaves, their daily life was familiar and predictable; on the other hand, going to a new land that they had never seen would require them to use faith. They knew what was behind them, but they didn't know what was ahead. Do you think that fear took over? They had no idea of all they would encounter on their journey. Sometimes we are drawn back to familiarity and predictability. Some of the people were willing to trade their new freedom in order to return to a place where they had learned at least to survive. I wonder if that's why some people relapse. Many of us learned survival skills in the disease of addiction. Our Higher Power wants to teach us spiritual survival skills as we go forward to freedom.

Question for today: Am I willing to learn spiritual survival skills as I go forward to a new land?

Write about the most significant thing you experienced or learned yesterday.

Prayer for today

I pray that I will learn and apply spiritual survival skills in my walk toward the land of "Sobriety."

10-17-08

Dear Matt,

I prayed for you this morning.

I was devastated by the loss of rank and losing the engine room that I'd been in charge of. My once promising navy career was a wreck. At that time, I was unable to see how the chain of events started by my drinking and gambling had placed me in the position I found myself. The navy was no longer a place I wanted to be. I wanted to quit, run, disappear. I put in for a transfer to another ship in order to run from my debts. My request was denied, and I became angry and resentful toward the navy for not doing what I wanted. I then decided that I wanted out, but it's not like a job that you can just quit. I needed to come up with a plan.

About the same time, some shipmates began playing a game that went like this: two guys would place their forearms together and place a lit cigarette where their arms joined. The first person who pulled away lost. There was usually a five- to ten-dollar bet involved. I entered the game and never lost. I began to be recognized as a guy who could stand a lot of pain. Then the plan came into my mind. I'll convince the navy that I think pain feels good. Perhaps they will believe I'm crazy and discharge me. I began to implement the plan. I would walk around the ship with a lit cigarette on my arm and tell guys that pain really felt good.

When that didn't get the response I was looking for, I began cutting myself with a razor blade. I'd get a crazy look on my face and tell the guys how good that felt. I received strange looks, but nobody was doing anything. One day in the engine room I cut my calf deeper than I'd intended. It was bleeding badly, so I went to the ship's corpsman to get it taken care of. He asked how I'd cut myself, and I replied, "Just like this," as I took another swipe with the razor blade.

That afternoon I was admitted to a lockdown psychiatric unit at Tripler Army Hospital. I really did not believe anything was wrong with me. This was just a plan I'd concocted. The hospital was a wonderful place. The food was great; we played games, spent time with a psychiatrist, and did ceramics. The pressure was off.

After three months, the psychiatrist decided that I was well enough to go back to a ship. My disappointment was tremendous. The navy assigned me to a different ship in the same squadron. That ship happened to be at sea when I was discharged from the hospital, so I received temporary orders to report to some barracks at Pearl Harbor. I did not want to go back to a ship. After arrival at the barracks, I requested liberty. It was granted, and I headed for Hotel Street with one thing in mind. This time I will convince them.

After getting very drunk, I returned to the barracks, got out a razor blade, stripped down, and went into the showers. I turned the water on and began to cut. The following day I was returned to Tripler. I had had many meetings with a psychiatrist my first stay at Tripler, and now I had to see him again. When I met with him he was very angry, and in a loud voice he said, while pointing his finger at me, "Do you want to know what your problem is?" Then he answered his own question. "You're a self-centered SOB, and you don't care about anyone in the world but you." His statement went right over my head, but to this day, I can still see his face as he spit those words at me.

Eleven years later, I was sitting in an AA meeting and the topic was self-centeredness. I flashed back to the psychiatrist's face, and the light came on. I finally understood. After my second stay at Tripler, I received a General Discharge Under Honorable Conditions. That was nothing but grace. I was happy to be free and to be headed back home. All through that entire process, I never believed that anything was wrong with me. My alcoholism and mental illness blinded me to who I was. When I returned to Oregon I was still not twenty-one, but I'd been able to hang on to my fake ID card. I could hardly wait to hit the bars.

Here's another meditation from *Rooted in God's Love*:

> We all have root systems. Roots are life-lines. They seek out and drink in water and nutrients. And they provide stability in times of wind and erosion.
>
> Unfortunately, many of us are rooted in the soil of shame. Roots in this rocky soil become bound. They cannot sustain growth. They are not able to provide nourishment or stability.
>
> Recovery for many of us is like being transplanted. It is the process of allowing God first to pull us out of the parched and rocky soil of shame and then to plant us in the soil of His love. In the rich soil of His love our fragile roots can finally begin to stretch, grow and take hold. It is a soil in which real nourishment and real stability are possible.
>
> But transplantation is not a simple matter. No matter how gently God pulls us up out of the soil of shame, there will be distress. And sinking roots in new soil will feel like an unfamiliar and risky adventure.

As our roots sink deeper and deeper in the soil of God's love, however, we will begin to experience growth that never could have been possible in the soil of rejection and shame. We will become "rooted and established" in love.

Prayer

My roots are in poor soil, Lord. They do not nourish. They provide no stability. My roots are bound, Lord. Transplant me. Give me a grace-full soil, Lord. Sink my roots deeply. Give me stability. Nourish me in your love. Amen. [41]

Keep looking up!
Gary L.

Ephesians 3:17–19: And I pray that Christ will be more and more at home in your hearts as you trust in him. May your roots go down deep into the soil of God's marvelous love. And may you have the power to understand, as all God's people should, how wide, how long, how high, and how deep his love really is. May you experience the love of Christ, though it is so great you will never fully understand it. Then you will be filled with the fullness of life and power that comes from God.

Day 30 Date ___________________

Today I will look at all the ways that my Higher Power has worked in my life since being in treatment.

I asked a group of people what they would want him to be if they could create a Higher Power. Following is a partial list of the characteristics they mentioned: loving, caring, forgiving, kind, gentle, powerful, understanding, compassionate, just, accessible, guiding, dependable, honest, generous, fatherly, and full of grace. I then asked them, if they wanted God to have those characteristics, if they supposed that maybe He wanted to begin working those traits into their lives as they grew spiritually. "One day at a time." There is an old saying: "If you need love, start loving someone else; if you want people to care for you, start caring for them; if you want to be a receiver of grace, then be a person that gives grace; if you want acceptance, start accepting." In other words, do what you need.

Question for today: Am I willing to look at my responsibility to others, or does everything still have to come my way?

Write about the most significant thing you experienced or learned yesterday.

Prayer for today

I pray that I will become a person that will share my experience, strength, and hope with others.

10-18-08

Dear Matt,

I prayed for you this morning.

After being discharged from the navy and my arrival at home, I partied until my mustering-out money was gone. Through influence from Dad, I got a job as a choker-setter for a small logging operation. We worked ten hours a day five days a week. I was paid two dollars per hour. This was in Gold Beach, Oregon, and I stayed in a place where I received room and board for twenty dollars a week. It was the hardest work I had ever done, and by the end of the day I was wiped out. But, in spite of that, after showering and eating, I headed for the bars to drink. With very few hours of sleep, I worked the next day, tired and hung over. The next day I'd do it again. I worked for the company less than a month, and one day just walked off the job. When I received my final paycheck, I went on a run until the money was gone.

One day, out of the blue, I received a phone call from my biological father's sister. I had not seen her since the divorce when I was four. She had seen a discharge notice in the local newspaper and wanted to meet with me. For some reason she took an interest in my life. During our first meeting she explained the importance of getting an education and offered to pay my tuition at a community college. I registered for classes, but after a week I withdrew and received a refund of the tuition. I drank until the money was gone. My aunt was disappointed but didn't write me off. She then said that if I wasn't ready to get an education she would train me to be a bartender in her nightclub as soon as I turned twenty-one.

I was extremely excited about the opportunity! The question in my mind was, "Why would I go to school when I can be a bartender?" As I said in an earlier letter, my values were really skewed. I could hardly wait to begin. When I wrote earlier that right things seemed wrong and wrong things seemed right, this was certainly an example of that.

I wrote to your chaplain to find out the procedure for getting books to you, but I haven't heard back yet. I think *As Bill Sees It* would be helpful. I read the following this morning.

Dependence—Unhealthy or Healthy

Nothing can be more demoralizing than a clinging and abject dependence upon another human being. This often amounts to the demand for a degree of protection and love that no one could possibly satisfy. So our hoped-for protectors finally flee, and once more we are left alone—either to grow up or to disintegrate.

We discovered the best possible source of emotional stability to be God Himself. We found that dependence upon His perfect justice, forgiveness, and love was healthy, and that it would work where nothing else would.

If we really depended upon God, we couldn't very well play God to our fellows, nor would we feel the urge to rely wholly on human protection and care. [42]

That is a great piece of wisdom.

Blessings,
Gary L.

Colossians 2:6–7: "And now, just as you accepted Christ Jesus as your Lord, you must continue to live in obedience to him. Let your roots grow down into him and draw up nourishment from him, so you will grow in faith, strong and vigorous in the truth you were taught. Let your lives overflow with thanksgiving for all he has done."

10-19-08

Dear Matt,

I prayed for you this morning.

I worked part time as a bartender for my aunt for several months and learned a lot of tricks of the trade. I needed to work full-time, and she didn't need me that much so she introduced me to a friend of hers who owned a very nice bar. After being interviewed by him, he hired me full time. I felt like the luckiest guy in the world! I couldn't imagine doing anything else. My shift was from 6:30 PM to 2:30 AM.

After I closed up the bar, I would go to another bar. It was also closed for the night, but the owner invited bartenders and cocktail waitresses to come to an after-hours party. It was illegal to do that, but we never got busted. I would drink until around 6:00 AM, and then some of us would go out for breakfast. After breakfast, most of the people would go home. Instead of going home, I would go to a bar that opened at 7:00 AM and drink until noon or so. After that, I'd go home, sleep five or six hours, and then go to work and do the same routine over again. I thought I had the greatest life.

The bar where I worked had a great system for employees. We could charge drinks and food to an account. At the end of the month, our employer would take 50 percent off our bill and subtract the remainder from our paycheck. That was a sweet deal. On my days off, I would drink there, eat steaks every day, buy drinks for others, and act like a big shot. When I received my first paycheck, after deducting my bar bill, there was not enough money to cover the taxes due. In other words, it was payday, and I didn't have any money coming. That continued for several months. My boss tried to talk to me about my drinking, but I wasn't interested in what he had to say.

After several months, he fired me. I again felt like such a victim. What right did he have to tell me what to do on my days off? Soon after I was fired I was hired in a hotel bar and restaurant. It was also a very nice place. I had been working there for a couple of months and the owner approached me with an offer. He had been negotiating with Greyhound Bus Co. to use the hotel lobby as a bus station. He asked if I was interested in becoming a Greyhound ticket agent. In addition to that, he said that he would also like me to work part time in the bar. It sounded like a great deal to me. Between both jobs, I would be making more money than I ever had before.

A Greyhound representative came and trained me for a week and I was set. Between working both jobs, I still managed to drink every day. With my increased income, my big-shot-ism really took over. When I was out drinking,

I would often buy a round of drinks for everyone in the bar. I really thought I was something. Even working two jobs, I did not make enough money to drink like that.

One day while making out the bank deposit for Greyhound, I "borrowed" twenty dollars with the idea of returning it on payday. The first time I took money was so easy. I paid it back on payday, but it wasn't long before I "borrowed" again. Before long, I was taking money almost every day. I lost track of what I had taken and then began to falsify numbers on my bookwork to cover what I was taking. Changing numbers was much easier than keeping track, because by that time I had no intention of paying the money back.

One day my boss approached me and said that a Greyhound auditor was going to be there the following week to audit the books. He said that was standard procedure, and it was done every three months. A sense of panic went through me, and I knew I was in big trouble. Oh, the webs we weave sometimes that we get trapped in. I needed to come up with a plan, and fast! I remember thinking that if my boss paid me what I deserved, I wouldn't be in this predicament. There was so much dishonesty and self-deception in my thinking, but that enabled me to not see my part and take any personal responsibility.

I'll continue this part of my story in my next letter.

Blessings
Gary L.

10-20-08

Dear Matt,

I prayed for you this morning.

I had about a week to come up with a plan to clean up the mess I'd created at Greyhound. One night while drinking and mulling over my dilemma, I had a vision. Beware of visions while drinking/using! In the vision, I saw myself in Reno. I was gambling and got extremely lucky. I won at everything I tried. Streams of money were flowing my way. I saw a look of excitement and delight on my face as I continued to win. After seeing that vision I thought, "That's my answer. After I return home with my winnings I can pay back Greyhound, and everything will be wonderful."

The problem all of that presented was that I had very little money at the time. So I had to come up with another plan. I then remembered where the money from the bar was hid after closing. It made sense to me to "borrow" from the cash box, because I would just pay that back too. I had a key to the bar, and after it had closed for the night, I returned and let myself in. I then went to the cash box, removed all of the cash, counted it, and then wrote out an IOU for the amount and placed it in the box. I then went to the lobby of the hotel and made out a Greyhound ticket to Reno. I routed the ticket through Portland because an early-morning bus went to Portland, and it was due any time. The bus arrived, and I was on my way. When I arrived in Portland, I changed to a bus going to Reno. After arriving in Reno, I registered at the Riverside Hotel.

After taking my belongings to my room, I headed for the casino to make my fortune. I really believed that was going to happen. A caveat to gambling was that waitresses kept bringing me free drinks. I thought it was the most wonderful place in the world until my money began to disappear. What happened to the great luck I was going to have? I began gambling with a sense of desperation, but nothing was working. I lost track of time. The days became a blur. After five or six days of losing, I awoke in my room. My watch and ring were gone along with extra clothes I had taken. I found receipts from pawnshops in my pocket. The only cash I had was some pocket change. Then the fear hit. I needed a drink but was afraid to leave the room. I owed the hotel money. "What am I going to do?" I wondered.

My fear and anxiety leapt within me when there was a knock on the door. In my mind, I saw two or three big guys on the other side of the door, coming to collect. I had heard horror stories about what happened to people that were in my position. I didn't answer the door. I wanted to run but there was no place to go. I felt trapped. Later that morning there was another knock on the door. I thought that I might just as well face the music. When I opened the door, there were two big guys. The larger one was in the three-hundred-pound range. The other was at least two hundred pounds.

Fortunately for me it was my dad and brother-in-law. Mom was down in the lobby. When I made out my bus ticket I'd left a paper trail, so they knew I was somewhere in Reno. When they arrived in Reno, they began searching for me. When they showed a picture of me to the desk clerk at the Riverside, they knew they had found me. Mom and Dad paid my bill, and we headed back to Oregon. That was a long, silent trip. A warrant for my arrest had been issued, so when we arrived back in Coos County, they took me to the county jail, and I turned myself in.

That was a long time ago, but it seems to me I was in jail a couple of weeks before I went before the judge. During that time, I did not have one visitor, not even Mom and Dad. I had never felt so alone. I was full of self-pity. I was only twenty-two at the time and wanted to die. Prison even sounded like a better alternative than the way I was living.

I like the following reading from *Twenty-Four Hours a Day.*

A.A. Thought for the Day

We are living on borrowed time. We are living today because of A.A. and the grace of God. And what there is left of our lives we owe to A.A. and to God. We should make the best use we can of our borrowed time and in some small measure pay back for that part of our lives which we wasted before we came into A.A. Our lives from now on are not out own. We hold them in trust for God and A.A. And we must do all we can to forward the great movement that has given us a new lease on life. *Am I holding my life in trust for A.A.?*

Meditation for the Day

You should hold your life in trust for God. Think deeply on what that means. Is anything too much to expect from such a life? Do you begin to see how dedicated a life in trust for God can be? In such a life miracles can happen. If you are faithful, you can believe that God has many good things in store for you. God can be Lord of your life, controller of your days, of your present and your future. Try to act as God guides and leave all results to Him. Do not hold back, but go all out for God and the better life. Make good your trust.

Prayer for the Day

I pray that I may hold my life in trust for God. I pray that I may no longer consider my life as all my own. [43]

Blessings,
Gary L.

10-21-08

Dear Matt,

I prayed for you this morning.

One of the consistent things in my recovery journey has been God revealing to me the ways of thinking or beliefs that kept me attached not only to alcohol, but also to a self-destructive way of living. Romans 12:2, which I've written about several times, is about being transformed by new ways of thinking. I read a book recently, which was first published in 1952, that has many stories about people whose lives have changed by God working in their belief systems. William James said, "The greatest discovery of my generation is that human beings can alter their lives by altering their attitudes of mind." The book that quote comes from is *The Power Of Positive Thinking*, by Norman Vincent Peale. The following story from that book is a great example of a changed life.

> I know a business executive, a modest man, but the type of individual who is never defeated. No problem, no setback, no opposition ever gets him down. He simply attacks each difficulty with an optimistic attitude and a sure confidence that it will work out right, and, in some strange way, it always does for him. He seems to have a magic touch on life—a touch that never fails.
>
> Because of that impressive characteristic, this man always interested me. I knew there was a definite explanation of his being this way and of course wanted to hear his story, but in view of his modesty and reticence, it was not easy to persuade him to talk about himself.
>
> One day when he was in the mood he told me his secret, an amazingly simple but effective secret. I was visiting his plant, a modern up-to-date structure, much of it air-conditioned. Latest type machinery and methods of production make it a factory of outstanding efficiency. Labor-management relations seem as nearly perfect as is possible among imperfect human beings. A spirit of good will pervades the entire organization.
>
> His office is ultra-modernisticly (sic) decorated and furnished

with handsome desks, rugs, and paneled with exotic woods. The decorating scheme is five startling colors blended together pleasantly. All in all it is the last word, and then some.

Imagine, then, my surprise to see on his highly polished white mahogany desk an old battered copy of the Bible. It was the only old object in those ultramodern rooms. I commented upon this seemingly strange inconsistency.

"That book," he replied, pointing to the Bible, "is the most up-to-date thing in this plant. Equipment wears out and furnishing styles change, but that book is so far ahead of us that it never gets out of date.

"When I went to college, my good Christian mother gave me that Bible with the suggestion that if I would read and practice its teachings, I would learn how to get through life successfully. But I thought she was just a nice old lady"—he chuckled—"at my age she seemed old—she wasn't really, and to humor her, I took the Bible, but for years practically never looked at it. I thought I didn't need it. Well," he continued slangily, "I was a dope. I was stupid. And I got my life in a terrible mess.

"Everything went wrong primarily because I was wrong. I was thinking wrong, acting wrong, doing wrong. I succeeded at nothing, failed at everything. Now I realize that my principle trouble was wrong thinking. I was negative, resentful, cocky, opinionated. Nobody could tell me anything. I thought I knew everything. I was filled with gripes at everybody. Little wonder nobody liked me. I certainly was a 'washout.' "

So ran his dismal story. "One night in going through some papers," he continued, "I came across the long-forgotten Bible. It brought up old memories and I started aimlessly to read it. Do you know it is strange how things happen: how in just a flashing moment of time everything becomes different. Well, as I read, a sentence leaped up at me, a sentence that changed my life—and when I say changed, I mean changed. From the minute I read that sentence everything has been different, tremendously different."

"What is this wonderful sentence?" I wanted to know, and he quoted it slowly, "'The Lord is the strength of my life…in this I

> will be confident' " (Psalm 27:1, 3).
>
> "I don't know why that one line affected me so," he went on, "but it did. I know now that I was weak and a failure because I had no faith, no confidence. I was very negative, a defeatist. Something happened inside my mind. I guess I had what they call a spiritual experience. My thought pattern shifted from negative to positive. I decided to put my faith in God and sincerely do my best, trying to follow the principles outlined in the Bible. As I did so, I began to get hold of a new set of thoughts. I began to think differently. In time my old failure thoughts were flushed out by this new spiritual experience and an inflow of new thoughts gradually but actually remade me."
>
> So concluded the story of this businessman. He altered his thinking, and the new thoughts which flowed in displaced the old thoughts which had been defeating him and his life changed. [44]

That kind of story has been repeated countless times by those who surrender their lives to God. I've been in the process of change for a long time, and it's been an exciting journey. I pray that you will experience that kind of transformation.

Blessings,
Gary L.

Psalm 37:3–5: "Trust in the Lord and do good. Then you will live safely in the land and prosper. Take delight in the Lord, and he will give you your heart's desires. Commit everything you do to the Lord. Trust him, and he will help you."

10-22-08

Dear Matt,

I prayed for you this morning.

Deuteronomy 30: 15–16: Now listen! Today I am giving you a choice between prosperity and disaster, between life and death. I have commanded you today to love the Lord your God and to keep his commands, laws, and regulations by walking in his ways. If you do this, you will live and become a great nation, and the Lord your God will bless you and the land you are about to enter and occupy.

Boy, that's a tall order. I have to admit that sometimes I come up real short with the command, "Walk in His ways." but God understands I cannot do that without His help. Oftentimes I try to do life with my power and really miss the mark. God has been so gracious to understand and forgive. Every day I get a chance for a fresh start.

Today I read the following on page 131 in *As Bill Sees It*:

Obstacles in Our Path

We live in a world riddled with envy. To a greater or lesser degree, everybody is infected with it. From this defect we must surely get a warped yet definite satisfaction. Else why would we consume so much time wishing for what we have not, rather than working for it, or angrily looking for attributes we shall never have, instead of adjusting to the fact, and accepting it?

Each of us would like to live at peace with himself and with his fellows. We would like to be assured that the grace of God can do for us what we cannot do for ourselves.

We have seen that character defects based upon shortsighted or unworthy desires are the obstacles that block our path towards these objectives. We now clearly see that we have been making unreasonable demands upon ourselves, upon others, and upon God. [45]

Ouch! Sometimes Bill's writings really take my inventory.

Gary L.

10-23-08

Dear Matt,

I prayed for you this morning.

Back to my story. While sitting in my cell I reviewed my life and didn't like what I saw. In one sense, the idea of going to prison was appealing, as I remembered my stay in the psyche unit while in the navy. I had come to an awareness that I didn't know how Dad to live in society without alcohol.

Mom and Dad had hired an attorney, and, without my knowledge, some plea bargaining was going on. When I finally appeared before the judge, the charge was larceny by embezzlement, and I pleaded guilty. I thought, "Let's just get this over with and lock me up." Rather than sentence me to prison, the judge placed me on probation for five years. There were two conditions of probation—pay restitution and not drink alcohol. I was full of fear and anxiety when I was released.

After being released, I moved in with Mom and Dad. They had always been my ace-in-the-hole. No matter how bad I messed up my life, they were always there to pick up the pieces. The sad thing was I had no appreciation for that because I thought it was their job. You may have heard the term "sense of entitlement." I really had it. I had no awareness of how I should treat them, or how I was affecting them. I sure had an awareness of how I believed they should treat me.

Because of Dad's influence I was hired at a sawmill. My shift ended at 1:00 AM. A few of the guys I worked with invited me to join them for some drinks after work one night. The bars closed at 2:30 AM. I declined their invitation for a couple of nights, but then decided to join them. After all, I would only have an hour or so to drink. Surely, I could do that without getting into trouble. I really believed what I was thinking.

Drinking several drinks after work worked for a while. But when I received my first paycheck, I was off to the races again. When I didn't show up for work or call in the following Monday, I was fired. I continued to drink until the money was gone. Mom and Dad were devastated, disappointed, and angry, but didn't kick me out. I went "on the wagon" again. I applied at another sawmill and was hired, but after getting paid, I went on another run and lost that job. I then talked to Mom and Dad and begged for another chance. I recognized that something was terribly wrong with me, and I didn't know how to fix it. I asked if I could just stay at home for a while and see if I could figure things out. Something was different the last time I drank. I drank when I was determined not to, but the obsession was so great that I could not overcome it with my will or determination. I contacted my probation officer and got honest with him, knowing I would end up in prison if he chose to revoke my probation. He consulted with my victim to see if restitution could be delayed. My victim agreed to wait. Alcohol had changed from being what I considered my best friend, and had become a terrible foe. I felt so lost. "Would life ever work for me?" I wondered. Have you ever asked yourself that question?

Blessings,
Gary L.

10-24-08

Dear Matt,

I prayed for you this morning.

After I'd been at Mom and Dad's for several days, I decided to walk to a neighborhood grocery store that was a few blocks away to get a candy bar. I walked outside, but when I reached the sidewalk in front of their home, I froze. I was unable to make my leg step out onto the sidewalk. I tried again to no avail. I stood back and wondered, "What in the world is wrong? Why can't I step out onto the sidewalk?"

As I returned to the house, a feeling of panic went through me. I didn't say anything to Mom and Dad when they arrived home from work. I was sure they wouldn't understand what had happened anymore than I did. The challenge before me became to get to the store, so I tried again the following day with the same result. On the third day, I stepped onto the sidewalk and felt elated. I strode boldly toward the store, but when I had gone twenty or so steps, I froze again and could not continue. Finally, after approximately two weeks, I made it to the store. It felt like a great victory.

One day Dad invited me to join him at practice with a barbershop chorus he was a member of. The chorus was part of the SPEBSQSA Inc., which stands for the Society for the Preservation and Encouragement of Barbershop Quartet Singing in America. He'd been a member of the chorus for some time, and since singing had been such a large part of my life while growing up, he thought I would enjoy it. I loved it! I eagerly looked forward to each practice. I didn't realize it at the time, but singing barbershop became a fix for me just like alcohol had been.

I had been living with Mom and Dad for about six months when I felt that I would be able to work. I applied for a job at a department store and was hired as a trainee in the women's and children's shoe department. I enjoyed the work and began paying restitution for my crime.

Just before Christmas, after I'd been working for about a year and a half, I had to work until nine o'clock one night. We were open late because of the Christmas rush. A gift-wrap station had been set up in the shoe department, and a young lady was working it. I introduced myself and asked where she lived. I didn't have a car and if she lived close to Mom and Dad, I was going to try and bum a ride from her. She quickly informed me that she was married and that she had ridden to work with her sister-in-law, who was working at another gift-wrap station.

After the store closed, she introduced me to her sister-in-law and said that I was looking for a ride. I was stunned by her blue eyes, and the first thought in my mind was, "You're going to marry her." Mind you, I was a totally committed bachelor at the time and had made a vow as a teenager that I would never get married. Growing up I had never known people who were happily married. Mom and Dad seemed happy for short periods of time, but for the most part, they spent a lot of time arguing. Sometimes their arguing turned into screaming matches. I wanted no part of that. But then I met Patsy that night. Something about her blue eyes absolutely captivated me.

The following night we dated after work, and on our third date, I proposed. Six weeks after meeting, we were married in my parents' home. The reception was also at their home, and many family members, friends from work, and barbershop buddies attended. Someone mixed up a huge bowl of punch and spiked it with alcohol. I wanted a drink so bad, but something inside said that if I took a drink I could kiss my marriage goodbye. I made it through that crisis, and we went to Eugene for a five-day honeymoon.

I have to say that very few people gave our marriage a chance. We settled in a small apartment to begin a journey together that has spanned over forty-six years. She is my angel, and I thank God every day for her. I have to say that I am passionately in love with her. That is from a man who did not have the capacity within himself to love another human being that way when we got married. If every man was blessed with a wife like Patsy, the word divorce could be taken out of the dictionary. I tear up as I think of the blessing she has been in my life.

Life was really coming around for me. I was married; I'd paid restitution for my crime and was part of a barbershop quartet. As we practiced and improved, we were invited to sing on shows. I loved the applause when we performed. But something was happening under the great life I had; I began to envy my friends in the quartet who were normal drinkers.

After many shows where we performed, there would be what is called an afterglow. It was usually held in a banquet room at a restaurant. The performers from the show would gather with friends, family, and audience members who wanted to hear some more singing. It was a show after the show. It seemed to me that people who drank at the afterglow were having more fun than me. I wondered, "Why can't I drink the way they do?" I remembered back when the feeling that alcohol gave me was like magic. That kind of thinking continued for about a year before I bought the first six-pack.

By this time, I had gone four and a half years without a drink. At the same time, my probation officer requested from the court that I be taken off probation six months early because I was doing so well. Little did he know what was going on with my thinking. I reasoned, "If drinking doesn't work, I'll just quit again."

Blessings,
Gary L.

10-25-08

Dear Matt,

I prayed for you this morning.

I still remember the day I bought the six-pack. Patsy and I were buying our weekly groceries at a Safeway store in North Bend. We had been talking about it for some time, and she wondered if it was a good idea. Up to then she'd never seen me drink. I reasoned that I was older and wiser, and if it bothered me as it had in the past, I'd just quit. I told her that I didn't want to drink in the bars. All I wanted to do was have a couple of beers when I got home from work to help me relax and take the edge off the day. I really believed those words as I said them. Neither of us knew anything about alcoholism at the time. I'd had problems with alcohol but didn't see myself as a real alcoholic. To me, alcoholics were people like my grandpa who couldn't hold a job, threw up in bed, messed his pants, and needed to drink every day. I certainly wasn't like that.

When Patsy and I arrived home from shopping I opened the first beer. At some level, I knew I was in trouble as I recalled the magical feeling that alcohol gave me the day I took my first drink. That same magic was there again. Through sheer determination, I only drank one beer that day, but I wanted to drink all of them. The six-pack lasted a few days, and it was torture for me. I had promised Patsy that I would not drink in the bars, but within a couple of weeks I was calling from work saying that I had to work late. I didn't have to work late. I wanted to drink. So I'd head for a bar, drink fast and hard for a couple of hours, and then go home.

As soon as I arrived at home, I'd rush to the refrigerator, open a beer, take a big drink, and then kiss Patsy, trying to convince her that was the first drink of the day. A couple of months after drinking that first beer, it was as if I had never gone four and a half years without a drink. Dishonesty and deception became a way of life again, and I took Patsy through hell for almost five years. I had many periods of abstinence during those years, but the obsession to drink was always there, and I would eventually succumb to the bottle. I had no resources within me to ward off the obsession. I have no ideas how many promises I broke during those years. I was a slave to alcohol again, and I could not get back a desire to not drink.

I continued to sing with the quartet but became undependable. I never missed a show, but many practice nights I would call the guys and tell them I had to work late. The truth was that I was going to a bar. I felt trapped and alone, and a feeling of hopelessness would visit me often. I wondered, "Why can't I stop drinking?" I would find the answer to that question some years later in the rooms of Alcoholics Anonymous.

Bill W. said the following in 1958 during one of his talks. "AA was born out of trouble, one of the most serious kinds of trouble that can befall an individual, the trouble attendant upon this dark and fatal malady of alcoholism. Every single one of us approached AA in trouble, in impossible trouble, in hopeless trouble. And that is why we came." 46

Keep looking up,
Gary L.

10-26-08

Dear Matt,

I prayed for you this morning.

1 John 4:7–8: "Dear friends, let us continue to love one another, for love comes from God. Anyone who loves is born of God and knows God. But anyone who does not love does not know God—for God is love."

The quartet eventually caught on to what was happening and confronted me. I told them I would change and not miss practices. Here I was, on the wagon again and hating every minute of it. Eventually I would drink again, and the undependability would be right back. We continued to sing in shows all over the Northwest, and three consecutive years we qualified to represent the Evergreen District at the International Contest. The first year was in Los Angeles, then Boston, followed by Chicago. The community we lived in generously helped us financially in order to go to the contests. We never won, but just to get there was an honor. Forty-five quartets competed, but approximately twelve hundred tried to get there.

After going through the cycle several more times—drink, become undependable, confrontation, and go on the wagon—the guys informed me that they decided to disband. On one hand, I was disappointed, but on the other, it was kind of a relief. The quartet was interfering with my drinking. The evening after they informed me of their decision, I stopped by the home where we practiced to pick up some sheet music and records that I'd left there. When I stepped onto the porch, I heard a quartet singing. On further examination, I discovered that the Bayshore Four Barbershop Quartet had replaced me. They didn't disband! I was so angry. How could they do that to me? Rage began to consume me, and I wanted to get even.

One way I did that was by character assassination. I would see people, and they would ask me why I was no longer with the quartet, and then the lies would flow. I became bitter and would say anything to make them look bad. Through all of that process, I was unable to see my part. That victim part of me took over. All I could think about is what they did to me.

Three major events happened in 1969—loss of the quartet, our second daughter was born, and I was injured while working in a tire store. After Patsy and I got married, and up to the time I was injured, I changed jobs many times. In 1964, I took a position in a department store as the manager of the shoe department. That job lasted about a year. I had a falling out with the owner and quit. Of course, it was all his fault. Ha! Ha! I then sold Singer sewing machines for a while with limited success. It was shortly after working for Singer that I returned to drinking. A man I knew through barber shopping owned a tire store. His business was growing, and he needed someone to help him. I didn't have any experience, but he said that he would train me. It was a great opportunity for a new career, and I jumped on it. We really hit it off. Part of the reason for that was that he liked to drink as much as I did. Another thing was that he would let me miss work when the quartet had a singing engagement.

I'll continue this part of my story in my next letter.

I liked the meditation in the *Twenty-Four Hours a Day* book for yesterday.

Meditation for the Day

We should work at overcoming ourselves, our selfish desires and our self-centeredness. This can never be fully accomplished. We can never become entirely unselfish. But we can come to realize that we are not at the center of the universe and that everything does not revolve around us at the center. I am only one cell in a vast network of human cells. I can at least make the effort to conquer the self-life and seek daily to obtain more and more of this self-conquest. "He that overcomes himself is greater than he who conquers a city."

Prayer for the Day

I pray that I may strive to overcome my selfishness. I pray that I may achieve the right perspective of my position in the world. [47]

Blessings,
Gary L.

10-27-08

Dear Matt,

I prayed for you this morning.

From 1966 to 1969 I worked at the tire store two different times. The first time was for approximately a year, but an opportunity came up for me to buy a Richfield service station. I didn't have the money, so I convinced my parents that if they would loan what I needed that I'd pay them back. I don't know how many times we'd ventured down that road without me paying them back, but they loaned me the money anyway.

Several weeks later, I took over the station. Wow! I was in business for myself! My grandiosity and big-shot-ism immediately took over. I opened the station at 7:00 AM and closed it at 9:00 PM. Those were long days, but I wanted to succeed. After closing, I would take a wad of money from the till, head for the bars and play like a big-shot businessman. I dined on steak and lobster regularly, bought drinks for everyone in the bar, and felt like I was really somebody. The expression, "Get drunk and be somebody" was what I lived. Many nights I would not arrive home until 2:00 or 3:00 AM, sleep a few hours, and go open the station. Day after day, seven days a week I kept that pace until I could go no longer, and then I'd stop drinking for a few days. After resting up, I'd do it all over again. After nine months of that, I went broke. When a check I wrote to Richfield for a load of gas bounced, I was shut down the following day.

Again, I could not see my part in the failure. That big oil company was doing it to me. It was so easy to slip into the victim role. I made a lot of money during those nine months, but not enough to support my big-shot-ism.

A competitor across the street hired me as an assistant manager. He was a great boss, but after several months I resigned and returned to the tire store. I was hired back with the title manager, which was kind of funny because it was just a two-man store. My grandiosity really liked the sound of manager. Through those years of job changes and upheaval, and my many promises to stop drinking, Patsy hung in there. That was not only the grace of God, but also the grace of Patsy. Her life was hell at the time. I was rarely around except to sleep, and she had two small children to care for. At times I would have pangs of guilt but would somehow suppress the feeling. I often wondered, "Why do I keep doing this?" I would not find the answer to that question until I ended up in the rooms of AA.

Sometimes it's difficult to revisit the dark times.

Gary L.

Psalm 32:1–5:

Oh, what joy for those whose rebellion is forgiven, whose sin is put out of sight! Yes, what joy for those whose record the Lord has cleared of sin, whose lives are lived in complete honesty! When I refused to confess my sin, I was weak and miserable, and I groaned all day long. Day and night your hand of discipline was heavy on me. My strength evaporated like water in the summer heat. Finally, I confessed all my sins to you and stopped trying to hide them. I said to myself, "I will confess my rebellion to the Lord." And you forgave me! All my guilt is gone.

10-28-08

Dear Matt,

I prayed for you this morning.

A major event of 1969 was when I was injured while working at the tire store. I was breaking down a truck tire, and while swinging a sledgehammer I missed my mark. My feet flew out from under me, and I landed on a tire rim that was behind me. I was unable to stand up. I yelled for my boss, and he helped me up. Even after getting up, I could not straighten up. When I tried to move, I had incredible pain. Somehow, I drove home and went to bed.

The following morning I was unable to get up without Patsy's help. I went to the emergency room and was admitted to the hospital. I was given pain pills and placed in traction. I filed for workers' comp and began receiving weekly checks. The amount I received was almost as much as my take-home pay. I thought, "This is a great deal." I didn't have to work and still got paid.

Another benefit was that my creditors could not touch my state comp. Because of my irresponsibility, we had numerous creditors who had turned our bills in to collection agencies. I wouldn't pay them either, and consequently they had sued us. When I drank, the last thing I wanted to do was pay bills. When the collection agencies would call, I'd be real rude and inform them that there was nothing they could do. I did not want to return to work because the collectors were waiting for that. In order not to return to work, I did not follow my doctor's instructions and deliberately did things to my back to make sure it didn't get better. A five-gallon bucket full of water was behind our garage, and I would grab the handle and quickly straighten up in order to wrench my back.

My doctor could not understand why I wasn't getting better and referred me to a specialist in Medford. I didn't follow his instructions either. I had a sweet deal going and didn't want to give it up. Meanwhile, my drinking progressed. My doctor then referred me to Vocational Rehabilitation after determining that I was not able to do physical labor. I enrolled in a community college and began taking classes. Most days after class I would stop at a bar and drink. Somehow, I managed to keep up with my schoolwork and actually received pretty good grades.

That Christmas was a very difficult time. Because of my drinking, we did not have money to buy our daughters any gifts. I had confided with one of my professors how broke we were but did not tell her the reason. I know now that this was all manipulation. She took pity on me, as I thought she would, and just before Christmas, she gave me a sack of toys for our daughters. Some of the toys were used and had been stored in her attic, but the kids were happy to receive gifts.

Through all of this process I was beginning to get glimpses of who I'd become. I didn't like what I saw but would assuage the guilt by drinking, which, of course, created more guilt. It became a vicious cycle. Along with the guilt came deep depression. (It might have been self-pity. They look similar.) Drinking would no longer lift me from that place. I desperately tried to get alcohol to work as it had in the beginning, to no avail. I no longer wanted to drink—I had to. Patsy didn't know what to do; neither did I.

Patsy and I lived eleven miles south of Coos Bay in a small community called Greenacres. By this time our only vehicle was a beat-up '52 Ford pickup. Many times, I would call Patsy from Coos Bay and tell her that something was wrong with the pickup and that I'd be late. A lot goes wrong with an old truck like that.

One night I was drinking and did not call Patsy. On the way home, I needed to come up with a reason for being late. I stopped at a service station at the edge of town and had them fill an empty gallon jug with gasoline. About a quarter mile from home, I pulled off on a wide shoulder on the road, opened the hood of the pickup, poured the gasoline on the engine, lit a match, and threw it in.

There was a whoosh of sound, and the flames leapt at me, burning my face and arms. I ran up the road and knocked on the door of Patsy's brother who lived next to us. He got Patsy and rushed me to the hospital. Fortunately, when the flames hit me I jumped back quickly enough that my burns were just on the surface. It could have been worse.

When I decided that night to pour gasoline on the engine, it made perfect sense to me. I would tell Patsy I'm late because the pickup caught on fire. In spite of that incident, I continued to drink. The pickup was destroyed.

I began to think about suicide. Life was not working, and it seemed that I was unable to do anything about it.

On a Friday early in February I went to Coos Bay to do some things and promised Patsy that I would be home in time for dinner. After completing what I needed to do, I looked at my watch. I decided that I had plenty of time to stop for a couple of beers and would be able to be home by dinnertime. Something I've discovered since being in recovery is that when I put that much alcohol in me it changes the way I think. After two beers, my mind said, "Have another." I arrived home around 3:00 AM. Patsy was angry and disappointed, and so was I. I was determined that I would only have two beers. I didn't know it at the time, but I was getting closer to the rooms of AA.

Sometimes it's darkest just before the light.

Gary L.

Gary L.

Colossians 3:9–10: "Don't lie to each other, for you have stripped off your old evil nature and all its wicked deeds. In its place you have clothed yourselves with a brand-new nature that is continually being renewed as you learn more and more about Christ, who created this new nature in you.

10-29-08

Dear Matt,

I prayed for you this morning.

Now back to the end of my last letter, where I'd arrived home after closing up the bars. When I went to bed early that morning I thought about the state of my life and began to cry. The crying turned into deep sobs that came in waves. In the midst of the sobbing I cried out to the God that my Grandma had introduced me to when I was five; I don't remember the words I said, but I remember the desperation I felt.

When I awoke later that morning, I wanted to drink. I had forgotten the sobbing, the prayer, and the desperation. The fire in me got started the night before and needed to be fed. That morning was the first of the month. Every month I'd walk about an eighth of a mile to where our landlord lived to pay the rent. We'd been renting from him for over a year. We never had a real conversation other than greeting each other. After our greeting, I'd give him the rent, and he'd give me a receipt.

Walking to Frank's house that morning I had several lies that I was playing with in my mind. I was going to ask him to take a half month's rent, because my plan was to go to Coos Bay and drink. I wanted as much cash as I could get. Frank was in his front yard. When I got close to him he looked at me, and our conversation changed that morning. With a stern look on his face, he pointed at me and asked, "Are you having a problem with the jug?"

Before I could think I answered, "Yes." I never wanted to take a word back so much in all my life, but it just popped out. He then said, "I'm a member of Alcoholics Anonymous, and it hasn't been necessary for me to take a drink in over ten years. Would you like to go to a meeting?" I lied to him and said, "Yes," again. He said that there was a meeting that night, and he would pick me up at seven thirty.

On the way home I wondered, "What in the world have I done to myself?" At the time, I did not know what AA was, but I knew I did not want to go to some kind of meeting. One thing he said "It hasn't been necessary for me to take a drink in over ten years," kept playing through my mind. How could someone possibly go ten years without a drink? I could not wrap my mind around that.

When I arrived home, I told Patsy what had happened, but she barely responded. By this time, there had been so many false starts and broken promises that she was afraid to hope. In one of my conversations with Frank later, I asked how he had the boldness to question me that morning. He said,

"There were too many late nights and early mornings that I heard your car speeding up the road, and I knew I had to say something." The amazing thing about all of that is that he had the boldness to ask the same morning I said a prayer of desperation. I will always believe that Frank was God's response to my prayer.

So here I was heading to my first AA meeting, full of fear and anxiety.

There was a great meditation on 8–3–08 from Max Lucado's book *Grace for the Moment.*

A Raging Fire

Resentment is the cocaine of the emotions. It causes our blood to pump and our energy level to rise. But, also like cocaine, it demands increasingly large and more frequent dosages. There is a dangerous point at which anger ceases to be an emotion and becomes a driving force. A person bent on revenge moves unknowingly further and further away from being able to forgive, for to be without the anger is to be without a source of energy.

Hatred is the rabid dog that turns on its owner.
Revenge is the raging fire that consumes the arsonist.
Bitterness is the trap that snares the hunter.
And mercy is the choice that can set them all free. [48]

When I began to make the choice to forgive those who had offended me in some way (real or imagined), that was a beginning to a journey of freedom.

Blessings,
Gary L.

James 1:19: "My dear brothers and sisters, be quick to listen, slow to speak, and slow to get angry. Your anger can never make things right in God's sight."

10-30-08

Dear Matt,

I prayed for you this morning.

Proverbs 10:1: "A wise child brings joy to a father; a foolish child brings grief to a mother."

Proverbs 19:26: "He who robs his father and drives out his mother is a son who brings shame and disgrace."

The above scriptures are descriptive of who I was while growing up. I caused so much grief for my parents.

One of the things that was woven into much of my life was the way I emotionally blackmailed my parents. For some reason I thought they owed me something. Every time I got into some kind of trouble, I felt it was their responsibility to help me out, and many times they did. Many times I would ask them for financial help, and they would initially deny me. Their denial meant nothing to me because I had always been able to wiggle around that and get them to say yes.

Several months before I went to my first AA meeting I'd asked for a "loan," and they refused. I tried everything I could to get them to change, but this time they wouldn't budge. Christmas was coming up, and I needed help. When it finally settled in that they were not going to help, I got very angry. My thought was, "You'll never see your grandkids again," and I stormed out. Another thought was, "I'll show you."

When that thought comes into my mind it's a red flag that says, "You're about to do something real stupid," and many times I did. I heard a guy at an AA meeting talk about playing the same game with his parents. He said that one time his mother refused to give him some money, and the thought that came into his mind was, "I'll show you. I'll kill me, and you're going to feel real bad." I understand that kind of insanity. It seems that every time in my life I got even with someone, it cost me more than them.

My parents' refusal that time was one of the best things they ever did for me, because during February following that Christmas I ended up in the rooms of AA. They had always been my ace in the hole and had finally decided that wasn't helpful to me. Today I see that as a great gift.

As Bill Sees It, page 58:

When we harbored grudges and planned revenge for defeats, we were really beating ourselves with the club of anger we had intended to use on others. We learned that if we were seriously disturbed, our very first need was to quiet that disturbance, regardless of who or what we thought caused it. [49]

Blessings,
Gary L.

10-31-08

Dear Matt,

I prayed for you this morning.

Well, here I was headed to an AA meeting. I knew nothing about AA and was full of fear and anxiety. My life at the time was like a big jigsaw puzzle that had been dumped on a table, and no picture was on the box. My life since that first AA meeting has been about God slowly putting the puzzle together.

My wife Patsy loves to do puzzles. I watch her when she dumps the puzzle out. Then she turns all the pieces right side up. The next step is to sort out the border pieces and begin putting them together. It's a slow, tedious process. Eventually, piece by piece, a picture begins to emerge. Occasionally I'll look for a piece. The pieces of a puzzle cannot put themselves together. They need an outside source. Just like a lump of clay on a potter's wheel cannot become anything without a potter.

Many of the pieces of my puzzle have been put together, but the final piece won't be in place until the day I see my creator. It's then that I will understand that all of the pieces were important, even the ones that made no sense to me.

Very early in recovery my sponsor, Hugh, said, "Gary, some people grow up; some people grow old. Which way do you want to do it?" His gaze pierced my soul as he said those words. He spoke the truth in love. At the time he said those words I was physically thirty-one years old but about fifteen emotionally. Since I had been using alcohol to deal with life since age fifteen, I'd had no opportunity to mature emotionally. I was still reacting to life like I had as a teenager. I was really scared by what I was seeing, but I knew Hugh was right. Fear again raised its ugly head.

As Bill Sees It, page 51:

The Coming of Faith

In my own case, the foundation stone of freedom from fear is that of faith: a faith that, despite all worldly appearances to the contrary, causes me to believe that I live in a universe that makes sense.

To me, this means a belief in a Creator who is all power, justice, and love; a God who intends for me a purpose, a meaning, and a destiny to grow, however little and haltingly, toward His own

> likeness and image. Before the coming of faith I had lived as an alien in a cosmos that too often seemed both hostile and cruel. In it there could be no inner security for me.
>
> When I was driven to my knees by alcohol, I was made ready to ask for the gift of faith. And all was changed. Never again, my pains and problems notwithstanding, would I experience my former desolation. I saw the universe to be lighted by God's love; I was alone no more. [50]

I can certainly say amen to what Bill wrote.

Gary L.

11-1-08

Dear Matt,

I prayed for you this morning.

I'll never forget the first AA meeting I attended. I had no idea what to expect. The chairs at the meeting were set up theatre style, and the chairperson sat behind a desk in front. The chairperson that night was a broken-down retired logger who had been in numerous car and logging accidents. He was a small man who had difficulty standing straight, and he walked really slowly. His nickname was Speed. I didn't see the humor of that for some time.

At the start of the meeting, Speed asked if anyone was there for their first meeting, and if so to introduce themselves by their first name. I was in the back row and introduced myself. Speed looked at me, pointed his finger at me, and said words that I'll never forget: "Gary, you're the most important person in the room tonight. We're so glad you are here. Hope you hear something that will make you want to come back." I was stunned by his statement. I felt like I was the least important person in the world that night.

Speed then said, "Let's open the meeting with a moment of silence followed by the Serenity Prayer." When he said that a sense of panic went through me, and I thought, "Oh no, I'm in a room with a bunch of religious fanatics." By the time the prayer was concluded, the sense of panic had eased, and I thought the words sounded kind of interesting. Most of the people who spoke that night told how their life was before AA, what happened and how their life was currently. I heard miracle stories! Again, I was stunned. They seemed to know all about me. I wondered if they had been talking to Patsy. I left the meeting with something that hadn't been present in my life for a long time: hope! After hearing stories of miracle changes in people's lives I thought, "Perhaps there's a chance for me."

For a long time I had believed that there were no answers for me and that I would drink until I was locked up or dead. After the meeting, I got on an emotional roller coaster. One moment I wondered why I ever drank, and in the next moment, I thought about suicide. I had great difficulty focusing. I tried to read the Big Book, but after reading the same paragraph over and over, I would forget what I just read. I was unable to pull the words off the page.

Some days I'd go into our bedroom, close the door, and pace back and forth thinking, "Is this ever going to get better?" Patsy was afraid because my emotions were all over the place. Sleep was almost impossible. When my head hit the pillow, my fear, worry, and anxiety escalated. Somehow, through all of the emotional turmoil, I continued to attend classes at the community college and AA meetings.

One night after an evening class, fear overwhelmed me, and I was afraid to leave the campus. It was the same kind of fear that gripped me when I was unable to step out on the sidewalk at Mom and Dad's home some years before. I went to the student union to get a cup of coffee and to think. I could not bring myself to drive home. A custodian was working, and I asked him if I could spend the night there. In spite of that being against school policy, he allowed me to stay. I called Patsy and told her what was going on. Her fear was that I was going to drink, and this was just another lie. I slept on a sofa that night, and by morning, the fear was gone. I drove home, and Patsy was so relieved when she realized that I had been truthful. My guess is that she did a lot of praying that night.

After about three and a half weeks on the emotional rollercoaster, I decided to drink again. I could not see any other way to get relief from my mental and emotional turmoil. The little bit of hope that I had at my first meeting was gone. I felt so alone.

Blessings,
Gary L.

11-2-08

Dear Matt,

I prayed for you this morning.

I don't remember exactly how many days it was after the incident at the college, but one morning I awoke and knew I was going to drink. The term "slip" is often used when people drink. The word to me gives the idea of accident. I did not have a "slip" that day. It was not an accident that I drank. I left home early that morning with the intent that as soon as I got into Coos Bay I was going to drink. I stopped at one of my favorite taverns and started to drink. I turned into an ugly drunk that day.

I had never been kicked out of a bar up to this time, but that day I was asked to leave two different bars. I had always been able to give the impression that I was having a great time, but the great times were way back in the past. On the inside I might be dying, but the outside looked different. That day the inside came out. I was obnoxious, angry, belligerent, and offensive.

That evening I ended up in a bar called Deb's Club in North Bend. The more I drank, the more I felt darkness closing in on me. I still remember looking at a clock over the bar, and it was ten fifteen. I then made a decision. On the way home, I was going to get our station wagon going as fast as possible, find a post or guardrail, and check out. I was so tired of the fight. I came to the conclusion that drinking no longer worked, nor did not drinking. Another thing I thought about was the AA meetings I'd attended, the people who had befriended me there, and how hurt Patsy and the kids would be. I rationalized that they and the whole world would be better off if I wasn't around. The despair and despondency were overwhelming. I just wanted all of the pain to go away, and I was so tired of disappointing those who loved me. I continued drinking until I heard those dreaded words from the bartender, "Last call." Well, it was time to carry out my plan.

Deb's was a downstairs bar. I started up the steps to leave, and the next thing I recall was opening the back door of our home twelve miles away. I'd gone into a blackout, which wasn't unusual for me. Many times, I would wake up at home and wonder how I had gotten there. Patsy was crushed. The look on her face was devastating to me. I went to bed, and later that morning when I awoke, the battle began—go back to AA or go drink and finish what I had planned the night before. All that day the battle raged within me. I felt like I was a hopeless loser and wondered how I could ever face again the people in AA who had reached out to me. Guilt, shame, regret, fear, hopelessness, and despondency were like dark clouds that surrounded me. There was also a huge chunk of self-pity.

That evening I told Patsy that I was going to give AA another try, but part of me was thinking that this was a good way to get out of the house. As soon as I got to Coos Bay I would drink and finish the job. Driving to Coos Bay the battle intensified. I finally parked in front of the AA meeting place, but when I tried to open the door, I was unable to do it. I remembered back to the time I had been unable to step out onto the sidewalk at Mom and Dad's. I then decided to drive to a tavern that was nearby, but after placing the key in the ignition, I was unable to turn it. Inside I cried, "What in the world is wrong with me?"

I began to see the insanity of my alcoholism in a way I had never seen it. In the rooms of AA I had heard stories of transformed lives, of people living in freedom. At the bar was nothing but heartache, disappointment, and death. I thought, "Why is this such a difficult decision?" A sane person, if given the choice of life or death, would choose life without hesitation, but I was struggling with the decision. I wondered, "Am I totally insane?" There aren't enough words to describe the darkness I felt that night.

Perhaps you've felt that darkness.

Gary L.

11-3-08

Dear Matt,

I prayed for you this morning.

The night I sat in my car outside the AA meeting was March 2, 1971. Because of what God began to do in my life that night, I've not had a drink since then. When I think of that, I can only be grateful.

After being unable to open the car door or turn the key in the ignition, I had what I can only describe as a vision. It was as if I was watching a video. To the left of me was a road that was gray. It was a straight road that descended, and as it descended, the road became darker and darker until it turned into absolute blackness. While viewing that road, I envisioned years of unhappiness for Patsy, Trina, and Kelly. There was nothing but heartache on that road.

Then I saw another road to the right of me that also started out gray, but it ascended and as it did it became brighter and brighter until it turned into the brilliance of an arc weld. On that road I saw happiness for Patsy, Trina, Kelly, and myself.

I then said a prayer to the God I had known as a child, in spite of the belief that I was sure He didn't want anything to do with me: "God, give me the strength to go into that AA meeting." I tried the door again, and it opened easily, and I walked into the beginning of a new life that night. When I confessed to my friends that I had gotten drunk, they seemed to understand, and some were not surprised. Perhaps some saw something in me that I was unable to see in myself the few weeks I had attended meetings. I felt love, acceptance, forgiveness, and no judgment. Their response spoke volumes to me. And so the journey began.

What I believe today is that when I said the prayer that night, steps one through three fell into place. On page 30 in the Big Book it states:

> The idea that somehow, someday he will control and enjoy his drinking is the great obsession of every abnormal drinker. The persistence of this illusion is astonishing. Many pursue it into the gates of insanity or death.
>
> We learned that we had to fully concede to our innermost selves that we were alcoholics. This is the first step in recovery. The delusion that we are like other people, or presently may be, has to be smashed. [51]

For sixteen years I had had the "great obsession." It was removed, and that night I was fully convinced without any reservation that I was a real alcoholic and would never in my lifetime be able to drink successfully. Step One was finally in place after a sixteen-year war. I also understood that night that God could restore me to sanity, which is the essence of Step Two. I have made a daily decision since that night to let Him (Step Three). I heard a short version of steps one through three at a meeting one night: (1) I can't, (2) God can, (3) I think I'll let Him.

I wish I could say that life got wonderful at that time, but it didn't. On page 58 of the Big Book it states: "There are those, too, who suffer from grave emotional and mental disorders, but many of them do recover if they have the capacity to be honest."52 Because of my "grave emotional and mental disorders," the first year or so was extremely difficult. The miracle was that going through the most difficult emotional turmoil I had ever experienced, I never wanted to take a drink. I saw the miracle of that.

> Twenty-Four Hours a Day
>
> We in A.A. are offering an intangible thing, a psychological and spiritual program. It's a wonderful program. When we learn to turn to a Higher Power, with faith that that Power can give us the strength we need, we find peace of mind. When we reeducate our minds by learning to think differently, we find new interests that make life worthwhile. We who have achieved sobriety through faith in God and mental reeducation are modern miracles. It is the function of our A.A. program to produce modern miracles.
>
> **Prayer for the Day**
>
> I pray that I may feel deeply that all is well. I pray that nothing will be able to move me from that deep conviction. [53]

I'm often amazed how God pulls things together. In this letter I wrote about the night outside the meeting and the vision I saw. Today in my daily Bible reading I read the following from Deuteronomy 30:29: "Today I have given you the choice between life and death, between blessings and curses. I call on heaven and earth to witness the choice you make. Oh, that you would choose life, that you and your descendants might live! Choose to love the Lord your God and to obey Him and commit yourself to him, for He is your life."

I was not even aware of those verses that night, but that is what happened.

Blessings,
Gary L.

11-4-08

Dear Matt,

I prayed for you this morning.

Matt, my mind was so messed up when I first got sober. I was full of fear, anger, shame, resentments, and guilt. The night after my last drunk, Hugh took me under his wing and began to mentor me. Over and over, he would remind me just to live "one day at a time." Another time he said that a person can put up with just about anything for one day with God's help. Speed kept saying, "Gary, better things are in store," and I'd ask, "When?" I had difficulty focusing, and when my head hit the pillow at night my mind would race in many directions. I couldn't stop it. Many mornings when I awoke, I was just as tired as when I went to bed. I thought about buying over-the-counter sleeping pills, but something inside said, "That's probably not a good idea." I complained to Hugh about my lack of sleep. In his "sympathetic" way he said, "I've never seen a death certificate that listed lack of sleep as the cause of death. One of these nights you'll sleep." I said a prayer, "God, I'd like to go to bed some night, go to sleep, and wake up when it's morning."

It finally happened when I'd been sober about six months. I got excited! Another thing that Hugh told me was, "Gary, when you get up in the morning, give your drinking problem to God for the day. He's big enough to handle it, and you're not." He added, "Then go out and live your life for the day, and say thank you at night." I followed his suggestion.

What happened when I began doing that was that God got between me and the bottle. The bottle had to get through God to get to me, and He wouldn't let that happen. When it was just me against the jug, the jug always won. About the time I had my first good night's sleep it dawned on me that never once, going through the most intense emotional turmoil I'd ever experienced, not once did I want to drink. What a miracle!

There's a great promise in the Big Book on page 64: "When the spiritual malady is overcome, we straighten out mentally and physically." 54 In the process of a loving God working through the 12 Steps, and the spiritual growth as a result of that, we begin to change. My belief is that the process of change will continue until the day I see my Lord and Savior, Jesus Christ. Philippians 1:6: "Being confident of this, that He who began a good work in you will carry it on to completion until the day of Jesus Christ." That is another great promise to us.

Rooted in God's Love:

The process of recovery restructures our lives in some very fundamental ways. We had learned silence, and in recovery we learn to speak the truth. We had learned not to feel, and in recovery we learn to feel. We had learned either not to need other people at all or to be excessively dependent on other people, and in recovery we learn to need other people in healthy ways. These are significant changes. But, they are not irreversible changes. We can go back to silence, emotional numbness and unhealthy relationships. Recovery is necessarily therefore a new way of life. It is a daily pressing on. It is the day-at-a-time practice of the disciplines of recovery that makes it possible for us to continue to heal, grow and change.

Prayer: Lord, you have brought me so far. Thank you. I am grateful for all I have gained. But, I want to press on. I want to continue to grow. I want to continue to learn. Help me to press on. Help me to do today's recovery today. Help me to press on toward you. Take hold of me with your love. Amen. [55]

Blessings,
Gary L.

Colossians 3:15–16: "And let the peace that comes from Christ rule in your hearts. For as members of one body you are all called to live in peace. And always be thankful. Let the words of Christ, in all their richness, live in your hearts and make you wise. Use his words to teach and counsel each other. Sing psalms and hymns and spiritual songs to God with thankful hearts."

11-5-08

Dear Matt,

I prayed for you this morning.

It was good to receive another letter from you. I appreciate your prayers. The Bible study course you are taking will be helpful. You can never go wrong from studying God's word. Pour yourself into God's word, and He will pour Himself into you.

When I got sober in 1971 there were not the treatment programs that we have today. At the time, there was only one detox center in the state, and it was in Grants Pass. There was a treatment place called Raleigh Hills that I learned of after being sober several years. It was very expensive, and they used a treatment technique called "aversion therapy." What I learned about their method is all secondhand, so I'm not sure how accurate my information is. But, I was told that their patients were made to drink alcohol, followed by other liquids that reacted to the alcohol. The person would vomit violently, and then the procedure would be repeated. The thinking was that people would get so sick of alcohol that when they just even saw it, they would be repulsed. I know a woman who went through treatment there and never took another drink. I doubt that it would have worked for me because I already knew how to throw up. In fact, there were times that I would go behind a tavern and make myself throw up so I could drink more.

Today, there are so many specialists working in the field of recovery: psychiatrists, psychologists, mental health therapists, and alcohol/drug counselors. I can just imagine what the diagnosis of me would be if I'd seen a professional in 1971. I believe I would have been given many labels: bipolar, anxiety disorder, sleep disorder, narcissistic personality disorder, anti-social traits. I would have walked around like a zombie with all the medications that would have been prescribed.

Because treatment and counseling were not available to me, my only option was to reach out to God and AA. Had treatment and counseling been available to me, the first few years of recovery might have been a lot easier. One thing I observed after treatment centers became common is that some people after thirty days of treatment had as many tools in their toolbox for living, as I had after a couple of years.

For me, and I know this isn't true for everybody, complete dependence on God and AA is exactly what was best for me. I know I will never forget the early years and the pain I went through. I am so grateful that as God began to heal the pain, He helped me to see how that might benefit others. Early in recovery, I viewed my alcoholism as a terrible curse on my life. I now see it as probably the greatest blessing in my life.

Alcoholics Anonymous, page 68:

> We never apologize to anyone for depending upon the Creator. We can laugh at those who think spirituality the way of weakness. Paradoxically, it is the way of strength. The verdict of the ages is that faith means courage. All men of faith have courage. They trust their God. We never apologize for God. Instead we let Him demonstrate, through us, what He can do. [56]

Blessings,
Gary L.

Psalm 28:7: "The Lord is my strength, my shield from every danger. I trust in him with all my heart. He helps me, and my heart is filled with joy. I burst out in songs of thanksgiving."

11-6-08

Dear Matt,

I prayed for you this morning.

After the obsession to drink was removed the night of my return to AA after relapsing, AA looked so different to me. During my first attempt at meetings, I went because I felt I had to. After relapsing, I began to attend because I wanted to. That was a significant shift for me. I was like a sponge trying to soak up everything I could. I still had difficulty sleeping. I was full of fear and anxiety, but I was also excited about some things I was learning in the meetings.

A major difficulty for me was listening. At times, I would get so caught up in my thoughts and what I was going to say when called on, that I missed a lot. But in spite of that, I was taking home valuable information from others. I heard someone say, "First, we have to learn to listen, and then we listen to learn."

I came up with a plan to help me listen. When I arrived at a meeting, I'd approach the chairperson and ask if I could be called early in the meeting. I explained that after saying what I had to say, I would be able to listen to others better. Another thing I began doing was concentrating on each person who spoke, and trying to repeat in my mind what they were saying. On the way home from the meeting I'd give myself a test. Who chaired the meeting? What was the topic? Who was at the meeting and where did they sit? What did each person say? Some nights I would have almost total recall of the meeting. I passed the test! I was learning to listen. Some nights on the way home, I could barely remember anything about the meeting. What that said to me is, "You just have to keep working at it."

I need to tell you more about Hugh. He was a godsend to me. He encouraged me at times, but more important than that, he was willing to tell me the truth as he saw it, even when I got angry. Hugh modeled carrying the message of recovery to other alcoholics. He said that if you want to keep it, you have to give it away. Very early in recovery he said, "If someone new is at the meeting, introduce yourself after the meeting, give them your phone number, and tell them that they can call you anytime of the day or night. If they need a ride to a meeting, tell them that you'll take them."

Hugh introduced me to the Twelve Steps as being more than ideas hung on the wall. He said they were a spiritual way of life. At times Hugh confronted me about my self-pity. Sometimes that was all I brought to a meeting. I really knew how to throw a pity party. "Woe is me; life isn't fair; I never got the breaks; my daddy abandoned me when I was four; my stepdad never loved me," I would repeat ad nauseam.

One day, while feeling particularly sorry for myself, I called Hugh to complain about the state of my life. Hugh's wife Margaret answered the phone and informed me that Hugh wasn't home. So I thought I'd tell her my tale of woe. I barely got started, and she interrupted me. She said, "Gary, I'm really busy right now, but I'll tell you what I'll do. Tomorrow I'll set aside fifteen minutes and feel sorry just for you." Then she hung up the phone. I was so angry, but later I realized that she said what I needed to hear.

Later, when I talked to Hugh, he wouldn't give me any sympathy either. He said that if I was looking for sympathy, I could find it in the dictionary somewhere around syphilis or sweat. Boy did that ever fry me! But, again, it was what I needed to hear. There were times I would be so angry and resentful toward Hugh that I'd avoid meetings where I knew he would be. Then I'd miss him so much that I would return like a whipped puppy.

Hugh taught me how to do a gratitude list. He acknowledged that there were many negatives in my life because of the wreckage I'd created, but he said there were also many positives. He said, "You still have your wife and children; everything physical is working, but the most important thing to be grateful about is that you're sober today." He then added that I needed to nurture an attitude of gratitude. Someone said that it's impossible to be grateful and unhappy at the same time, and grateful is better. As gratitude grew within me, it began to push out not only my self-pity, but also the deep depression I was in. I don't know if this is true, but I sometimes wonder if a lot of depression isn't really self-pity disguised.

As Bill Sees It, page 238:

Maudlin Martyrdom

> Self-pity is one of the most unhappy and consuming defects that we know. It is a bar to all spiritual progress and can cut off all effective communication with our fellows because of its inordinate demands for attention and sympathy. It is a maudlin form of martyrdom, which we can ill afford.
>
> The remedy? Well, let's have a hard look at ourselves, and still a harder one at A.A.'s Twelve Steps to recovery. When we see how many of our fellow A.A.s have used the Steps to transcend great pain and adversity, we shall be inspired to try these life-giving

principles for ourselves. [57]

Blessings,
Gary L.

Psalm 107:13–14: "Lord, help!' they cried in their trouble, and he saved them from their distress. He led them from the darkness and deepest gloom; he snapped their chains."

11-7-08

Dear Matt,

I prayed for you this morning.

One area of dishonesty that I had to face early in recovery was the way I'd abused the state compensation system. I had not followed the doctor's instruction, nor did I do the exercises that might have helped. The truth was that I did not want to get better because that would mean that I would need to get a job and face the financial wreckage I'd created. Hugh said I needed to face my creditors, tell them what I was trying to do, and as soon as I got a job to start paying them. It was a difficult decision for me because of my lack of integrity.

While mulling the decision over, a plan came into my mind that seemed like a lot easier solution. My plan was to buy renters insurance, burn down our house, collect the insurance money, and pay our creditors. The plan made perfect sense to me. And then I planned how I was going to do it. Our home had an oil stove, and I decided that I'd a crack the oil line open and then light the oil. As I thought my plan through, a thought entered my mind, "Gary, if you carry out your plan, save some of the insurance money to buy a jug." I answered that thought with, "But I don't want to drink." The next thought was, "It goes with the territory." In a flash, I saw the insanity. I prayed, "Oh God, help me to do this the right way."

My belief today is that God cannot honor dishonesty, and part of my process was to get honest with myself. My entire life I had not had integrity, and it had never bothered me, but now it did. More evidence of God working in me. God was stirring me inside and allowing me to see what was really there. It was so difficult in the beginning to travel that inward journey. I had always been so conscious of what was wrong in my life externally, that I'd never taken an honest look inside. That's where the giants were. As a cartoon character named Pogo would often say, "I has met the enemy, and he is me."

As Bill Sees It, page 124:

Freedom to Choose

Looking back, we see that our freedom to choose badly was not, after all, a very real freedom.

When we chose because we "must," this was not a free choice, either. But it got us started in the right direction.

When we chose because we "ought to," we were really doing better. This time we were earning some freedom, making ourselves ready for more.

But when, now and then, we could gladly make right choices without rebellion, holdout, or conflict, then we had our first view of what perfect freedom under God's will could be like. [58]

Blessings,
Gary L.

Psalm 5–7:"Who can be compared with the Lord our God, who is enthroned on high? Far below him are the heavens and the earth. He stoops to look, and he lifts the poor from the dirt and the needy from the garbage dump."

11-8-08

Dear Matt,

I prayed for you this morning.

I finally made the decision to get off state compensation and face my creditors. I had not worked for approximately eighteen months, and my creditors were waiting for me to get a job so they could go after my wages. I had just enrolled for the spring term at Southwestern Oregon Community College. That was paid for by Vocational Rehabilitation, and I could not undo that. However, I could look for employment and stop receiving state compensation.

My reputation was shot in the community, and I wondered who might take a chance on me. I made many visits to the State Employment Office to no avail. One day, while leaving the office I noticed a three-by-five card on their bulletin board. It said: Wanted—Manager Trainee—$400.00 a month plus commission. I knew I could not possibly make it on that salary but wondered what the commission might be. I talked to a staff person in the employment office, and he arranged for an interview. I was still unaware of what the job was. I just knew it was an office job without any physical labor.

I arrived for the interview, and it seemed to go well. I was then called back for a second interview and was hired. God really has a sense of humor. The office was a credit reporting and collection agency. I was one of the biggest deadbeats in the county, and they should never have hired me with my track record. I have to believe that God was involved. Part of their hiring process is to check the credit history of the applicant. When they checked on me, they were unable to find anything negative.

Approximately six months later, I found out why. A collector would work a file until it became evident that it was impossible to collect, and then the file would be moved to what they called pending files. My file had been moved, and when the manager checked my credit file he did not check the pending files. The reason he discovered it six months after I'd been hired was because I'd applied for credit, and when the credit reporter checked on me she also checked the pending files and discovered that they had a judgment against me. I was not aware of the file or that they had a judgment against me. When files were placed in "pending," they stopped sending notices.

All of our other creditors had continued to send notices, and I had contacted all of them and made arrangements to make payments. Without exception, they worked with me. By the time my file was discovered I had proven myself as an excellent collector and employee, and my manager did not want to fire me (which he should have), and so he worked out a reasonable payment plan with me.

You might ask how I was unaware of the judgment. The last year or so I drank, when bills arrived I just tossed them. When a process server showed up, I tossed those papers as well. I just didn't care. When I had worked for the company for nine months, the assistant manager resigned, and I was promoted to his position. It normally took two years with the company for that kind of advancement. Three months later, I was promoted to manager. I worked for that company for three years, and when I resigned all of our financial wreckage had been cleaned up.

When I had first viewed the mountain of debt, I was unable to see how it could possibly work out. I've discovered over and over that God will lead us to the top of the mountains we face if we're willing to take His hand.

As Bill Sees It, page 152:

Miraculous Power

Deep down in every man, woman, and child is the fundamental idea of a God. It may be obscured by calamity, by pomp, by worship of other things, but in some form or other it is there. For faith in a Power greater than ourselves, and miraculous demonstrations of that Power in human lives are facts as old as man himself. [59]

Blessings,
Gary L.

Psalm 9:9: "The Lord is a shelter for the oppressed, a refuge in times of trouble."

11-9-08

Dear Matt,

I prayed for you this morning.

Today, I look back on the first year of recovery and know that the only way I made it through was by God's grace. Think about it—a new job, a mountain of financial wreckage, college classes, wife and two daughters, grave emotional and mental disorders, and trying to stay sober.

An evening class I signed up for was Psychology 101. I thought I might find some answers to the ways my mind worked, or, more importantly, how it did not work. In one of my conversations with Hugh, I began to spout off some of the psychology terms I was learning and about the insights I was gaining. He was not impressed and one day said, "Gary, you need to stop analyzing yourself, because you're working with a quack." Then he chuckled. I was so angry.

Today, I see the humor in his remark, but it wasn't funny then. Hugh then talked about "paralysis of analysis," and brought me back to the Twelve Steps. He said that if I would practice the principles within the Twelve Steps "one day at a time," that everything would work out. I believe that I really tried to complicate recovery in those early days. I heard someone say at a meeting, "AA is a simple program for complicated people, not a complicated program for simple people."

The professor of the psychology class was a great guy. His name was Bob.

One evening after a class, I confided to him that I was new in recovery from alcoholism and was really struggling mentally and emotionally. He invited me into his office, and we must have talked for an hour or so. He was the gentlest man I had ever met. It became a ritual for us to meet after class. He was genuinely interested in how I was doing. We also occasionally met for lunch.

During one of our meetings, he told me some of his history. When he was younger, he'd been a minister and then went back to school to get a PhD in psychology. He then added that whenever I was ready to do Step Five (Admitted to God, to ourselves, and to another human being the exact nature of our wrongs), he would be willing to listen. Bob knew about the Twelve Steps! So, that's why he was so willing to spend time with me. He had some understanding of the process from when he was a minister. I filed that information in my mind because I had not as yet started Step Four. (Made a searching and fearless moral inventory of ourselves.) I'll write more about

Steps Four and Five in future letters when I share with you my experience with the steps.

I will be eternally grateful to God and the way he has placed people on my path just when I need them. I can't begin to imagine how it would be to try and recover without the people who have influenced my life in many ways. I tried to stop drinking for many years by my own efforts and always failed.

Matt, I pray that the Twelve Steps will become as important in your life as they have been in mine and that God will use you to influence others because of the way He has worked in your life.

Blessings,
Gary L.

Hosea 10:12: "I said, 'Plant the good seeds of righteousness and you will harvest a crop of my love. Plow up the hard ground of your hearts, for now is the time to seek the Lord, that He may come and shower righteousness upon you.'"

11-10-08

Dear Matt,

I prayed for you this morning.

Although I was working a new job, taking night classes, and trying to be a better husband and father, I attended as many AA meetings as I could. My mind was so busy, and meetings seemed to slow it down. Meetings were almost like a place of refuge for me. I felt safe there. It was evident to me that God was helping.

The first few weeks I attended meetings I really struggled with Step One. "We admitted we were powerless over alcohol—that our lives had become unmanageable" (Big Book, page 58). 60 My alcoholism has a voice, and it would remind of the times that I seemed to be in control—the times I drank a few and quit—the periods of abstinence that I had. Although those times were few and far between, that's where the voice would take me. Because of that, I carried some reservations into the rooms of AA. So much evidence in the past reflected powerlessness, but I didn't want to look at that.

It was after the last night I drank after being in AA for a few weeks that the reservations were removed. Up until then the idea of powerlessness really went against the grain of who I was. To admit powerlessness seemed like losing, and I already felt like a loser. After the last drinking episode, I began to see Step One differently. In reviewing my drinking history and being honest with myself, I saw so many incidences when I intended on just having a few and ended up closing the bars. And there were many days when I would leave for work, determined to not drink after work, and then end up getting drunk. I could not guarantee 100 percent what was going to happen when I picked up the first drink. My eyes were slowly being opened.

Life Recovery Bible commentary on page 313: "When we refuse to admit our powerlessness we are only deceiving ourselves. The lies we tell ourselves and others are familiar: 'I can stop any time I want to.' 'I'm in control; this one won't hurt anything.' And all the while, we are inching closer to disaster." [61]

The second part of Step One, that my life was unmanageable, also rubbed me the wrong way. If everyone around me would just straighten up and do what I wanted, I wouldn't have any problems. They were at fault. Some more self-honesty helped me to begin seeing my side of the street. I was a control freak and didn't know it. When I couldn't get everything under control, I would drink and then blame everything and everybody. It's amazing to me all the games I played to avoid taking any personal responsibility for the way my life was.

Gary L.

It was while sitting in my car outside the AA meeting the night after my last drunk that I saw the truth. Those first few weeks in AA were difficult because I just didn't want to admit I was powerless. When Step One fell into place that night, I had a sense that my battle with the bottle was over. The issue now became, how do I learn to live sober? I didn't know how and was scared to death. There was also a great feeling of relief when Step One was in place. Step One, to me, is the foundation for all the other steps. As long as I had reservations about whether I was a real alcoholic, I could not stay sober. Bill W. said that Step One is the only one we have to do perfectly.

Blessings
Gary L.

Galatians 5:22: "For the fruit of the Spirit is love, joy, peace, patience, kindness, goodness, faithfulness, gentleness, and self-control."

11-11-08

Dear Matt,

I prayed for you this morning.

Proverbs 3:5–6: "Trust in the Lord with all your heart; do not depend on your own understanding. Seek his will in all you do, and he will direct your paths."

Big Book, page 59: Step Two. "Came to believe that a power greater than ourselves could restore us to sanity." 62

After Step One was in place, it was time to look at Step Two. Step One helped me to see the insanity of my life. Being in recovery meant I had everything to gain. Continuing to drink meant that I had everything to lose. A sane person would not struggle with those choices. The Big Book, on page 44, says this: "To be doomed to an alcoholic death or to live on a spiritual basis are not always easy alternatives to face." 63

What that says to me is that I cannot live on a "spiritual basis" without the help of God. I had believed in God since age five when I asked Jesus into my heart. I completely walked away from God at age ten but did not stop believing in God. What I had a difficult time believing is that God wanted anything to do with me. I had violated almost every value I was raised with. I had cursed God and anyone who claimed to be religious. I was extremely rebellious toward God. I was spiritually bankrupt, but I was also desperate.

Today, I believe that's the soil where God can really work. When I finally realized that all of my best efforts to make life work ended in failure, it opened the door for God to begin. Big Book, page 84: "We will suddenly realize that God is doing for us what we could not do for ourselves." 64

Grace for the Moment, by Max Lucado

Spiritual Bankruptcy

God does not save us because of what we've done. Only a puny god could be bought with tithes. Only an egotistical god would be impressed with our pain. Only a temperamental god could be satisfied with sacrifices. Only a heartless god would sell salvation to the highest bidders.

And only a Great God does for his children what they can't do for themselves.

> God's delight is received upon surrender, not awarded upon conquest. The first step to joy is a plea for help, an acknowledgment of moral destitution, and an admission of inward paucity. Those who taste God's presence have declared spiritual bankruptcy and are aware of their spiritual crisis....Their pockets are empty. Their options are gone. They have long since stopped demanding justice; they are pleading for mercy. [65]

That meditation is a perfect description of where I was. I knew I could not recover without God's help. Someone said, "We came. We came to. We came to believe." One thing that helped me tremendously in the beginning was the stories I heard at the AA meetings. Many people who had been right where I was were no longer there. The stories in the Big Book were also helpful.

On page 64 of the Big Book it states, "When the spiritual malady is overcome, we straighten out mentally and physically."66 Step Two helped me to deal with my spiritual malady, which is described on page 62 of the Big Book.

> Selfishness—self-centeredness! That, we think, is the root of our troubles. Driven by a hundred forms of fear, self-delusion, self-seeking, and self-pity, we step on the toes of our fellows and they retaliate. Sometimes they hurt us, seemingly without provocation, but we invariably find that at some time in the past we have made decisions based on self which later placed us in a position to be hurt.
>
> So our troubles, we think, are basically of our own making. They arise out of ourselves, and the alcoholic is an extreme example of self-will run riot, though he usually doesn't think so. Above everything, we alcoholics must be rid of this selfishness. We must, or it kills us![67]

So there's the "spiritual malady." I either serve myself or God. BigBook, page 44: "But after a while we had to face the fact that we must find a spiritual basis of life—or else."68

There is great commentary about Step Two on page 1,343 of the *Life Recovery Bible.*

Saying that "We came to believe" suggests a process. Belief is the result of consideration, doubt, reasoning, and concluding. The ability to form beliefs is part of what it means to be made in God's image. It involves emotion and logic. It leads to action. What, then, is the process that leads us to solid belief and changes our life?

We start with our own experiences, and we see what doesn't work. Looking at the condition of our life, we realize that we don't have enough power to overcome our dependency. We try with all our might, but to no avail. When we are quiet enough to listen, we hear that still, small voice inside us saying, "There is a God, and he is extremely powerful."

Recognizing our internal weaknesses is the first step toward recovery. When we look beyond our self, we see that there are others who have struggled with addiction and recovered. We know that they, too, were unable to heal themselves, yet they now live free of addictive behaviors. We conclude that there must be a greater Power that helped them. Since we can see the similarities between their struggles and our own, we come to believe that our powerful God can restore us to sanity. This is where many people are when they get to Step Two, and it's a good place to be on the way to recovery.[69]

Blessings,
Gary L.

11-12-08

Dear Matt,

I prayed for you this morning.

Nahum 1:7: "The Lord is good. When trouble comes, he is a strong refuge. And he knows everyone who trusts him."

Big Book, page 59: Step Three. "Made a decision to turn our wills and our lives over to the care of God as we understood him."70

I've always been a people-watcher. That kind of intensified as I attended AA meetings. It seemed to me that there were two major camps in AA. In one camp I observed some people who were not drinking, but they seemed angry, sometimes bitter, negative, resentful, and seemed to have very little peace. They rarely spoke of hope or gratitude and seemed generally unhappy. On page 58 of the Big Book it says, "If you have decided you want what we have, and are willing to go to any lengths to get it, then you are ready to take certain Steps."71 Seldom did I hear them speak about the steps. I didn't want what they had because I already had it.

There was another group of people who were sober. They seemed to have some peace and happiness, and for the most part the words they spoke were positive and hopeful. I heard a lot of gratitude when they spoke. They talked about the steps and how they were experiencing changes on the inside. They talked about God or Higher Power and how that helped in their journey. They were involved in service work within AA, sponsored others, and reached out to newcomers. There were other differences between the two groups, but I think you get the point. There was a distinct difference.

As I continued observing the two groups I concluded that there is a big difference between just not drinking and being sober. Many in the first group could tell you almost to the hour how long they had been sober. It seemed like they were doing "time." The first group rarely spoke about God, but God was really important to the other group. Both camps spoke a loud message, and I needed to decide which camp I wanted to be part of. That is where Step Three came in.

I desperately wanted what the second camp had, and I knew that I needed God's help to be in that camp. To me, Step Two is about believing in a higher power or God, and Step Three is about surrendering to the God of my understanding. I suppose if a person stood on a busy street and asked the first one hundred people who went by, "Do you believe in God?" a high percentage would say yes. If those who said yes were then asked, "Would you be willing to turn your will and life over to God and allow him to be your manager?" Very few would answer in the affirmative.

In spite of believing in God, I still wanted to run my own show. But the wreck my life became indicated that I didn't know how to do that. Step Three, to me, is about surrender. Sometimes I don't do that very well. I've not always had a great prayer life, but as time has gone on, prayer has become more and more a part of my life. There's a Step Three prayer in the Big Book on page 63 that I say every morning: "God, I offer myself to thee—to build with me and to do with me as thou wilt. Relieve me of the bondage of self, that I may better do Thy will. Take away my difficulties, that victory over them may bear witness to those I would help of Thy power, Thy love, and Thy way of life. May I do Thy will always."

That is a great prayer! I suppose if that prayer was written today it would say, "Relieve me of my narcissism, rather than bondage to self." An ongoing challenge for me has been to stay out of my own way, and the prayer helps. Earlier in sobriety it became clear to me that God had a much better plan for my life than I had, and in order to do it His way my will needs to be aligned with His.

There is great commentary about Step Three on page 1,131 of the *Life Recovery Bible.*

> When our burdens become heavy and we find that our way of life is leading us toward death, we may finally be willing to let someone else do the driving. We may have worked hard at getting our life on the right track but still feel as if we always end up on dead-end streets.
>
> Proverbs tells us, "There is a path before each person that seems right, but it ends in death" (Proverbs 14:12). When we began our addictive behavior, we were probably seeking pleasure or looking for a way to overcome our pain. The way seemed right at first, but it wasn't long before it became clear that we were on the wrong track. By then we were unable to turn around on our own. Jesus said, "Come to me, all of you who are weary and carry heavy burdens, and I will give you rest. Take my yoke upon you. Let me teach you, because I am humble and gentle, and you will find rest for your souls" (Matthew 11:28–29).
>
> Taking on a yoke implies being united to another in order to work together. Those who are yoked together must go in the same direction; by doing so, their work is made considerably

> easier. When we finally decide to submit our life and our will to God's direction, our burdens will become manageable. When we let him do the driving, we will "find rest" for our soul. He knows the way and has the strength to turn us around and get us on the road toward recovery.[72]

I'll talk some more about Step Three in my next letter. I pray that things are going well for you.

Blessings,
Gary L.

11-13-08

Dear Matt,

I prayed for you this morning.

1 Peter 1:8: "You love him even though you have never seen him. Though you do not see him, you trust him; and even now you are happy with a glorious, inexpressible joy."

Commentary on the above scripture on page 1,522 in the *Life Recovery Bible*:

Turning our will and our life over to God is a critical step in the recovery process. During our most painful trials, we may fail to see God with us. Yet Peter suggests that, strange as it may seem at the time, surrendering to God in difficult times can be a joyful experience. If we trust that God will use our trials to further the process of healing in our life, even the tough times can become times of celebration.73

The above scripture catches the essence of Step Three; surrender and trust in a God who can't be seen. So in addition to surrender in Step Three, there is also the issue of trust.

Many battles were fought during World War II. After each battle either our enemy retreated or we did, knowing that later we'd be shooting at each other again. After surrender was signed, they knew and we knew that we didn't have to shoot at each other anymore. It was only after surrender that restoration could begin. There were conditions of surrender to which our enemies had to submit. As long as they complied, the restoration continued. I had retreated from alcohol many times during the sixteen years I drank but had never surrendered until the night after I took my last drink. When surrender finally happened is when restoration of my life could begin. I was finally able to say, "Okay, alcohol, you finally beat me." I needed to surrender to the power of alcohol before I could surrender to God. As long as I believed that I was going to beat the jug, I kept taking it on. Alcohol had been my god, and I didn't even know it. The reason ongoing surrender is so important to me is that the God I serve today is bigger than the god I served for sixteen years, but I'm not. In a place of surrender He is my warrior, while in a place of retreat it's just a matter of time until I'm in the fracas again.

Because of events during my life, trust has not been easy. Even today, after many years of sobriety, I still struggle with trust at times. I am a long way from trusting as I'd like, but way ahead from where I was. There is a risk in trusting; sometimes people will let us down. I have to take the risks anyway, if I want to continue to grow spiritually. Another part of trust is this—can I be trusted?—can people depend on me to keep my word? The first time someone trusted me with their Step Five I was stunned. That person trusted me, a person who until recovery began could not be trusted with anything.

The choice I was given when I got to Step Three was to either embrace the step or to continue to run my life by myself. My track record was abysmal and gave abundant evidence that I did not know how to do life sober. When I got sober, newcomers were often referred to as "babies," and I certainly qualified. I am so grateful for the people who taught and nurtured me in my infancy. I owe a debt of gratitude to so many people because they've been there to help me through many stages of growth. When Step Three talks about "the care of God" I know today what it feels like to be cared for. God has used many people to care for me, when in the beginning I was unable to care for myself.

There is additional commentary regarding Step Three in the *Life Recovery Bible* on page 695.

> The thought of turning our will and our life over can be attractive. When we give in to our dependencies and compulsions, aren't we giving control over to another power? Aren't we in some way giving up personal responsibilities for our life? When we are overwhelmed and want to escape, our addiction can make us feel strong, safe, attractive, powerful, happy. So, in a sense, we are very comfortable with the thought of giving up control of our will and our life.
>
> We can take steps to change our focus and turn our life over to God instead of reverting to the hiding places of the past. The apostle Paul touched on this contrast when he said, "Don't be drunk with wine, because that will ruin your life. Instead, let the Holy Spirit fill and control you" (Ephesians 5:18).
>
> When we are overwhelmed and in need of some kind of escape, we have a new place to turn. King David declared, "The Lord is a shelter for the oppressed, a refuge in times of trouble. Those who know your name trust in you, for you, O Lord, have never abandoned anyone who searches for you" (Psalms 9:9–10).

David also wrote, "From the ends of the earth, I will cry to you for help, for my heart is overwhelmed. Lead me to the towering rock of safety, for you are my safe refuge, a fortress where my enemies cannot reach me" (Psalms 61:2–3).[74]

Blessings
Gary L.

11-14-08

Dear Matt,

I prayed for you this morning.

August 20 in *Twenty-Four Hours a Day*, applies to issues around Step Three.

A.A. Thought for the Day

When many hundreds of people are able to say that the consciousness of the presence of God is today the most important fact of their lives, they present a powerful reason why one should have faith. When we see others solve their problems by simple reliance upon some Spirit of the universe, we have to stop doubting the power of God. Our ideas did not work, but the God-idea does. Deep down in every man, woman, and child is the fundamental idea of God. Faith in a power greater than ourselves and miraculous demonstrations of that power in our lives are facts as old as the human race.

Meditation for the Day

You should not dwell too much on the mistakes, faults, and failures of the past. Be done with shame and remorse and contempt for yourself. With God's help, develop a new self-respect. Unless you respect yourself, others will not respect you. You ran a race, you stumbled and fell, you have risen again and now you press on toward the goal of a better life. Do not stay to examine the spot where you fell, only feel sorry for the delay, the shortsightedness that prevented you from seeing the real goal sooner.[75]

Well, I've given you my initial and ongoing experience with Step Three. The Big Book and the book *Twelve Steps and Twelve Traditions* are probably the best resources for the steps. I'm going to take a break from sharing my experience with the Twelve Steps and continue my story tomorrow.

Psalm 32:8: The Lord says, "I will guide you along the best pathway for your life. I will advise you and watch over you."

Blessings,
Gary L.

11-15-08

Dear Matt,

I prayed for you this morning.

Early in my sobriety, there were only three meetings a week in Coos Bay. I was usually at all three. Then Hugh introduced me to meetings in Gardner, Myrtle Point, and Coquille, and sometimes we'd drive sixty to seventy miles to Gold Beach to attend a meeting at the city jail. At that time, when a person had been sober six months he could apply to the Oregon State Prison to attend meetings at the Mill Creek Group at the penitentiary on Sundays. When I was sober six months, Hugh encouraged me to jump through all the hoops so I could attend the meeting with him. He drove there about once a month. Hugh had been in jail more than forty times during his years of drinking and understood what it was like to be locked up.

Shortly after I received approval, we picked a Sunday to attend the meeting. We left Coos Bay early on a Sunday morning so that we could attend a morning meeting in Florence and then on to Salem. My first visit there reminded me how close I had been to being incarcerated there. After the meeting, I was filled with gratitude. From the prison, we went to the S.O.S. Alano Club in Salem, where Hugh had many friends. After that we headed to Eugene and another Alano club and then on to Coos Bay. We arrived home sometime in the evening, and I have to say, "That was a great day!"

One major thing I recognized early in sobriety was that the obsession, compulsion and even the desire to drink were gone. That is certainly evidence of God doing for me what I had never been able to do for myself. Going through days of fear and deep depression (it might have been self-pity), Hugh and other members of AA continued to encourage me.

Shortly after I got my first job in sobriety at the Credit Bureau, I was informed that I needed to go through a week of training at the company's central office in Salem. Training would begin early on a Monday morning, so it was necessary that I drive to Salem on Sunday. I began to experience tremendous anxiety. I had no desire to drink, but I was fearful the desire would come back. Here I would be in a strange town, on an expense account, and no one to be accountable to. That was the kind of situation I would have "died" for when I was drinking. I arrived at the motel late in the afternoon, checked in, and went to my room full of fear and anxiety. While in my room, I remembered what I had heard someone say at a meeting. He said that he was in a situation that he had always drank. A thought came into his mind that he attributed to God, "You don't have to drink." He said, "It was then I realized that I don't have to drink."

While in the motel room that day I began to repeat, "I don't have to drink." It was like a revelation. Had I not been at the meeting where the man shared that, I would have missed it. I left the motel in the evening to get something to eat. I walked by a tavern that had its front door open. I smelled the booze, heard the bar noise, and said to myself, "I don't have to drink." After stopping at a restaurant and eating a sandwich, I returned to the motel. When I entered my room, I went over to the bed, and when I lay down, I began to cry from the wave of gratitude I felt. The training went well that week. It concluded on Friday afternoon. I knew when I began to drive home that I would be going through Gardner about the time of the AA meeting. I was so excited to get to that meeting so I could declare, "I don't have to drink!" That week was such a valuable experience for me. I knew that my faith was growing.

As Bill Sees It, page 196: "As faith grows, so does inner security. The vast underlying fear of nothingness commences to subside. We of AA find that our basic antidote for fear is a spiritual awakening."76

I really like the meditation and prayer from the *Twenty-Four Hours a Day* book today.

Meditation for the Day

God's miracle-working power is as manifest today as it was in the past. It still works miracles of change in lives and miracles of healing in twisted minds. When a person trusts wholly in God and leaves to Him the choosing of the day and hour, there is God's miracle-working power becoming manifest in that person's life. So we can trust in God and have boundless faith in His power to make us whole again, whenever He chooses.

Prayer for the Day

I pray that I may feel sure that there is nothing that God cannot accomplish in changing my life. I pray that I may have faith in His miracle-working power. [77]

Psalm 73:22–24: "I was so foolish and ignorant—I must have seemed like a senseless animal to you. Yet I still belong to you; you are holding my right hand. You will keep on guiding me with your counsel leading me to a glorious destiny."

Blessings,
Gary L.

11-16-08

Dear Matt,

I prayed for you this morning.

Proverbs 15:30: "A cheerful look brings joy to the heart; good news makes for good health."

As I approached my first year sobriety birthday, several things became apparent to me. Going through some of the most intense emotional turmoil that I'd ever experienced, I had not wanted to drink. During times when thoughts of suicide would enter my mind, I did not want to numb out with a drink. My mind was slowing down, and after approximately six months, I was able to sleep well. I was becoming a better husband and father. I had moments of serenity. All of those things were miracles. I felt the grace of God in a way I never had previously. There was a purpose in my life to help other alcoholics. Hugh suggested to me early in sobriety that, whenever a newcomer came to a meeting, I introduce myself after the meeting and tell him that he could call me any time of the day or night if he needed to talk. Hugh said that if he needs a ride to meetings that it is to my benefit to provide that. *Hope began to grow!*

My home group did not give out recovery medallions until a person had been sober a year, unlike many groups that give them out at thirty, sixty, ninety days, etc. When a person celebrated one year, it was his responsibility to bring a cake to the meeting in order to thank the group for helping him stay sober. My home group meeting was on Saturday nights, and Patsy attended that meeting with me almost every week. She really got a lot out of the meeting. I will always be grateful for the way she has supported my recovery. Well, my birthday finally arrived. In my home group, the chairperson always called on the birthday people last. I don't think I heard much of what was said that night. I was so caught up in my own mind thinking about what I was going to say, that it was difficult to listen. When the chairperson called on me, I opened my mouth to speak and instead began to cry. It dawned on me that this hopeless, helpless, loser alcoholic had gone a year without a drink. As I cried, I had waves and waves of gratitude go through me. Words like hope, faith, peace, and freedom were meant for me! I had believed for so long that none of that was available to me.

Grace for the Moment 11/16, by Max Lucado.

God Knows the Answers

Thomas came with doubts. Did Christ turn him away?

Moses had his reservations. Did God tell him to go home?

Job had his struggles. Did God avoid him?

Paul had his hard times. Did God abandon him?

No. God never turns away the sincere heart. Tough questions don't stump God. He invites our probing.

Mark it down. God never turns away the honest seeker. Go to God with your questions. You may not find all the answers, but in finding God, you know the One who does.[78]

Blessings
Gary L.

11-17-08

Dear Matt,

I prayed for you this morning.

As I was walking on the treadmill this morning and thinking about what to write today, I thought back to an incident that happened sometime when I was sober six to eight months. That was a long time ago so I don't remember the exact time line. I might have told this to you in a previous letter. If that's the case, just indulge this forgetful old man.

A health teacher from Marshfield High School called the AA number to see if a member would be willing to talk to his class about their experience with alcohol. The group asked me if I would do it. Hugh had said to me one time that if AA asks you to do something, it would be to my advantage to say yes, so that's what I did.

Now I have to tell you why that was difficult. One of the biggest lifelong fears that I had up to then was speaking in front of people. On a list of fears that people have, public speaking ranks right next to fear of death. When I was given an assignment in school that required an oral report, I would try to bargain with the teacher. I might say, "I'll write a three-thousand-word essay, if you won't make me get up in front of the class." Sometimes that worked, and when it didn't I would take a failing grade. The thought of speaking in front of people brought total panic to me. I brought that fear into adult life, and when I agreed to speak at Marshfield High School, I wondered, "What have you just done to yourself?" The day selected to speak was several weeks out, and fear consumed me as I thought about it. I had nightmares and thoughts of canceling.

The day finally arrived, and I drove to the school. I was early, and after locating the classroom where I would be speaking, I began to pace the hallway waiting for the class bell to ring. When it rang, the students filed out followed by the teacher. We introduced ourselves, and he asked me to wait in the hall until he signaled me to come in. My palms and pits were sweating as I waited. He finally motioned for me to come in, and I said a quick prayer,

"God, if you're not with me, I'm dead." I walked to the front of the class, where I was introduced. When I opened my mouth to speak, all of the fear went away! It just disappeared! And since that time, I've had many opportunities to speak to groups, and the fear has never returned. What a miracle of God doing for me what I had never been able to do for myself! What a boost for my faith. As someone said, "Every time we go through a place of fear with God's help, our faith will grow."

Gary L.

Well, my friend, I hope your studies are going well. I won't be able to do it until next spring, but if you get me on your visitors list, I'll drive over to see you. I hope to see Jason at the same time.

Proverbs 12:25: "Worry weighs a person down; an encouraging word cheers a person up."

Blessings,
Gary L.

11-18-08

Dear Matt,

I prayed for you this morning.

It was good to receive another letter from you yesterday. Please don't feel that you have to write as often as I do. After I've completed my story, I won't write every day.

You said that you don't struggle with alcohol, but as you know, a drug is a drug. It's impossible for me to serve God and use chemicals. It's two distinct lifestyles, as I'm sure you're aware. When you say, "Tacoma would make me fall under again," I thought back to when a major shift of belief happened in me.

I had a false belief (old idea) for many years that said things outside of myself caused me to drink. I had many periods of abstinence, and then something would happen and I'd be on another run. At the time, no one could have convinced me that it was my fault that I was drinking again. And that again goes back to the false belief: something or someone caused me to drink. As long as I could blame something else, I didn't have to take responsibility for my actions. That's the primary reason that I was unable to maintain sobriety through the many times I quit "drinking forever." When the realization came that nothing could "cause" me to drink, I no longer had anyplace to stick the blame. I was shifted to a new level of responsibility that was kind of scary to me. All of a sudden, I realized that there were no longer any excuses to drink. I've experienced more losses in sobriety than when I was drinking—the death of my younger brother from this disease when he was twenty-seven—the death of my mother—the death of my stepfather who raised me—a business failure when I had been sober fifteen years, and Patsy and I lost everything. Through all of those losses there was never a thought of taking a drink because of the shift of belief from "things cause me to drink," to "I'm responsible, and there is no such thing as a valid excuse to drink for an alcoholic." When I believed that externals caused me to drink, I was always able to find something to drink at. Since the shift of belief happened, all of my excuses disappeared.

You ask about your struggle with reading the Bible. Ask the chaplain if there is an NLT available there. It is easy to read, and there is a lot of commentary that explains about each book. There is also a guide on working through the Twelve Steps and the scriptures that apply. I've been using the NLT for a long time, and it has really been helpful to me. You could also ask the chaplain about a Bible survey course. Let me know which version of the Bible that you're using. Some translations are difficult to read.

If you end up in this area at some point, I would gladly be your sponsor. Let me know if and when you're transferred. As far as the craving you wrote about, think the drug all the way to the end. Where did it always take you? The Big Book talks about "pitiful, incomprehensible demoralization." That's where the first drink always eventually took me. When you think it all the way through, the appeal will probably go away. Craving, to me, says that you need to revisit Steps One through Three. If I was to desire a drink, that would be evidence of insanity, given my track record with alcohol.

As Bill Sees It, page 33:

> **Foundation for Life**
>
> We discover that we receive guidance for our lives to just about the extent that we stop making demands upon God to give it to us on order and on our terms.
>
> In praying, we ask simply that throughout the day God place in us the best understanding of His will that we can have for that day, and that we be given the grace by which we can carry it out.
>
> There is a direct linkage among self-examination, meditation, and prayer. Taken separately, these practices can bring much relief and benefit. But when they are logically related and interwoven, the result is an unshakable foundation for life.[79]

It was so comforting to me when I began to understand that God was on my side and that He would help me through my struggles. When I fought my alcoholism with my power I always lost. Surrender, surrender, surrender.

John 14:27: "I am leaving you a gift—peace of mind and heart. And the peace I give isn't like the peace the world gives. So don't be troubled or afraid."

Blessings,
Gary L.

11-19-08

Dear Matt,

I prayed for you this morning.

During my second year of sobriety, I became involved in an organization called the Coos County Council on Alcoholism. This was a nonprofit corporation formed by a group of people who wanted to start an inpatient treatment center for alcoholics and addicts. The council had received some grant money to hire a person to head up the program. The person they hired was from San Francisco, and he had been instrumental in starting the first treatment center in that city. His name was Bill, and he was a mental health therapist. I liked him immediately when we met. He had a great ability to bring people together and to work for a common goal. Before long, because God had removed my fear of public speaking, I was speaking at various civic organization luncheons and banquets, explaining the goals of the council and our need for public support. Part of what I presented was how treatment was cost-effective for the community. A sober alcoholic or addict can contribute to the community. I was excited about what the council was doing, and it was such a privilege to be part of that. Then the company I worked for promoted me and transferred me to their Portland office. Career-wise it was a great opportunity. The office I managed had seven employees, and in the Portland office, I would be supervising approximately twenty collectors. The total number of employees in the office was around fifty. The opportunity was bittersweet in that I would be leaving the recovery community that had saved my life.

After discussing it with Hugh, he assured me that there was a lot of great AA where I was moving to. I accepted the promotion, and when it was time to move, Hugh not only helped us load the U-Haul truck, he also drove it to Battle Ground, Washington, where we had purchased a home near my parents. By the time we moved, I had celebrated two years of sobriety. What great changes had occurred during that time! After unloading the truck, I took Hugh to the Greyhound bus station in Portland. He wouldn't even let me pay for the ticket back to North Bend.

There were job pressures in an office of that size that I had difficulty dealing with, and part of me longed to be back in Coos County. I worked in the Portland office for nine months, but my heart wasn't in it. While looking in the help-wanted section of the newspaper, I saw an ad for an alcohol/addict counselor trainee position. The program was on the fifth floor of a hospital in Vancouver. I applied for the position, was interviewed, and was accepted into the program. I resigned from the Credit Bureau and accepted the position. The initial part of the program was that the trainee had to actually go through the twenty-eight-day program as a patient.

The date was set for me to report, and I had tremendous anxiety about it. I questioned, "Is this what God really wants me to do?" There would be extreme financial hardship for our family for the year it took to complete the training. The morning of the day I was to report, I received a call from Bill from the Coos County Council on Alcoholism. He informed me that the council had raised enough money to start a treatment center. They had leased a large ranch-style home outside of Coquille, and he asked if I would be interested in helping set up the program and being the director of the center. One thing I've learned in recovery is that God is never late; nor is He ever early. I got so excited while talking to Bill. Patsy readily agreed that taking the position was the right thing to do. If someone had told me when I first got sober that a little more than three years later I would be the director of a treatment center, I would have laughed. What a great God I serve! I called the treatment center in Vancouver and told them that I'd changed my mind. The man I spoke with was very gracious and wished me well.

At the time, 1974, Serenity Lane had been open for a short while; aversion therapy was available at a place called Raleigh Hills; a detox center was in Grants Pass, and that was about it in the state. Oregon has come a long way since then. In almost every community there is help available for the alcoholic/addict.

The agency that was going to oversee the new treatment center was the Coos County Mental Health Department. I was to report to work there on July 1, 1974, to meet with the director and with Bill. I reported for work, and that's when things got real sticky. I'll tell you about that in my next letter.

2 Corinthians 10:17–18: As the scripture says, "The person who wishes to boast should boast only of what the Lord has done." When people boast about themselves, it doesn't count for much. But when the Lord commends someone, that's different!

Blessings,
Gary L.

11-20-08

Dear Matt,

I prayed for you this morning.

When I arrived at the Coos County Mental Health Department to meet with the director and Bill (he was the man who hired me), I was in for a shock. After being ushered into his office, I sat down with him and Bill. The director was reviewing my resume. After a few moments he looked at me and said, "We can't pay you what was offered because you don't have enough education." I was stunned, as was Bill. He then looked at Bill and said, "You didn't have the authority to offer that much salary." As calmly as I could, I asked, "Well, how much can you pay me?" The amount he offered was so much lower than what I had been offered, and I would not be able to support my family on it. A feeling of rage began to develop within me, but I'd learned in AA to think things through to the end, and I intuitively knew that if I said the things going through my mind, I would do more harm than good. My emotions were going crazy, and I said to them, "I need to leave before I say or do something that I will regret," and I walked out.

I had just moved my family approximately two hundred miles to start a dream job, and it was all going up in flames. I didn't know what to do. Fear and confusion were like giants. I had a friend in AA who was building a new home at the time. He got sober a few months after me, and we had become good friends. I needed to talk to someone, so I drove to his home. When I arrived he was working on his new home. I explained what had happened. He was in the process of nailing off the floor of the first story of his home. I was wearing slacks, a sport coat, and tie. I took off the sport coat, grabbed a nail apron and hammer, and began driving nails with a vengeance. I was driving them as hard and as fast as I could. I don't think I was even holding a nail when I hit my thumb with the hammer. I really smashed it. But that diversion stopped my crazy thinking. We stopped working, and I was able to talk with my friend a little more rationally. I appreciated the fact that he didn't try to fix my situation, nor did he tell what to do; he just extended the gift of listening.

One of the blessings of adversity is that God can use it to help shape our trust. It's easy to trust God when life is cooperating. But when life goes sideways is when I really need to exercise trust. Believing is much easier for me than trusting. I wondered, "How is this ever going to work out?"

Once again, Patsy and I were in a place that we needed to trust God. We couldn't fix what was happening, but God could. I'll tell you about that in my next letter.

Blessings,
Gary L.

11-21-08

Dear Matt,

I prayed for you this morning.

Later, on the same day I smashed my thumb, Bill called me and said that he had called a special meeting with the board members of the Council on Alcoholism to see if they could work something out. The consensus with the board members was that the director of Mental Health had authority over policies and procedures of the Treatment Center, but not over who would be hired or what that person would get paid. Bill and the council then had a meeting with the director.

Several days went by, and then we received the good news from Bill. The council could hire me and pay the salary that I had been offered, and I could begin immediately in setting up the South Coast Recovery Center. Patsy and I were so relieved, and also thrilled by the opportunity ahead of us. The house that had been leased needed a lot of cosmetic work, primarily interior painting, which Patsy and I did. Then it was time to furnish the house. Other than a stove and refrigerator, the house was empty of furnishings. I contacted a friend who owned a hardware and furniture store. He provided all of the mattresses we needed, plus many kitchen items. Another friend who owned a manufactured-home business gave us sofas, chairs, and tables. We had other items donated, and, within several weeks, we welcomed our first patient. Patsy and I had not found a home to move into during the time we worked on the house and had slept in sleeping bags in one of the bedrooms.

We had to remain in the house for some time because there was not enough money to hire another staff person, and we could not leave our patient unsupervised. While in Coos Bay one day, I ran into a guy that I had given a ride to meetings when I first got sober. My friend had lost a leg when he was a child and was now on Social Security. I told him about what I was doing, and he said that he would be willing to be a night and weekend volunteer in exchange for room and board. He was a godsend to us. After he moved in, Patsy and I met with a real estate agent and began looking for a house to buy in Coquille.

Our first patient was only twenty-six when he arrived. He had been detoxed in a local hospital. He was separated from his wife and child and absolutely beat up by his addiction. He was depressed, felt hopeless, was full of fear and grief, and had considered suicide. In spite of all of that, he was willing to go to meetings and to explore the possibility of a Higher Power. After a couple of weeks, it seemed as if a light came on for him. That was exciting to see. He stayed with us for over two months and then was reunited with his family. He got a sponsor and became involved with meetings. What a change! A year or so after he got sober, he moved out of state. My hope is that he stayed on the path. We continued to get more patients, and eventually our census was twelve to fifteen. In my next letter I'll describe how primitive the program was compared to today.

Twenty Four Hours a Day. 11–21:

Meditation for the Day

You were meant to be at home and comfortable in the world. Yet some people live a life of quiet desperation. This is the opposite of being at home and at peace in the world. Let your peace of mind be evident to those around you. Let others see that you are comfortable, and seeing it, know that it springs from your trust in a Higher Power. The dull, hard way of resignation is not God's way. Faith takes the sting out of the winds of adversity and brings peace even in the midst of struggle.[80]

Ephesians 1:6–8: "So we praise God for the wonderful kindness he has poured out on us because we belong to his dearly loved son. He is so rich in kindness that he purchased our freedom through the blood of his Son, and our sins are forgiven. He has showered his kindness on us, along with all wisdom and understanding."

Blessings,
Gary L.

11-22-08

Dear Matt,

I prayed for you this morning.

The treatment program that we put together was based on the Twelve Steps. That was my only point of reference. The director of the Coos County Mental Health Department was accurate when he said that I did not have enough education for the position. What I did have was personal recovery, the Twelve Steps, and God. I also had passion in carrying a message of hope to alcoholics and addicts. In spite of my inexperience, some of the patients got sober and stayed sober. That had to be the "grace of God." Bill came to the center once a week and did group process. We began an AA meeting once a week at the house, which was strongly supported by the AA community. Several nights a week, I took our patients to outside AA meetings. I also spent a lot of one-on-one time with the patients. Patsy was hired as a cook and was paid minimum wage. We arrived at the center at 6:00 AM, and Patsy would go home around 6:00 PM. I was busy most evenings with AA meetings and would get home around 10:30 PM. The days were long, and I loved it.

In addition to working at the center, another responsibility I had was fund-raising and community education. I made presentations to civic organizations, city councils, and churches. There was a major setback for me the second year at the Center. Instead of hiring more staff at the center, the council hired a person to work in the council office. I desperately needed another staff person. I wasn't aware of the term burnout at the time, or the term self-care. In retrospect, I was heading for burnout.

One great benefit from hiring the person in the office was that I was no longer responsible for fund-raising or community education. Before the new person was hired, I had put together a fifteen-hour diversion program for the courts. People would attend a three-hour session for five weeks. A medical doctor lectured on the disease concept the first week. A psychologist spoke the second week, and that was followed by a person from the police department, and then an attorney. The last week was an AA speaker, usually me or Hugh. I was relieved of the responsibility of the diversion program when the new person was hired. The council was aware that I needed more staff, and the new office person knew how to do grant writing. Hopefully she would be able to get some grants to fund more staff. Well, she was successful at getting more funding, but rather than give me more staff, the council decided to set up a detox center. I was so angry about that decision.

Gary L.

After two and half years of Patsy and I being the only staff at the center, I was burned out/fried. My passion was gone. When I tendered my resignation I felt a great sense of relief, but along with that was a great feeling of loss. It was time to get honest with myself and look for my part in what happened.

Rooted in God's Love:

> We need to be reminded that we are not God. This seems pretty basic. You wouldn't think it would be hard to remember. But we get so caught up in proving ourselves by performing, achieving and rescuing that we forget that we are humans with real limits. We fill our time so full of frenzied activity that there is no stillness. And when there is no stillness, it is hard to remember who is God and who is not.
>
> Fortunately, God does not forget who is God and who is not. God invites us to quiet ourselves—to slow ourselves down. God invites us to be still long enough to regain perspective. "Be still," God says, "and know that I am God."
>
> In the stillness we can see again that there is a difference between our frenzy and God's kingdom. It is God's work to provide and protect and rescue. It is not our work. We can do our part. But our part needs to be respectful of our human limits. Our part needs to actively acknowledge our dependence on God. God is God, and we are not.
>
> Help me to slow down, Lord.
>
> Help me to be quiet.
>
> Help me to be still long enough to remember that you are God.
>
> Help me to remember who is creature and who is Creator.
>
> Let this truth free me, Lord, to accept my limits, Amen.[81]

One of the biggest challenges that I face, is how to stay out of God's way. Often I'm not even aware when I've taken the job of Conductor until the train wrecks. Through the years, I have been constantly reminded of His amazing grace. My biggest regret from those two and a half years was that I was not much of a dad to our daughters. Because of self-interest, my priorities were skewed.

Proverbs 3:5–6: Trust in the Lord with all your heart; do not depend on your own understanding. Seek his will in all you do, and he will direct your paths.

Blessings,
Gary L.

11-23-08

Dear Matt,

I prayed for you this morning.

I need to go back to when the Credit Bureau transferred me to Portland. As you might remember, we moved to Battle Ground, Washington. One day our doorbell rang. When I opened the door there was a young couple who said they were from a local church. They asked if we had a church home, and I quite smugly informed them that I believed in God and didn't need church. They asked if we had children who might want to attend Sunday school. They explained that the church had a bus that would pick them up and take them home. We asked Trina and Kelly if they'd like to go to Sunday School, and it sounded like a great adventure to them, so the couple said they would be picked up on the following Sunday.

We lived on a cul-de-sac and were the last stop on their route. When our daughters were brought home the first Sunday, the young couple got off the bus and came over to Patsy and me while we were working in our yard. They tried to witness to us about Jesus, and I smugly, perhaps rudely, rebuffed their efforts. They politely excused themselves. But when they started to get on the bus, the man said to me, "The scripture says that no man can come to the Father but through the Son." That phrase began to haunt me. Driving to work it would be in my thoughts. Sitting at my desk working it would invade my mind. I could shake it for a while, but then it would return.

After resigning my position and moving to Coquille to start my new job, Patsy and I met with a real estate agent in order to buy a new home. With the new night and weekend person at the center, it was time for us to move into a home. While driving up a street with the agent we passed a home that had her sign in the yard. I asked about it, but she said that there were other homes we might like better. We couldn't get that house out of our minds, and after looking at several homes we asked to see the one that she didn't think we'd be interested in. The house needed a lot of cosmetic repairs, but the foundation, wiring, and plumbing were good. We made an offer, and it was accepted.

Soon after we moved in, we noticed that a church was just across the street. We really hadn't noticed it before. One Sunday afternoon while Patsy and I were working in our yard, a car pulled up to the front of the church. When the driver got out of the car our daughter Trina yelled to him, "Hello, Mr. Steward." He looked our way and came over to introduce himself. He was Trina's schoolteacher. After initial introductions he invited Patsy and me to attend church. I smugly declined, but Trina and Kelly said they'd like to go to Sunday school. At the time, I was in kind of a dark place spiritually, and after talking it over with Patsy, we thought we'd give it a try.

I had a tremendous amount of anxiety the first Sunday we attended. We arrived at the church early enough to attend an adult Sunday school class. We were warmly greeted, which eased some of my anxiety. After the class, we were directed to the sanctuary for the main service. You might recall that when I was a child I attended a church with my grandma and had sung hymns on the church's radio program. So, many years later, attending church again, something absolutely amazing happened. They sang a hymn that morning that was one I had sung many years earlier in my grandma's church. I still remembered the words. "I come to the garden alone. While the dew is still on the roses. And the voice I hear, falling on my ear, the Son of God discloses. And He walks with me, and He talks with me, and He tells me I am His own. And the joy we share, as we tarry there, none other, has ever known." I just about came unstuck as the hymn was sung. What are the odds of them picking that hymn out of the hundreds in the book? God really got my attention that morning.

John 1:10–13: "But although the world was made through him, the world didn't recognize him when he came. Even in his own land and among his own people, he was not accepted. But to all who believed him and accepted him, he gave the right to become children of God. They are reborn! This is not a physical birth resulting from human passion or plan—this rebirth comes from God."

Blessings,
Gary L.

11-24-08

Dear Matt,

I prayed for you this morning.

By the time Patsy and I attended church the first time, I had been sober more than three years. Despite many exciting events during that time, I felt spiritually empty. The time I spent in prayer and meditation was minimal and unfulfilling. God seemed distant to me and much doubt had crept in. I wondered, "Has God been just a figment of my imagination?" But the Sunday the people sang the hymn I had sung as a child, the doubts disappeared. My faith was rekindled; once again, God's timing was perfect.

We began to attend the church weekly. We had been so welcomed by others, and new friendships developed. I had been so judgmental of organized religion and those who practiced it. God began to break down my prejudices. It was about the fourth week we attended that God touched me in a way I never expected. Pastor Grimes was preaching, and toward the end of his sermon he asked the question, "If you had to appear before God, and all of the sins during your lifetime were read to Him to be judged, would you plead guilty or not guilty?" I would have had to admit my guilt. My first Fourth Step clearly revealed to me my wrongs.

He then asked, "If you lived in a culture that the penalty for your sins was death by crucifixion, how would you feel when the guilty verdict was read?" I imagined the fear I would have felt. Then he asked another question, "What if just as they were getting ready to drive the first nail, someone approached the authorities and offered to be crucified in your place, that he would pay the price for your sins, allowing you to go free? How would you respond," he asked. I thought, "I would probably respond with overwhelming gratitude."

Pastor Grimes then added, "That's exactly what Jesus did for you. He took on himself the punishment for your sins, past, present, and future. If you accept what He did on your behalf, the penalty for your sins has been paid, and you get to go free." I heard the truth of what he was saying that morning in a way I'd never heard it before. The truth penetrated my soul. Pastor Grimes then asked the congregation to bow in prayer. With all bowed in prayer he asked the question "Is there anyone here today who would like to accept what Jesus did for you? If so, please raise a hand so I can lead you in prayer." With our eyes closed, Patsy and I raised a hand that morning. I don't remember the exact wording of the prayer he led us in, but it went something like this, "God, thank you for sending your Son to pay the price for my sins. I accept today what He did on my behalf, and I invite Him in as my Savior and Lord." Pastor Grimes then said that if we had prayed that prayer, that we were forgiven because the price had been paid in full. I realized that morning that there had been a big hole on the inside of me that I had tried to fill with many things—alcohol, money, acclaim, busyness, prestige, and relationships. I realized that morning that place in me had always been reserved for Him. When I asked Him to fill that place, I was finally free.

Bill W. suffered from depression and wrote about it often. In the book *Alcoholics Anonymous Comes of Age*, Bill writes on page 63:

> My depression deepened unbearably and finally it seemed to me as though I were at the very bottom of the pit. I still gagged badly on the notion of a Power greater than myself, but finally, just for the moment, the last vestige of my proud obstinacy was crushed. All at once, I found myself crying out, "If there is a God, let Him show Himself! I am ready to do anything, anything!"
>
> Suddenly the room lit up with a great white light. I was caught up into an ecstasy which there are no words to describe. It seemed to me, in the mind's eye, that I was on a mountain and that a wind not of air but of spirit was blowing. And then it burst upon me that I was a free man. Slowly the ecstasy subsided. I lay on the bed, but now for a time I was in another world, a new world of consciousness. All about me and through me there was a wonderful feeling of Presence, and I thought to myself, "So this is the God of the preachers!"[82]

Alcoholics Anonymous, page 64: "When the spiritual malady is overcome, we straighten out mentally and physically."83

Life has never been the same since that morning in 1974. God has not protected me from life in the ensuing years, but He has been faithful to help me through whatever life has placed on my path. As I wrote this letter, I had great waves of gratitude wash over me. Someone said, "It's impossible to be grateful and unhappy at the same time, and grateful is better."

Matt, count your many blessings this Thanksgiving week.

Psalm 40:11: "Lord, don't hold back your tender mercies from me. My only hope is in your unfailing love and faithfulness."

Blessings,
Gary L.

11-25-08

Dear Matt,

I prayed for you this morning.

I have a lot going on today so all I'll share with you today is another meditation and prayer from *Rooted in God's Love*:

Recovery As Seeing The Light

Isaiah 9:2: "The people who walk in darkness will see a great light—a light that will shine on all who live in the land where death casts its shadow."

We know what it is like to walk in darkness. We know what it is like to live in the shadow of death. But we also are beginning to experience what it is like to see. The darkness of denial is giving way to the light of honesty in our lives.

Of course, when you have lived in darkness as long as we have, the light can be painfully bright. We see the truth about ourselves and our self-destructive behavior. We see the truth about our refusal of love. We see the truth of our brokenness. We see old pain. We see current behaviors that damage ourselves and others. The light dawns. It is not a pretty sight.

But God does not send His light into our darkness to shame us. The exposure may trigger our deep shame, but this is not God's purpose. God's light is like the light of dawn. It is a light that signals that something new is happening. A new beginning is possible. The light that God brings into our dark world is a light of hope.

Recovery is God's light coming into our darkness. The light exposes. We begin to see clearly the ways we have sinned and the ways other people have sinned against us. And the light provides hope. In the light, we see the possibility for new beginnings.

Prayer

Lord, your light hurts my eyes. It is too bright. I see too clearly now. It is too painful for me. Help me to believe that your light is not to bring shame but to bring hope into my dark world. Light of heaven, embrace me with your warmth. Help me with your bright rays. Give me life. And hope. Amen.[84]

That meditation and prayer sets the stage for my next letter, where I'll be talking about my first experience with Step Four: "Made a searching and fearless moral inventory of ourselves" (Big Book, page 59).

I look forward to the day that we'll be able to see each other face-to-face.

Take care, my friend.

Blessings,
Gary L.

11-26-08

Dear Matt,

I prayed for you this morning.

It was somewhere around my sixth to eighth month of sobriety that I faced Step Four. I had a lot of anxiety because I was so afraid of what I might find. After a lifetime of living a lie, blaming others, making excuses, justifying behaviors, taking others' inventories, and irresponsibility, it was time to look at me. Many times Hugh had said to me, "Gary, you need to get honest with yourself." As difficult as Step Four was, it was an extremely important part of my journey. To set the stage for Step Four, I'll quote from the Big Book, *As Bill Sees It*, and the *Life Recovery Bible*.

Big Book, pages 63–64:

> Next we launched out on a course of vigorous action, the first step of which is a personal housecleaning, which many of us had never attempted. Though our decision was a vital and crucial step, it could have little permanent effect unless at once followed by a strenuous effort to face, and to be rid of, the things in ourselves that had been blocking us. Our liquor (drug) was but a symptom. So we had to get down to causes and conditions.
>
> Therefore, we started upon a personal inventory. *This was Step Four.* A business which takes no regular inventory usually goes broke. Taking a commercial inventory is a fact-finding and fact-facing process. It is an effort to discover the truth about the stock-in-trade. One object is to disclose damaged or unsalable goods, to get rid of them promptly and without regret. If the owner of the business is to be successful, he cannot fool himself about values. [85]

As Bill Sees It

> Page 111: We should make an accurate and really exhaustive survey of our past life as it has affected other people. In many instances we shall find that, though the harm done others has not been great, we have nevertheless done ourselves considerable emotional injury.

> Then, too, damaging emotional conflicts persist below the level of consciousness, very deep, sometimes quite forgotten. Therefore, we should try hard to recall and review those past events which originally induced these conflicts and which continue to give our emotions violent twists, thus discoloring our personalities and altering our lives for the worst.[86]
>
> Page 261: When A.A. suggests a fearless moral inventory, it must seem to every newcomer that more is being asked of him than he can do. Every time he tries to look within himself, Pride says, "You need not pass this way," and Fear says, "You dare not look!"
>
> But pride and fear of this sort turn out to be bogymen, nothing else. Once we have a complete willingness to take inventory, and exert ourselves to do the job thoroughly, a wonderful light falls upon this foggy scene. As we persist, a brand new kind of confidence is born, and the sense of relief at finally facing ourselves is indescribable.[87]
>
> Page 173: Moments of perception can build into a lifetime of spiritual serenity, as I have excellent reason to know. Roots of reality, supplanting the neurotic underbrush, will hold fast despite the high winds of the forces which would destroy us, or which we would use to destroy ourselves.[88]

In my next letter will be quotes from commentaries in the *Life Recovery Bible*. I can't emphasize enough how important a thorough inventory is.

1 Peter 5:5–7: "You younger men, accept the authority of the elders. And all of you serve each other in humility, for God sets himself against the proud, but he shows favor to the humble. So humble yourselves under the mighty power of God, and in his good time, he will honor you. Give all your worries and cares to God, for he cares about what happens to you."

Blessings,
Gary L.

11-27-08

Dear Matt,

I prayed for you this morning.

Psalm 100:1–5: "Shout with joy to the Lord, O earth! Worship the Lord with gladness. Come before him, singing with joy. Acknowledge the Lord is God! He made us, and we are his. We are his people, and the sheep of his pasture. Enter his gates with thanksgiving; go into his courts with praise. Give thanks to him and bless his name. For the Lord is good. His unfailing love continues forever, and his faithfulness continues to each generation."

The above scripture sure fits this Thanksgiving Day. Our oldest daughter and her family are coming for Thanksgiving dinner. Our youngest daughter is with her husband's family today. I am so grateful for the relationship I have with our daughters. During my time of prayer and meditation this morning, I wondered what kind of relationship that I'd have with them if I hadn't gotten sober. That's a frightening thought. I believe that all of us have negative things we deal with, but there are also many positives to be thankful for. The opportunity to recover is such a great blessing to alcoholics and addicts. Many never find the path.

The *Life Recovery Bible* has a lot of great commentary relating to Step Four. *Alcoholics Anonymous*, page 59: "We made a searching and fearless moral inventory of ourselves."

Life Recovery Bible

> Page 9: Many of us have spent our life in a state of hiding, ashamed of who we are inside. We may hide by living a double life, by using drugs or other addictions to make us feel like someone else, or by self-righteously setting ourselves above others. Step Four involves uncovering the things we have been hiding, even from ourselves.
>
> When the real person inside us comes out of hiding, we will have to deal with some dirt! Making this inventory is a good way to "wash the inside"; some of that washing may involve bathing our life with tears. It is only by uncovering the hidden parts of our self that we will be able to change the outer person, including our addictive/compulsive behaviors.[89]

Page 595: Most of us falter at the prospect of making an honest personal inventory. Rationalizations and excuses for avoiding this step abound. The bottom line is that we know there is an enormous amount of sadness awaiting us, and we fear the pain that facing the sadness will bring.

When we set out to face the pain and sadness of making a moral inventory, we will need the "joy of the Lord" to give us strength. This joy comes from recognizing, even celebrating, God's ability to bring us out of bondage and care for us as we pass through the sadness toward a new way of life.[90]

Page 597: As we make our moral inventory, we will probably find ourselves listing our destructive habits, our defects of character, the wrongs we have done, the consequences of wrong choices that we now live with, and the hurts we have caused others. It's like sifting through all the garbage in our past. This is painful, but it is a necessary part of throwing away those rotten habits and behaviors that, if not dealt with, will almost certainly spoil the rest of our life.

The idea of confession (Step Five) involves not only owning up to one's sins but being truly sorry for them as well. Sins are offenses against God, including any transgression against His will. The natural follow-up to true confession, after owning up to our sins and bemoaning them before God, is to turn from them. We can list the occasions of our offenses, our destructive habits, and the consequences we have brought into our life and the lives of others. Then, after accounting for all the garbage, we can "take out the trash."[91]

Page 1,125: There have probably been times when we have ignored our own sins and problems and pointed a finger at someone else. We may be out of touch with our internal affairs because we are still blaming others for our moral choices. Or perhaps we avoid self-examination by making moral inventories of the people around us.

We also may avoid our own problems by evaluating and criticizing others. Jesus tells us, "And why worry about a speck in your friend's eye when you have a log in your own? Hypocrite! First get rid of the log from your own eye; then perhaps you will see well enough to deal with the speck in your friend's eye." (Matthew 7:3–5)

While doing this Step, we must constantly remember that this is a season of *self*-examination. We must guard against blaming and examining the lives of others. There will be time in the future for helping others after we have taken responsibility for our own life.[92]

Page 1,401: We all have to deal with sorrow. We may try to stuff it down and ignore it. We may try to drown it by giving in to our addiction or avoid feeling it by intellectualizing. But sorrow doesn't go away. We need to accept the sorrow that will be part of the inventory process.

Not all sorrow is bad for us. We can learn to accept our sorrow as a positive part of recovery, not as punishment.[93]

Page 1,577: We may wish we could avoid taking moral inventory; it's normal to want to hide from personal examination. But in our heart, we probably sense that a day will come when we will have to face the truth about ourselves and our life.[94]

Well, that's a lot of information to chew on. In my next letter I'll share with you my first experience with Step Four.

Blessings,
Gary L.

11-28-08

Dear Matt,

I prayed for you this morning.

I don't know about you, but it had always been easier for me to take everyone else's inventory, but the steps tell me that I need to take mine. The Big Book, beginning on the bottom of page 63, tells how to do an inventory. The first thing suggested is that we go back through our life and write down our resentments—who or what we resent, what happened, how it affected us, and then what our part was. It was easy for me to do the first three columns, but the most important part was the last column. What was my part? The Big Book tells us that in many cases we did something to "get the ball rolling." I needed to get real honest about my part.

For example, on my resentment list was the IRS. What happened? After losing my service station, I went to work at another station just across the street. My boss paid once a month, and when I approached him on payday to get my check, he said, "Gary, I have some really bad news. An IRS agent came in today and took your paycheck." I asked, "The whole thing?" and he nodded, "Yes." I was enraged as I drove to the IRS office. I'm sure you've heard the term "going postal." That's how I felt. I went into the office like a madman. I understand why they have those tall counters. The agent who had taken my check came out, and I asked him if I could have some of the money back, and he said, "No." I said, "I have a wife and two children. How am I supposed to feed them?"

He responded, "That's not my problem." I thought my mind was going to explode. I carried that resentment until I got to Step Four some years later. I felt like such a victim. The word "resent" comes from a Latin word; re-centari, which means to re-feel. I had re-felt that so much that it had become a giant. When I got to the last column describing what my part was, I needed to get real honest. The nine months that I had my own service station I made a lot of money, but because of big-shot-ism, I spent more than I made. While in business, I neglected to pay withholding on employees, nor did I pay quarterly estimates on earnings. So, although I ended up going broke, I owed a considerable amount of taxes. An IRS agent met with me and my accountant and worked out a payment plan that was more than reasonable. The problem was that I was still drinking. When I drank, paying bills was not a priority. When I missed a payment to the IRS, the agent would call me, and I'd stall or lie. Well, I missed making a payment three months in a row, and the agent just did his job. As painful as it was to look at the truth, that is what I needed to see. Had I been responsible and taken care of business, the

IRS would never have been involved in my life. As I continued through my resentments, I began to see my side of the street. I not only saw my side of the street, but I also saw the character defects and flaws under the behaviors. I not only needed to inventory what I had done, but needed to also inventory who I was. I did not like what I was seeing as I continued to write. After so many years of playing the victim, I began to see the part I'd played in my life.

After we've completed the resentment inventory, the Big Book suggests that we list our fears. I really didn't understand for a long time that much of my life was ruled by fear. The Big Book pages 67-8 states:

> This short word somehow touches about every aspect of our lives. It was an evil and corroding thread; the fabric of our existence was shot through with it. It set in motion trains of circumstances which brought us misfortune we felt we didn't deserve. But did not we, ourselves, set the ball rolling? Sometimes we think fear ought to be classed with stealing. It seems to cause more trouble.
>
> We reviewed our fears thoroughly. We put them on paper, even though we had no resentment in connection with them. We asked ourselves why we had them. Wasn't it because self-reliance failed us? Self-reliance was good as far as it went, but it didn't go far enough. Some of us once had great self-confidence, but it didn't fully solve the fear problem, or any other. When it made us cocky, it was worse.
>
> Perhaps there is a better way—we think so. For we are now on a different basis; the basis of trusting and relying upon God. We trust infinite God rather than our finite selves. We are in the world to play the role He assigns. Just to the extent that we do as we think He would have us, and humbly rely on Him, does he enable us to match calamity with serenity.
>
> We never apologize to anyone for depending on our creator. We can laugh at those who think spirituality the way of weakness. Paradoxically, it is the way of strength. The verdict of the ages is that faith means courage. All men of faith have courage. They trust their God. We never apologize for God. Instead we let Him demonstrate, through us, what He can do. We ask Him to remove our fear and direct our attention to what He would have us to be. At once, we commence to outgrow fear.[95]

After completing the resentment and fear inventory, the Big Book suggests we do a sexual inventory.

As Bill Sees It, page 270:

Honesty and Recovery

> In taking an inventory, a member might consider questions such as these:
>
> How did my selfish pursuit of the sex relation damage other people and me? What people were hurt, and how badly? Just how did I react at the time? Did I burn with guilt? Or did I insist that I was the pursued and not the pursuer and thus absolve myself?
>
> How have I reacted to frustration in sexual matters? When denied, did I become vengeful or depressed? Did I take it out on other people? If there was rejection or coldness at home, did I use this as a reason for promiscuity?[96]

Well I need to tell you that doing that first inventory was painful but so necessary. You'll understand when I tell you my experience with Step Five. I almost forgot; *Twelve Steps and Twelve Traditions* can be a great help in doing Step Four.

Blessings,
Gary L.

11-29-08

Dear Matt,
I prayed for you this morning.

Big Book, page 72:

Having made our personal inventory, what shall we do about it? We have been trying to get a new attitude, a new relationship with our creator, and to discover the obstacles in our path. We have admitted certain defects; we have ascertained in a rough way what the trouble is; we have put our finger on the weak items in our personal inventory. Now these are about to be cast out. This requires action on our part, which, when completed, will mean that we have to admit to God, to ourselves, and to another human being, the exact nature of our defects.[97]

That is the Fifth Step.

Big Book, pages 73–74: We must be entirely honest with somebody if we expect to live long or happily in this world. Rightly and naturally, we think well before we choose the person or persons with whom to take this intimate and confidential step.[98]

Wow! Telling another person about the things I discovered in Step Four was frightening to me. As I wrote in a previous letter, my psychology professor had offered to listen to my Step Five when I was ready. Bob had become a good friend, and I was fearful that if I did my Step Five with him, he would tell me that he didn't want to have anything to do with me anymore. I intuitively knew that I was supposed to do it with him in spite of my fear.

As Bill Sees It, page 164:

A Saving Principle

The practice of admitting one's defects to another person is, of course, very ancient. It has been validated in every century, and it characterizes the lives of all spiritually centered and truly religious people.

But today religion is by no means the sole advocate of this saving principle. Psychiatrists and psychologists point out the deep need every human being has for practical insight and knowledge of his own personality flaws and for a discussion of them with an understanding and trustworthy person.

So far as alcoholics are concerned, AA would go even further. Most of us would declare that without a fearless admission of our defects to another human being, we could not stay sober. It seems plain that the grace of God will not enter to expel our destructive obsessions until we are ready to try this.[99]

Page 248:

We Need Outside Help

It was evident that a solitary self-appraisal and the admission of our defects based upon that alone wouldn't be nearly enough. We'd have to have outside help if we were surely to know and admit the truth about ourselves—the help of God and of another human being.

Only by discussing ourselves, holding back nothing, only by being willing to take advice and accept direction could we set foot on the road to straight thinking, solid honesty, and genuine humility.[100]

The *Life Recovery Bible* has much commentary regarding Step Five.

Page 57: Admitting our wrongs to ourselves can be the most difficult part of Step Five. Denial can be blinding! How can we be expected to admit to ourselves those things we are blind to? Here's a clue that can help us. We will often condemn in others the wrongs most deeply hidden within ourselves.[101]

Page 1,035: We may be sorely aware of the deep shame, trouble, and pain we inflicted on our family when we were controlled by our addiction. We may be afraid to admit the exact nature of our wrongs because we don't understand how God could love someone who is so bad.

We may be asking, "How could God (or anyone) still love me?" There is absolutely nothing we can do or confess to God that would cause him to stop loving us. (See Romans 8:38–39.)[102]

Page 1,345: All of us struggle with our conscience, trying to make peace within our own heart. We may deny what we have done, find excuses, or try to squirm out from beneath the full weight of our conduct. We may work hard to be "good," trying to counteract our wrongs. We do everything we can to even out the score. In order to put the past to rest, however, we must stop rationalizing our sins and admit the truth.

We are all born with a built-in alarm that alerts us when we do wrong. God holds everyone accountable: "In their hearts they know right from wrong. They demonstrate that God's law is written within them, for their own consciences either accuse them or tell them they are doing what is right" (Romans 2:14–15).

In Step Five we set out to stop this internal struggle and admit that wrong is wrong. It is time to be honest with God and our self about our cover-ups and the exact nature of our wrongs. We need to admit the sins we have committed and the pain we have caused others. We may have spent years constructing alibis, coming up with excuses, and trying to plea-bargain. It is time to come clean. It is time to admit what we know deep down inside to be true: "Yes, I'm guilty as charged."

There is no real freedom without confession. What a relief it is to finally give up the weight of our lies and excuses. When we confess our sins, we will find the internal peace we lost so long ago. We will also be one step closer to recovery.[103]

"Confess your sins to each other and pray for each other so that you may be healed." (James 5:16)

Well, it was time to call Bob.

Blessings,
Gary L.

11-30-08

Dear Matt,

I prayed for you this morning.

Big Book, page 59: Step Five. "Admitted to God, to ourselves, and to another human being the exact nature of our wrongs."

It was time to call Bob and set a time for me to do Step Five. Anxiety and fear were overwhelming. We decided to meet at his home on a Saturday morning. When I arrived he invited me into a travel trailer parked in his driveway. The coffee was on, and we sipped it while chatting. He then asked if I was ready to start Step Five. My expectation was that it would probably take me about thirty minutes to tell Bob my inventory. But after I began speaking things began to come out of me that I didn't expect. I not only spoke of harms I had done, but I also talked about the character defects under my behaviors. I became very emotional and cried almost uncontrollably at times. Bob just sat and listened for the most part but would occasionally ask a question to get clarification about something.

As all of the darkness in me began to come out, I thought, "When I'm done with this, Bob will probably never want to see me again." After approximately three gut-wrenching hours I was an emotional wreck. Bob then asked, "Is there anything else?" When I looked into his eyes as he asked the question, all I could see was love, acceptance, forgiveness, and no hint of judgment.

Big Book, page 75:

> We pocket our pride and go to it, illuminating every twist of character, every dark cranny of the past. Once we have taken this step, withholding nothing, we are delighted. We can look the world in the eye. We can be alone at perfect peace and ease. Our fears fall from us. We begin to feel the nearness of our creator.[104]

As Bill Sees It, page 126:

Admitted to God

> Provided you hold back nothing in taking the Fifth Step, your sense of relief will mount from minute to minute. The damned-up emotions of years break out of their confinement,

> and miraculously vanish as soon as they are exposed. As the pain subsides, a healing tranquility takes its place. And when humility and serenity are so combined, something else of great moment is apt to occur.
>
> Many an A.A., once agnostic or atheist, tells us that it was during this stage of Step Five that he first actually felt the presence of God. And even those who already had faith often become conscious of God as they never were before.[105]

That was my experience that day. When I left Bob I felt like a tremendous load had been lifted from me, and I knew I no longer needed to carry all the things from the past that I felt so much shame and guilt about. It was so liberating.

As Bill Sees It, page 318:

> **Forgiveness**
>
> Through the vital Fifth Step, we began to get the feeling that we could be forgiven, no matter what we had thought or done.
>
> Often it was while working on this Step with our sponsors or spiritual advisers that we first felt truly able to forgive others, no matter how deeply they had wronged us.
>
> Our moral inventory had persuaded us that all-round forgiveness was desirable, but it was only when we resolutely tackled Step Five that we inwardly knew we'd be able to receive forgiveness and give it, too.[106]

1 John 1:8–9: If we say we have no sin, we are only fooling ourselves and refusing to accept the truth. But if we confess our sins to him, he is faithful and just to forgive us and to cleanse us from every wrong.

Blessings,
Gary L.

12-1-08

Dear Matt,
I prayed for you this morning.

As Bill Sees It, page 291:

> In every A.A. story, pain has been the price of admission into a new life. But this admission price purchased more than we expected. It led us to a measure of humility, which we soon discovered to be a healer of pain. We began to fear pain less, and desire humility more than ever.[107]

I experienced a lot of pain when I did my first Fifth Step. I saw parts of me that I had been either blind to or in denial about. I saw my self-centeredness, selfishness, pride, my lack of concern for others, the way I'd gone through life using people and then discarding them when they were no longer a benefit to me, and how the bottom line with everything in life was, "How is that going to affect me?" I saw my dishonesty, deceitfulness, sense of entitlement, and my incapacity to truly love another human being. As difficult as it was to look at those defects in my character, I felt a great sense of relief after completing Step Five. I finally saw the part I'd played in my life.

Alcoholics Anonymous: Page 62:

> So our troubles, we think, are basically of our own making. They arise out of ourselves, and the alcoholic (addict) is an extreme example of self-will run riot, though he usually doesn't think so. Above everything, we alcoholics (addicts) must be rid of this selfishness. We must, or it kills us! God makes that possible. And there often seems no way of entirely getting rid of self without His aid. Many of us had moral and philosophical convictions galore, but we could not live up to them even though we would have liked to. Neither could we reduce our self-centeredness much by wishing or trying on our own power. We had to have God's help.[108]

Gary L.

In spite of the ugliness I saw about who I had become, I had hope, because by the time I did the Fifth Step I believed that God was helping me in my life. I knew that I could not by making a decision become a different person. I had heard so many stories in the rooms of AA of people who had been just like me, and they were changing. Most attributed the changes they had experienced to God. A transformed life is strong evidence to pay attention to. I also saw small changes that had happened to me early in sobriety, and I knew I was not the author of those changes.

I realized the day I did my Fifth Step that if I did not invite God into all the areas of my character that I saw, I would either die drunk or be locked up somewhere. It was very clear to me. God, working through the Twelve Steps, would be what would change me. To me, a lot of the process of change in my character has been the principles within Steps Six and Seven. Just as Steps One, Two, and Three are everyday steps for me, so are Six and Seven. I believe that process will continue as long as I live.

> Big Book, page 60:
>
> We are not saints. The point is, that we are willing to grow along spiritual lines. The principles we have set down are guides to progress. We claim spiritual progress rather than spiritual perfection.[109]

> *As Bill Sees It*, page 294:
>
> It seems to me that the primary object of any human being is to grow, as God intended, that being the nature of all growing things.
>
> Theology helps me in that many of its concepts cause me to believe that I live in a rational universe under a loving God, and that my own irrationality can be chipped away, little by little. This is, I suppose, the process of growth for which we are intended.[110]

Blessings,
Gary L.

12-2-08

Dear Matt,

I prayed for you this morning.

I read a great meditation this morning in Max Lucado's book *Grace for the Moment.*

God Is for You

God is for you. Turn to the sidelines; that's God cheering your run. Look past the finish line; that's God applauding your steps. Listen for him in the bleachers, shouting your name. Too tired to continue? He'll carry you. Too discouraged to fight? He's picking you up. God is for you.

God is for you. Had he a calendar, your birthday would be circled. If he drove a car, your name would be on his bumper. If there's a tree in heaven, he's carved your name in the bark....

"Can a mother forget the baby at her breast and have no compassion on the child she has born?" God asks in Isaiah 49:15 (NIV). What a bizarre question. Can you mothers imagine feeding your infant and then later asking, "What was that baby's name?" No. I've seen you care for your young. You stroke the hair, you touch the face, you sing the name over and over. Can a mother forget? No way. But "even if she could forget....I will not forget you," God pledges (Isa 49:15.[111]

I'll add to the above: If He had a billfold, your picture would be in it.

Twenty-Four Hours a Day. Dec. 2.

Meditation for the Day

Many of us have a sort of vision of the kind of person God wants us to be. We must be true to that vision, whatever it is, and we must try to live up to it, by living the way we believe we should live. We can all believe that God has a vision of what He wants us to be like. In all people there is a good person whom God sees in us, the person we could be and that God would like us to be. But many a person fails to fulfill that promise, and God's disappointments must be many.

Prayer for the Day

I pray that I may strive to be the kind of a person that God would have me be. I pray that I may try to fulfill God's vision of what I could be.[112]

With the meditations and prayer for today, I'll begin to set the stage for Step Six. Big Book, page 59: "Were entirely ready to have God remove all these defects of character."

By the time I'd completed Step Five I was ready to begin the process of change. I knew that I could not change myself by my effort alone and that I needed to daily surrender to God. In my next letter I'll share some more thoughts about Step Six and my ongoing experience with it.

Blessings,
Gary L.

12-3-08

Dear Matt,
I prayed for you this morning.
The *Life Recovery Bible* has some great commentary on Step Six.

Page 1,261: How can we honestly say that we are entirely ready for God to remove our defects of character? If we think in terms of all or nothing, we may get stuck here because we will never feel entirely ready. It is important to keep in mind the Twelve Steps are guiding ideals. No one can work them perfectly. Our part is to keep moving, to get as close as we can to being ready.

For us, "entirely ready" may mean getting as close to the hope of healing as we can in our crippled condition. When we do, God will meet us there and take us the rest of the way.[113]

Page 1,437: Getting "entirely ready" to have God remove "all" our defects of character sounds impossible. In reality we know that such perfection is out of human reach. This is another way of saying that we are going to do our best to work toward a lifelong goal that no one ever reaches until eternity.

We will need to practice these steps the rest of our life. We don't have to demand perfection of our self; it is enough to keep moving ahead as best we can. We can look forward to our rewards with the hope of becoming all that God intends us to be. God will strengthen and encourage us as we do.[114]

Page 31: The pathway to recovery and finding new life also involves the death process. The different means we used to need to help us cope were "defective," but still, they did give us comfort or companionship. Giving them up is often like suffering the death of a loved one.

As we journey on in our new life, we will necessarily lose some of our defective ways of coping. When this happens, we need to stop and take time to give our losses a proper burial. We need to put them away, cover the shame, and allow ourselves to grieve the loss of something very familiar to us. When the time of grieving is over, we, too, can journey on.[115]

Page 689: If we have sincerely practiced the previous steps, we have probably found enough pain inside our self to break our heart. Facing the fact that brokenness is part of the human condition can be crushing. But if we have arrived at this point, it is probably a sign that we are ready for God to change us.

Jesus taught that "God blesses those who mourn, for they will be comforted" (Matthew 5:4). God isn't looking for evidence of how good we are or how hard we try. He only wants us to mourn over our sins and admit our brokenness. Then he will not ignore our needs but will forgive us, comfort us, and cleanse us.[116]

I would add "change us."

Page 863: People tell us to repent and stop thinking the way we do. Most of us would give anything to do this. If it were only that simple to stop our obsessive thoughts! When we are starving emotionally, it is almost impossible to stop thinking about what has fed that hunger, even when we realize it doesn't satisfy.

We fight our addiction on two fronts: dealing with the hunger deep inside us and changing our thoughts of doing wrong. Neither battle is easily won; each requires our daily readiness and willingness to allow God to satisfy our hunger and help us overcome our defects of character.[117]

Page 1,063: When we are upset, we often depend on our addiction to make us feel better. As we get rid of our addiction, we face the deeper character defects that God wants to heal. Our addiction functions as a place of "shelter" from our pain. But when that "shelter" is removed, deep anger may surface, exposing even deeper character flaws that need healing.

The removal of our sheltering addiction may expose deeper problems. This may spark defensive anger as God touches our deepest hurts. It is all right to let the anger out. But it is also important to let God take care of the real problem.[118]

That's a lot of information to "chew on."

Blessings,
Gary L.

12-4-08

Dear Matt,

I prayed for you this morning.

Well, my friend, I've given you a lot of information regarding Step Six. In Step Four we discover our character defects and shortcomings, and talk to "God, ourselves, and another human being" in Step Five. Step Six, to me, is ongoing readiness for God to work in our character, and then there is a natural transition to Step Seven: "Humbly asked Him to remove our shortcomings" (*Alcoholics Anonymous*, page 59).

To me, there are two key words in Step Seven: "Humbly and Him." In my opinion the major block to Step Seven is pride. Not the kind of pride that happens when we take on a task, give it our best, and complete it successfully. There is another kind of pride that I call self-centered pride. This kind of pride says that it's all up to me; I don't need anyone's help, and I'm certainly not going to ask God for help. That's the kind of pride that kills alcoholics and addicts. When I humbly ask God for help, I'm acknowledging that I can't remove my flaws by myself. Steps Four and Five helped me to see how broken I was on the inside. Steps Six and Seven showed me that God is the healer of the brokenness. The word "humbly" also says to me that God will work in my defects according to His timetable, not mine.

For example, I was a thief growing up and took things that didn't belong to me. When I stole something and didn't get caught, I had a sense of power. As I wrote in a previous letter, I embezzled from an employer as an adult. When I got sober that defect was still there. I desperately wanted it gone. Someone said that opportunity knocks on the door, but temptation leans on the doorbell. In spite of me wanting that gone, the temptation to steal was there. I realized that I needed to stop the behavior if I wanted to remain sober, so I did. God helped me stop stealing, but I still wanted to.

One day, Patsy and I were in a restaurant, and when I paid the cashier she gave me change for a twenty-dollar bill. I had paid with a ten. Without thinking, I said to her, "You gave me too much change." I realized in that moment that I no longer wanted something that didn't belong to me. I was no longer a thief! What a miracle that was! The recovery journey for me has been one of growing in God's grace. It is He who is making the changes in me as I depend on Him, which is the second key word in Step Seven.

My belief is that God's grace is that part of Him that covers all the areas in my life that He hasn't changed yet. I see God as a perfect God who knows what is best for me more than I do. On one end of the spectrum is God's perfection, and on the other end is my imperfection. The chasm between those two places is vast, but it's not larger than His grace. For many years I filled that chasm with self-condemnation, self-judgment, and self-hate. God's grace is better. One short definition of grace is "unmerited favor." In other words grace cannot be earned or bought; it's God's gift to us.

The following is adapted from a book titled *More Sowers Seeds*. It's a true story. Two Italian sculptors named Donatello and Michelangelo were contemporaries. Donatello had ordered a three-ton block of marble, and when it was delivered he examined it with the help of the sun shining on it. He saw many cracks and flaws in it, so he rejected it. The workers, rather than move it back to the quarry, decided to take it to Michelangelo, who was known to be a little absentminded. They hoped that he wouldn't remember that he hadn't ordered it. Well, it was quite a job moving it because they had to move it on log rollers. When they arrived at Michelangelo's studio, he examined it, saw all the same cracks and flaws that Donatello had, but then to the delight of the workers he accepted it. Out of that flawed block of marble he created what is considered one of the world's greatest art treasures; the statue of David.

God is our sculptor. He looks at our cracked and flawed lives, our brokenness, and declares, "I want to make something beautiful out of that life." So, as we surrender to the Great Sculptor he begins to chip away at our flaws and character defects. The block of marble could never have turned itself into the statue of David; it needed a sculptor. On those same lines, a lump of clay on a potter's wheel cannot become a vase; it needs a potter. That to me is the essence of Steps Six and Seven. What a great God who can look down at the broken lives of alcoholics and addicts and say, "I can work with that." I have no hope in my ability to sculpt my life, but great hope in Him. As I write those words tears come to my eyes, because I know the life I have today is because of what He has done in me, and will continue to do as promised in Philippians 1:6:

"Being confident of this, that He who began a good work in you will carry it on to completion until the day of Jesus Christ."

Blessings,
Gary L.

12-5-08

Dear Matt,

I prayed for you this morning.

2 Thessalonians 2:16–17: "May our Lord Jesus Christ and God our Father, who loved us and in his special favor gave us everlasting comfort and hope, comfort your hearts and give you strength in every good thing you do and say."

I need to add some thoughts to my last letter. One of the things I neglected to write was the Seventh Step prayer found on page 76 of the Big Book. I say this prayer every morning as part of my God time. "My creator, I am now willing that you should have all of me, good and bad. I pray that you now remove from me every single defect of character which stands in the way of my usefulness to you and my fellows. Grant me strength, as I go out from here, to do your bidding. Amen."119

Two of the principles found in both the third and seventh prayers are surrender and service. It's so important for us to pass on the message of hope we've been given. As Hugh would say, "If you want to keep it, you have to give it away." My experience has been that I cannot out-give God, and every time I share the message of recovery, it becomes stronger in me.

I wrote about grace in my last letter, and I'll expand on that some. I was praying and meditating on the concept of grace one day, and the thought came: Grace: God—Removing—All—Condemnation—Eternally. That is very comforting to me. One thing that the grace of God does not do—grace does not always stop consequences that come because of our choices. A big part of grace, to me, is forgiveness. Some people believe they can do just about anything they want, because God just keeps extending grace. They take scripture out of context to support their position. When I ask God to forgive me He does, but there may still be a consequence. For example; if I rob a bank and end up in jail and ask God to forgive me, He will. But, I'll still be in jail.

I believed for a long time that if God really loved me, it was His job to clean up my messes, and when He didn't I'd moan, "God doesn't really love me." That's a real self-centered approach to God. God's job is not to protect me from life or the consequences of my choices. His job is to help me work through life's terms when they stink and the consequences of my behaviors or choices. I had huge financial wreckage when I got sober (consequences), and God didn't pay one of those bills. What He did was open doors to employment, and He also gave me a desire to clean up the wreckage. He began to change my belief systems about money and possessions. That's the grace piece. Because of that I began making better decisions about money. That has been an ongoing process to this day. What it boils down to is this: another example of God doing for me what I had never been able to do for myself.

I hope that my experience with the first Seven Steps will be helpful to you. In my next letter I'll take a break from the steps and get back to my story.

Blessings,
Gary L.

12-6-08

Dear Matt,

I prayed for you this morning.

When I resigned from the treatment center I applied for a job at a plywood mill. My interview went well, and I was hired. There was a contingency, however; I had to pass a physical exam that included a back x-ray. Remember, some years prior to this I had injured my back while working in a tire store. At that time the doctor said that I would never be able to do strenuous physical labor. I was apprehensive as I waited for the doctor's report. The x-ray showed no evidence of an injury to my back! Wow! God came through again.

I reported for work and was assigned to a carpenter crew because I'd had some experience swinging a hammer. I really enjoyed going around the mill doing repairs. Some union members complained that the carpenter job should have been put up for bid. Because of that I was taken off the job and assigned as a cleanup man. I was given a wheelbarrow, pitchfork, scoop shovel, and an area of the mill to keep clean. I loved the job. I worked ten hours a day five days a week and sometimes on Saturday. What was great about the job was that I didn't have to deal with people or do much thinking. It was just hard physical labor. It was just the break my mind and emotions needed after the intensity of the treatment center. By this time Patsy and I were very involved in the church we attended, and I was also opening up an AA meeting in Coquille. Life was good, but I was beginning to feel a spiritual unrest. I didn't understand what was happening at the time. I ended up in a spiritual desert. My spiritual life became empty and dry. I was doing all of the things I knew to do, and nothing seemed to be working. It was in that desert experience that God gave me some understanding.

When I first accepted Christ as my savior, I was flooded with his grace. But slowly, without realizing it, I began to walk out from under His grace and began to take credit for the blessings in my life. That self part of me reared its ugly head again. I began to judge other Christians and my AA friends by standards I believed I was living up to. Every time the church doors were open I was there. I prayed and read my Bible every day. I was faithful to attend AA meetings and sponsor others. I wanted to be a "good" Christian and needed ways to measure that, so I began to look at and judge externals. My spiritual vitality and joy left. Growing in my love for God and others is the true way to measure. We are cautioned in Proverbs to not compare ourselves with others. I need to be on guard against doing that.

A place where I've learned some of my most valuable lessons has been the desert. I hate to admit it, but God has had to take me there many times during my journey. The desert always brings me to the place of more inventory of myself. One interesting aspect to a desert is that a few days after a rain the desert comes alive with color. Many of the plants were just waiting for some moisture in order to bloom. God has been faithful to "rain" on me in the desert and bring forth new life and understanding.

Big Book, page 417:

Shakespeare said, "All the world's a stage, and all the men and women merely players." He forgot to mention that I was the chief critic. I was always able to see the flaw in every person, every situation. And I was always glad to point it out, because I knew you wanted perfection, just as I did. A.A. and acceptance have taught me that there is a bit of good in the worst of us and a bit of bad in the best of us; that we are all children of God and we have a right to be here. When I complain about me or about you, I am complaining about God's handiwork. I am saying that I know better than God.[120]

The *Twenty-Four Hours a Day* book on September 8 is good.

A.A. Thought for the Day

Another of the mottoes of A.A. is "But for the Grace of God." Once we have fully accepted the program we become humble about our achievement. We do not take too much credit for our sobriety. When we see another suffering alcoholic in the throes of alcoholism, we say to ourselves: "But for the Grace of God, there go I." We do not forget the kind of people we were. We remember those we left behind us. And we are very grateful to the grace of God which has given us another chance. the *Am I truly grateful for Grace of God?*

Meditation for the Day

A consciousness of God's presence as One who loves you makes all life different. The consciousness of God's love promotes the opening of your whole being to God. It brings wonderful relief from the cares and worries of our daily lives. Relief brings peace and peace brings contentment. Try to walk in God's love. You will have that peace which passes all understanding and a contentment that no one can take from you. Feel sure of God's unfailing love and care for you and for all His children. There is freedom and serenity in those who walk in God's love, held safe in His loving care.

Prayer for the Day

I pray that I may walk in God's love. I pray that, as I go, I may feel the spring of God's power in my steps and the joy of His love in my heart.[121]

1 John 4:9–10. "God showed how much he loved us by sending his only Son into the world so that we might have eternal life through him. This is real love. It is not that we loved God, but that he loved us and sent his Son as a sacrifice to take away our sins."

Blessings,
Gary L.

12-7-08

Dear Matt,

I prayed for you this morning.

After working in the plywood mill for approximately two years, a position opened in the company's chemical plant. It was a great opportunity, so I turned in an application. The person getting the position would be trained as a resin operator. The plant made resin for plywood, particle board, and other wood products. The job would entail working with dangerous chemicals and large chemical reactors. I was interviewed, and several days later was notified that the job was mine. I was so excited. Instead of being a laborer in the plywood mill, I would learn a trade. The pay was much more than I'd been earning, and there was a tremendous benefits package.

The primary difficulty of the job was that it involved working rotating shifts. The cycle began with working seven-day shifts, followed by one day off, and then seven swing shifts and a day off, and that was followed by seven graveyard shifts. A good thing about the schedule was that after the seven graveyard shifts I would get five days off. It took my body a long time to adjust to different sleep times each week. It was also hard on family life because I wasn't available to them as they needed.

It was the best job I'd ever had with regard to pay and benefits. Even though the treatment center was more fulfilling, I believed I would work at the chemical plant until retirement. God had a different plan than mine. In 1979 the economy was in a free-fall. Interest rates were soaring, housing starts were way down, and the need for wood products plummeted. An all-staff meeting was scheduled, and it was there that the bomb was dropped. The manager informed us that the plant was being shut down, that it had been sold to the country Borneo. Only two employees would be retained; the plant manager and the man who would be transferred to Borneo to help reassemble the plant and train others on how to operate it. We were given the option to help disassemble the plant and to crate it for shipment. That meant about six months of work at a reduced wage without any benefits. I was devastated by the announcement but agreed to help in the disassembly. It was difficult to tell Patsy what had happened, and I wondered, "Where are you, God, in all of this?"

After we completed getting the plant ready for shipment I got a general contractor's license and started my own business. In spite of the economy at that time, my new business prospered. I began to get so many jobs that I was working fifty to sixty hours a week. The income was good, but I had no sense of fulfillment. One of the things I've discovered in my walk with God is that sometimes God will move us in directions that we'd never considered. One day this thought came into my mind: "Go to Bible college and become a minister." I tried to shake the thought, but it persisted. Closing my business and moving my family so I could go to school made no sense to me. How would we survive financially?

About the time all of this was going on, I received a call from a former coworker at the chemical plant. He had been hired by a large company in Rock Springs, Wyoming. He said that it was a better job than the chemical plant and that they were expanding and would be hiring more people. Patsy and I drove to Rock Springs, and, through my friend's influence, I was granted an interview. This was early spring, and I was told that new people would start work on July first. I was hired and told to call once a week. There was a possibility of starting earlier than July. Patsy and I drove back home, and I began my weekly calls. I was not at ease with the decision to move to Wyoming. Occasionally the thought of Bible college would come into my mind, but I would dismiss it. Patsy and I prayed about the move but couldn't seem to get any clarity. On the surface the job seemed ideal, but, again, was that where God wanted me?

We were at a home fellowship group one night, and I asked a friend to ask God to give us some peace about the decision. When he prayed for me one of the things he prayed was, "God, if this isn't the right thing, close the door." The following day I made my weekly call and was informed that the company had changed its plans and would not be hiring. The door was slammed shut! Okay, God, what's next?

1 John 4:16: "We know how much God loves us, and we have put our trust in him. God is love, and all who live in love live in God, and God lives in them."

Blessings,
Gary L.

12-8-08

Dear Matt,

I prayed for you this morning.

After the door was slammed shut in Wyoming we continued to pray. I was willing to continue my business if that was God's will, but something inside me said that He had something else for me.

One day while reading a Christian magazine an advertisement caught my eye. It was an ad for a Bible school called ICHTHUS Training Center in Salem. (It is now called Salem Bible College.) The ad described the first year curriculum as being designed for a person's personal spiritual growth. The second year was geared toward ministerial preparation. Patsy and I talked about it and what kind of impact that would have on our family. We discussed it with friends and our pastor. He believed God had placed a call on my life to ministry and encouraged me to pursue it. Patsy and I drove to Salem to talk with the pastor who had started the school. I knew if we decided to move that it would be a faith journey. We asked our church to pray for us.

After a Sunday service, an elderly lady we knew approached us and said that she would pay the first-year tuition if I decided to go. Although I was still kind of dragging my heels, that woman's offer seemed strong confirmation that we were supposed to move. We lived in a small home that we'd fixed up and had some equity in it, but the housing market was really bad at the time. It seemed that nothing was selling. We listed the house with a real estate agent she showed it to one man, and it was sold within a week. More confirmation! After all costs were taken out, we ended up with approximately $3,000 to help us move.

I moved to Salem first and lived with friends from Coquille who had also enrolled in the school. After three months I found a house to rent that was near the school. I went back to Coquille on a weekend, and friends from our church helped us make the final move. By the time we settled into our home we had about $2,000 left, and neither of us had a job.

The following two years God provided for us in remarkable ways. The first job we found was cleaning a small office once a week for $60 a month. We then got a job cleaning a restaurant late at night after it had closed. Then Patsy started a day care in our home. One of our biggest surprises came from our church in Coquille. Once a month we received a check ranging from $300 to $500 donated by friends from our church in Coquille. The donation was anonymous, so we never knew who had contributed. What a blessing our friends were to us! One weekend we drove to Coquille to visit friends and to attend church. At the end of the service our pastor said that there were some things in the foyer for us to take back to Salem. The church had surprised us with a food shower. During the service some members of the church had moved the food into the foyer in order to surprise us. There was so much food that we were unable to get it all in our car, so a friend filled the back of his pickup with the rest and followed us back to Salem. Wow!

Even with our part-time jobs, the day care, and help from our friends, our savings finally ran out, and we didn't have enough money coming in to meet our obligations. As we looked at our budget we realized that we were about one hundred dollars a week short. The next day while I was in class, a teacher announced that a Christian home builder was looking for someone part time who had some construction experience. I was the only person in class who had experience in carpentry. After I arrived home from school I called the home builder to be interviewed. He said that he needed someone twenty hours a week and that he would pay five dollars per hour. There was the one hundred dollars per week we needed! So for the two years I was in school God provided for us in miraculous ways! When God leads, He also provides. We were so excited when I finally graduated. Think for a moment, just thirteen years earlier I had been suicidal, convinced that life would never work for me, angry at God (if there really was a God), drinking myself to death, and disappointing the people in my life who loved me. I had just graduated from Bible school! If someone had said to me at my first AA meeting that all of that would happen, I would tell them they were totally insane. As I said earlier, God had a better plan for my life than I did.

As Bill Sees It, page 8:

A New Life

Is sobriety all that we are to expect of a spiritual awakening? No, sobriety is only a bare beginning; it is only the first gift of the first awakening. If more gifts are to be received, our awakening has to go on. (Spiritual Growth) As it does go on, we find that bit by bit we can discard the old life—the one that did not work—for a new life that can and does work under any conditions whatever.

Regardless of worldly success or failure, regardless of pain or joy, regardless of sickness or health or even of death itself, a new life of endless possibilities can be lived if we are willing to continue our awakening, through the practice of AA's Twelve Steps.[122]

Hebrews 11:1: What is faith? It is the confident assurance that what we hope for is going to happen. It is the evidence of things we cannot yet see.

Blessings,
Gary L.

12-9-08

Dear Matt,

I prayed for you this morning.

It was great to receive another letter from you. Pendleton is a lot closer than Ontario. When you first wrote to me you asked if I would help you with the Twelve Steps. So far, I've shared with you my experience with Steps One through Seven. I have some questions regarding your experience with Step One. Do you truly see your powerlessness over drugs, or do you believe that at some time you will be able to control them? Would you give me some examples in your past that demonstrate your powerlessness? Do you believe that you can overcome your addiction with determination or your own willpower? Do you believe you can have it both ways; taking drugs and living a spiritual way of life? I've seen many people try that, and I've never seen it work. Addiction is a lifestyle, and there is no room for a spiritual way of living while using. The questions I've asked are important because my experience is that those who have reservations about their addiction try using again unless the reservations are removed.

If you find that within you there are reservations, ask God to remove them. The *Life Recovery Bible* has some great commentary regarding Step One.

> Page 313: When we refuse to admit our powerlessness we are only deceiving ourselves. The lies we tell ourselves and others are familiar: "I can stop any time I want to. I'm in control; this one won't hurt anything." And all the while we are inching closer to destruction.[123]
>
> Page 455: It can be very humiliating to admit that we are powerless, especially if we are used to being in control. We may be powerful in some areas of our life, but out of control in terms of our addictive/compulsive behaviors. If we refuse to admit our powerlessness, we may lose everything. That one unmanageable part of our life may infect and destroy everything else.
>
> There is no instant or easy cure. The only answer is to admit our powerlessness, humble our self, and submit to the process that will eventually bring recovery.[124]

Page 1,183: For many of us in recovery, memories of childhood are full of the terrors associated with being powerless. If we were raised in a family that was out of control, where we were neglected, abused, or exposed to domestic violence and dysfunctional behavior, the thought of being powerless might be very frightening. We may have silently vowed never again to be as vulnerable as we were when we were children.

In any society, children are the most dependent members. They have no inherent power for self-protection—no means to ensure that their lives will be safe, comfortable, or fulfilling. Little children are singularly reliant on the love, care, and nurture of others for their most basic needs. They must cry out even though they may not know exactly what they need. They must trust their lives to someone who is more powerful than they, and, hopefully, they will be heard and lovingly cared for.

We, too, must admit that we are truly powerless if our life is to become healthy. This doesn't mean we have to become victims again. Admitting our powerlessness is an honest appraisal of our situation in life and a positive step toward recovery.[125]

Page 1,395: We may be afraid to admit that we are powerless and that our life is unmanageable. If we admit that we are powerless, won't we be tempted to give up completely in the struggle against our addiction? It doesn't seem to make sense that we can admit powerlessness and still find the power to go on. This paradox will be dealt with as we go on to Steps Two and Three.

Once we recognize the paradox of powerlessness, we can be quite relieved. We don't have to always be strong and pretend to be perfect. We can live a real life, with its daily struggles, in a human body beset with weakness and still find the power from above to keep going without being crushed and broken.[126]

Twenty-Four Hours a Day, December 9:

Meditation for the Day

We are all seeking something, but many do not know what they want in life. They are seeking something because they are restless and dissatisfied, without realizing that faith in God can give an objective and a purpose to their lives. Many of us are at least subconsciously seeking for a Power greater than ourselves because that would give meaning to our existence. If you have found that Higher Power, you can be the means of leading others aright, by showing them that their search for meaning to life will end when they find faith and trust in God as the answer.

Prayer for the Day

I pray that my soul will lose its restlessness by finding rest in God. I pray that I may find peace of mind in the thought of God and His purpose for my life.[127]

Hebrews 2:18: "Since he himself has gone through suffering and temptation, he is able to help us when we are being tempted."

Blessings,
Gary L.

12-10-08

Dear Matt,

I prayed for you this morning.

When I graduated from Bible school, it never occurred to me to ask God for the next step. I thought it was all planned out; I would be hired by a church as an associate pastor and begin a new career. It seemed very plain to me. Wrong! Wrong! Wrong! I didn't realize it at the time, but I was not equipped spiritually to be a pastor. There was still way too much of me in the way, although I didn't know it then. God knew I wasn't ready, and as a result doors to ministry did not open.

The homebuilder I worked for went out of business, and I ended up getting a job at a company that manufactured modular buildings. After several months, their business slowed and many of us were laid off. My next job was with a house framing crew. After framing several homes our wages were cut, and I quit. By this time I was disillusioned, discouraged, and disappointed. After all of that I thought, "Perhaps I need to talk to God and ask for direction." What an idea!

A place called the Christian Renewal Center is near Silver Creek Falls. I decided that I would go there and fast and pray in order to get some direction. I was assigned a small cabin surrounded by large fir trees. There was a woodstove for heat. After settling in, I got on my knees to pray. While praying, something came out of my mouth that stunned me, "God, give me a vision of hell." Why did I ask that? When I turned out the lights that first night it was pitch black. I had a difficult time going to sleep and a great feeling of despair.

When I awoke the following morning I began to pray again. It seemed that God had disappeared. I could get no sense of His presence. My prayers seemed to be going nowhere. "Where are you God?" I cried. There was no response. By the time I went to bed that night in that dark, dark room, my despair had turned into despondency. The next day was more of the same, and when I went to bed that night I felt totally abandoned by God. I awoke the next morning to a snow-covered landscape. I started a fire to get warm and had decided that I was through praying—what's the point? It continued to snow for a while, and then it stopped.

As I was sitting and looking through the patio door at the beauty, the clouds parted. A beam of sunlight shone through the door, and I felt that it was wrapped around me. A feeling of gentleness and Presence filled the cabin. I began to weep. And then God spoke to me, "Those days without my

Presence is what hell will be like." I realized at that moment that God had given me a vision of what it would be like to have no chance of a relationship with Him. I'd like to report that God then gave me clear direction of what I was supposed to do next, but that didn't happen. I don't know if this is true, but it seems that sometimes God has not given me clear direction in order that I can see that left to my own devices, I can still "wreck the train."

One day I heard of an opportunity to start my own business selling term life insurance and securities. It seemed like a great opportunity, and some who worked for the company had achieved financial independence within a few years. Without asking God or anyone else, I jumped in feet first. I took an insurance and securities course, passed the state exams, and began my own business. I was determined that I would be one of the success stories. I put blinders on to everything else in order to reach my goals.

Life Recovery Bible, page 780, commentary on Proverbs 23:4–5:

> Perhaps the most common and unrecognized addiction in our culture today is greed or materialism. Many people weary themselves trying to get more and more money so they can buy more goods and do more things. The pleasure that money buys is only temporary; it doesn't satisfy the longings of our heart. The wise learn the secret of delayed gratification and resist the greedy impulses that bring quick and fleeting pleasure. Instead they seek to have their needs met through a healthy relationship with God and with others.[128]

I was not wise. It took two and a half years for the train to wreck. I'll tell you about it in my next letter.

Alcoholics Anonymous, page 127: "Although financial recovery is on the way for many of us, we find we could not place money first. For us, material well-being always followed spiritual progress; it never precedes."129

Proverbs 23:4–5: "Don't weary yourself trying to get rich. Why waste your time? For riches can disappear as though they had the wings of a bird."

Blessings,
Gary L.

12-11-08

Dear Matt,

I prayed for you this morning.

James 1:5: "If you need wisdom—if you want to know what God wants you to do—ask him, and he will gladly tell you. He will not resent your asking."

Life Recovery Bible commentary on above:

> Page 1,512: How many times have we scolded ourselves for making unwise decisions? All of us have made wrong choices that have led us into trouble, ultimately affecting our relationship with God and with others. When we ask God for wisdom, he is more than willing to give it. Since God is the source of all wisdom, we can make fewer unwise decisions by turning to him for guidance. In recovery we are told to improve our conscious contact with God so we can better know his will for us. This can be achieved by studying God's Word and praying regularly.[130]

I didn't ask God for direction or wisdom when I began my new business. For the following two and a half years I worked as hard as I had ever worked. Fifty- to sixty-hour workweeks were not uncommon. After the first two years it dawned on me that I probably would not be one of the success stories. My sales had slowed to the place that I began using credit cards to pay bills. After another six months I'd exhausted our credit lines, and the business failed, leaving us with a huge mountain of debt. We would never have survived without Patsy's day-care income. She often took care of ten to twelve children. Some days our daughter Kelly helped out. My dreams of financial independence were shattered. Once again, disillusionment, disappointment, and despair. We never stopped being part of a church through the years in business, and my involvement in AA never wavered, but my spiritual life was really empty. Patsy was also burned out from taking care of so many children. By the time the weekend came around she would be exhausted. We heard about a company that processed cherries and berries that was hiring. We applied and were hired. Patsy closed her day-care business, and we reported to work on the graveyard shift. Our youngest daughter, Kelly, was also hired.

I vividly remember the first night as I stood at a conveyor belt picking off rotten strawberries. Across the belt from me was Patsy. She had not had to work outside our home after our daughters were born. It was difficult to see what my choices had done to her. Guilt, shame, remorse, and regret were my companions. When the berry and cherry season ended, we were hired at a cannery that processed vegetables. We earned $4.24 per hour, which was not much more than minimum wage. Our combined income barely covered our living expenses.

That's when the calls from our creditors began. I explained to the collectors our situation and attempted to work out arrangements that we could meet. What they wanted and what we could do was worlds apart, and they would not budge. Then the calls became threatening. Kelly answered the phone one day, and a collector brought her to tears. I was so angry. This was not her fight. When she told me what happened I sought help from an attorney. As a result of meeting with him, we ended up in bankruptcy court. We could not see any other solution.

After the vegetable season ended at the cannery, Patsy was able to get a job for a manufacturing company that made lockboxes for real estate agents. She started right at the bottom but was grateful just to have a job. A friend of mine who worked at a State of Oregon juvenile correction facility called Hillcrest school said that they had openings for temporary employees. The duration of employment was six months. I applied for a position and was hired. We both had jobs. Perhaps there was a light at the end of the tunnel.

Christmas that year was extremely difficult. It would be the first Christmas in our teenage daughters' lives that they wouldn't receive a gift from us. We just didn't have the money. We did decide that we would have a big Christmas dinner, although it would take most of our weekly food budget. When we sat down to eat, I was going to pray and ask God to bless our meal. Instead of praying, I began to cry. Trina and Kelly came behind me, placed their hands on me, and prayed for me.

After praying they said things like, "Dad, we don't need presents. Look at all we have." I realized at that moment the deep work God had done in their lives. Because of what God has done in my life, I can look back on the Christmas without presents and thank Him for the gift of His Presence.

We still look back on that Christmas with fond memories.

Blessings,
Gary L.

12-12-08

Dear Matt,

I prayed for you this morning.

A thought that came into my mind many times during my life before recovery was, "I wish I could just start my life over." Perhaps you've felt that way at times. It seemed that I just kept making messes. Although I was so good at blaming others for my problems, at some level I knew I was part of the problem. I never wanted to look at that. It was much easier to blame, justify, and rationalize.

As Bill Sees It, page 20:

Light from a Prayer

> We treasure our "Serenity Prayer" because it brings a new light to us that can dissipate our oldtime and nearly fatal habit of fooling ourselves.
>
> In the radiance of this prayer we see that defeat, rightly accepted, need be no disaster. We now know that we do not have to run away, nor ought we again try to overcome adversity by still another bulldozing power drive that can only push up obstacles before us faster than they can be taken down.[131]

I began to understand early in recovery that God wanted to help me clean up the wreckage I'd created, but more important than that, He wanted to work in my life in such a way that I would depend on Him for guidance. I haven't always done that very well as you've learned by now—my business failure being a prime example. In spite of the times that I've wrecked the train, God's grace has been sufficient to bring me back to Him. So, as I repent (change direction) and ask for forgiveness, He gives me a fresh start. That is truly "Amazing Grace." When I accepted Christ as my Savior, that did not mean that the self part of me died and that all of my character defects and flaws were gone. It did mean that as I began to get honest with myself, He would begin working in my character. That is a lifelong process. I am so grateful for His grace.

Big Book, page 59: Step Nine. "Made a list of all persons we had harmed, and became willing to make amends to them all."

Step Eight was easy for me. All I needed to do was go back to my Step Four inventory and write down the names of those I had harmed. Making the list was not difficult; what was difficult was seeing the truth about the person I had been. I think of the harm that I caused my parents while growing up. The sleepless nights Mom had expecting another call from the police or, worse yet, the hospital or morgue. I continued to harm my parents as an adult: "If you don't help me with this mess, you'll never see your grandkids again." I borrowed money from them with no intention of paying it back. I had no consideration for them. I harmed employers by stealing from them and at times not giving an honest day's work for an honest day's wage. I harmed Patsy and our daughters by not being the husband and father they needed. I harmed people with lies and character assassination. I harmed the community through acts of vandalism. I harmed my country by not being a responsible, productive member of society. I harmed myself by violating many of the values I was raised with. I harmed friends as I violated their trust. I harmed creditors by not paying them. I harmed members of the barbershop quartet that I was part of, by not being dependable and telling lies about them when they replaced me. All of those things were difficult to look at, but as Hugh told me many times, "Gary, you need to get honest with yourself."

When I viewed my list, it seemed that I was facing a huge mountain of amends. I realized that I could not do it without God's help. Step Eight is the foundation for Step Nine. We will face many mountains as we journey through life. Climbing a mountain alone is not a good idea. I've never climbed a real mountain, but if I decided that I wanted to climb Mount Hood, I would ask experienced climbers to help me. How foolish I would be if I took on the mountain without help. I've known many people who have tried to climb the "Recovery Mountain" alone, only to perish. The experienced climbers in the "recovery community" have been so important to me. I would never have been able to climb this far alone.

Well, Matt, I hope you have your climbing boots on. Climbing the mountain can be a great adventure. Just think of how the view expands the higher you climb. Oh, another thing about mountain climbing: it is really hard work, but with the help of God and others we can do it.

Zephaniah 3:17: "For the Lord your God has arrived to live among you. He is a mighty savior. He will rejoice over you with great gladness. With His love, He will calm all your fears. He will exult over you by singing a happy song."

Blessings,
Gary L.

12-13-08

Dear Matt,

I prayed for you this morning.

Well, it's on to Step Nine. Big Book, page 59: "Made direct amends to such people wherever possible, except when to do so would injure them or others."

As Bill Sees It, page 145:

To Take Responsibility

Learning how to live in the greatest peace, partnership, and brotherhood with all men and women, of whatever description, is a moving and fascinating adventure.

But every A.A. has found that he can make little headway in this new adventure of living until he first backtracks and really makes an accurate and unsparing survey of the human wreckage he has left in his wake.

The readiness to take the full consequences of our past acts, and to take responsibility for the well-being of others at the same time, is the very spirit of Step Nine.[132]

Life Recovery Bible, page 147: It is natural to hope that the people we have hurt will think better of us once we have sought to make amends. We may fear that there are some who will never upgrade their opinions about us, no matter what we do.[133]

Page 47: Returning to someone we have hurt is a scary thing. The passing years, lack of communication, and memories of anger and hateful emotional exchanges can all create tremendous anxiety.[134]

Page 1119: We all suffer brokenness in our life, in our relationship with God, and in our relationships with others. Brokenness tends to weigh us down and can easily lead us back into our addiction. Recovery isn't complete until all areas of brokenness are mended.

> Much of recovery involves repairing the brokenness in our life. This requires that we make peace with God, with ourself, and with others whom we have alienated. Unresolved issues in relationships can keep us from being at peace with God and ourself. Once we go through the process of making amends, we must keep our mind and heart open to anyone we may have overlooked. God will often remind us of relationships that need attention. We should not delay going to those we have offended and seeking to repair the damage we have caused.[135]
>
> Page 1,239: When we are feeding our addiction, it is easy to become consumed by our own needs. Nothing matters except getting what we crave so desperately. We may have to lie, cheat, kill, or steal; but that doesn't stop us. Within our family and community we become known as "takers," trampling over the feelings and needs of others.
>
> Making amends includes paying back what we have taken whenever possible. Some of us may even seize the opportunity to go further, giving more than we took. As we begin to see the needs of others and respond by choice, our self-esteem will rise. We will realize that we can give to others, instead of just being a burden.[136]
>
> Page 1,525: At this point in recovery, most of us have experienced some major changes in our attitudes. At one time, we were so consumed by our addiction that we thought only of ourselves, failing to show any consideration for others. This step focuses on the interests and needs of others. This step can be very difficult as we face the painful consequences of past actions.[137]

That's a lot of foundational information regarding Step Nine. In my next letter I'll write about my experience with Step Nine.

Proverbs 8:17: I (wisdom) love those all who love me. Those who search for me will surely find me.

Blessings,
Gary L.

12-14-08

Dear Matt,

I prayed for you this morning.

Step Nine was an important part of my journey. It gave me opportunity to set right the damage I had done to others. The idea of going to people and making amends was frightening to me. I wondered how they would respond. I knew it was important to do regardless of how they might react. I had to clean up my side of the street.

My parents were grateful that I was sober but also wary. Remember, I had stayed sober four and a half years earlier and then went back to drinking. I had been sober approximately three years this time before my stepdad stopped thinking that I was just running another "deal." I had burned them so many times through the years. Although I made amends to them during my first year of recovery, they remained cautious, and I understood that.

As I went to others to make amends it became obvious that people could be more gracious than I thought. A great example of that were the guys from the barbershop quartet. I knew it was time to face them, and after finding out which night they practiced I set out to see them. I approached the home where they practiced with great anxiety. I rang the doorbell and was greeted by Paula, our lead singer's wife. She was surprised to see me but invited me in. I told her that I needed to see the guys, and she led me back to the room where they practiced. They were surprised to see me and asked what I wanted. Prior to going to Jerry's home I had visions of making amends and them telling me that they never wanted to see me again.

With those thoughts in mind, I told them what I had done to them by character assassination. With tears in their eyes, each of them embraced and forgave me. They said, "We didn't know what to do. We wanted to help you but didn't know how." Some years later the Coos Bay Barbershop Chorus had their twenty-fifth anniversary show. The guys in the quartet called me and asked if I would like to practice with them, work on some of our old songs, and then sing on the show. Wow! If someone had told me when I got sober that those guys would someday be my friends again and that we would sing on a show, I would never have believed it. What a miracle! That was a typical response as I continued to make amends. That's not always true for some people. Sometimes an amends will be rebuffed, but we can't do anything about that. Another part of making amends, to me, is ongoing living amends to those I love, to my country, and to society. I do this by keeping my side of the street clean with God's help. I do that by being responsible and trying to serve my fellow man. Someone said, "The truly happy people are those who have discovered the gift of service" (author unknown).

We are told in Step Nine to not make amends if it will cause more harm to others. When in doubt I need to consult with my sponsor, pastor, or counselor. Bill W. cautions us on page 70 in *As Bill Sees It*:

> Just how and when we tell the truth—or keep silent—can often reveal the difference between genuine integrity and none at all.
>
> Step Nine emphatically cautions us against misusing the truth when it states: We made direct amends to such people wherever possible, except when to do so would injure them or others." Because it points up the fact that the truth can be used to injure as well as to heal, this valuable principle certainly has a wide-ranging application to the problem of developing integrity.138

Exodus 34:6: He passed in front of Moses and said, "I am the Lord, I am the Lord, the merciful and gracious God. I am slow to anger and rich in unfailing love and faithfulness."

Blessings,
Gary L.

12-15-08

Dear Matt,

I prayed for you this morning.

2 Corinthians 1:4: He comforts us in all our troubles so that we can comfort others. When others are troubled, we will be able to give them the same comfort God has given us.

The above scripture really defines the AA and NA (Narcotics Anonymous) message. As God comforts and helps us, we learn to pass that on to those who come in behind us. I would not be alive today if others had not reached out to me. People cared for me when I was unable to care for myself. They loved me when I hated myself. Early in recovery when I thought about suicide, they encouraged me. They taught me by their example that there was a way to stay sober and that the mountains I faced could be climbed with their help and the help of God. They shared their hope with me when I felt hopeless. They taught me that if I would pass on to others what was being passed on to me, I would stay sober.

Well, so far I've taken you through my early experience with the first nine steps. It was quite a journey the first time through. I was so resistant at times, because the principles within the steps clashed with the ways I did life. Big Book, page 58: "Some of us have tried to hold onto our old ideas (belief systems) and the result was nil until we let go absolutely."139 As I said in an earlier letter, "If my belief systems don't change, the way I live life won't change, so the results will not change either."

I fought the idea of powerlessness and unmanageability in Step One, and it was difficult to admit insanity in Step Two. My issue with Step Three was not as much about believing in God, but in believing that God wanted anything to do with me. Step Four was difficult because it had to do with self-honesty, and I had not been honest with myself my entire life. I struggled with Step Five, because in spite of the wreckage of my life, my ego and self-centered pride were still huge. (I didn't know that then). Step Five is a direct assault on our ego and self-centered pride. I didn't struggle as much with Steps Six and Seven, because I really wanted to be changed, and I knew that only God could change me on the inside. That process continues as we stay on the path of recovery. We never arrive. Someone said, "Recovery is a journey, not a destination." Step Eight was not difficult, but Step Nine was another assault on my ego and self-centered pride.

Right after Step Nine commentary in the Big Book, we are given some great promises, on pages 83 and 84:

> If we are painstaking about this phase of our development, we will be amazed before we are half way through. We are going to know a new freedom and a new happiness. We will not regret the past nor wish to shut the door on it.
>
> We will comprehend the word serenity and we will know peace. No matter how far down the scale we have gone, we will see how our experience can benefit others. That feeling of uselessness and self-pity will disappear. We will lose interest in selfish things and gain interest in our fellows. Self-seeking will slip away. Our whole attitude and outlook upon life will change. Fear of people and of economic insecurity will leave us. We will intuitively know how to handle situations which used to baffle us. We will suddenly realize that God is doing for us what we could not do for ourselves.
>
> Are these extravagant promises? We think not. They are being fulfilled among us—sometimes quickly, sometimes slowly. They will always materialize if we work for them.[140]

One constant in my recovery journey is God doing for me what I can't do for myself. My dependence is on Him. Matt, what do you think your life would look like if all of the promises came true for you? Reflect on the "promises," and imagine that they all came true.

The Bible also gives us many promises, but the one found in Galatians 5:22–23 is wonderful. "But when the Holy Spirit controls our lives, He will produce this kind of fruit in us: love, joy, peace, patience, kindness, goodness, faithfulness, gentleness, and self-control." All of those attributes are part of who God is, and He wants to work in our life in such a way that they become part of who we are. It is He who works those into the fabric of who I am as I surrender to Him daily. The more I grow in my relationship with Him, the more the fruit is evident in my life. Sometimes my ego, self-centered pride, self-centeredness and selfishness, raise their ugly heads. When that happens, the "fruit of the spirit" is just words. I then have to ask for forgiveness, clean up my side of the street, and allow God's grace to move me forward. The Big Book on page 60 says this: "We are not saints. The point is, that we are willing to grow along spiritual lines. The principles we have set down are guides to progress. We claim spiritual progress rather than spiritual perfection."141 That statement gives me great hope.

Blessings,
Gary L.

12-16-08

Dear Matt,

I prayed for you this morning.

Well, Matt, I've been jumping back and forth between my story and the Twelve Steps for a while, but today I'll continue my story.

After my business failure and working in the cannery, Patsy and I were grateful when doors opened for new careers. Although my new job at Hillcrest School was just a temporary position for six months, I was hopeful that a permanent position might open. After I'd been there for two months that did happen. I applied for the permanent position, was interviewed, and several days later was notified that it was mine. That was exciting to Patsy and me, because it meant I would get a great benefits package. We had not had health insurance for a long time.

My new job was working a graveyard shift that began at 11:00 PM and ended at 7:00 AM. The cottage I worked on had seventeen students. When I arrived at work all of the guys were already locked in their rooms, and my responsibility was to shine a flashlight through a window in their door every hour to make sure they were okay. At 6:00 AM a second staff would arrive; we'd get the boys up so they could clean their rooms and the cottage. At 7:00 AM the second staff would take them to breakfast, and I would leave. I had seven hours of solitude every night. It was during those early-morning hours that God began to heal me from the pain of my failed business and how that had affected my family.

I did an autopsy of the business and discovered how my self-will had taken over. I saw how I had not asked God for direction when I started the business. It was all about me and my drive for financial independence.

As Bill Sees It, page 259:

Servant, Not Master

In A.A., we found that it did not matter too much what our material condition was, but it mattered greatly what our spiritual condition was. As we improved our spiritual outlook, money gradually became our servant and not our master. It became a means of exchanging love and service with those about us.[142]

Page 177:

Although financial recovery is on the way for many of us, we find we cannot place money first. For us, material well-being always follows spiritual progress; it never precedes.[143]

In regard to my spiritual growth, the business failure was so valuable, because it moved me back to the path of serving Him and others. If the business had succeeded as I had hoped, I would not have the life I have today. I would not know you or be writing to you. Out of what I considered a colossal failure, God worked good. What a tremendous example, again, of His marvelous grace. Romans 8:28: "And we know that God causes everything to work together for the good of those who love God and are called according to His purpose for them." That is a great promise! Had it not been for the failure, my relationship with money would have remained skewed.

Twenty-Four Hours a Day, December 16:

Meditation for the Day

Life is not a search for happiness. Happiness is a by-product of living the right kind of a life, of doing the right thing. Do not search for happiness, search for right living and happiness will be your reward. Life is sometimes a march of duty during dull, dark days. But happiness will come again, as God's smile of recognition of your faithfulness. True happiness is always the by-product of a life well lived.

Prayer for the Day

I pray that I may not seek happiness but seek to do right. I pray that I may not seek pleasure so much as the things that bring true happiness.[144]

Ephesians 2:8–10: God saved you by his special favor when you believed. And you can't take credit for this; it is a gift from God. Salvation is not a reward for the good things we have done, so none of us can boast about it. For we are God's masterpiece. He has created us anew in Christ Jesus, so that we can do the good things he planned for us long ago.

Blessings,
Gary L.

12-17-08

Dear Matt,

I prayed for you this morning.

Proverbs 3:5–6: Trust in the Lord with all your heart; do not depend on your own understanding. Seek his will in all you do, and he will direct your paths.

I settled into my new job, and one night while working the thought came into my mind that I should volunteer at an alcohol/drug treatment center in Salem called White Oaks. I approached the director, told her my background, and said I would be willing to volunteer four hours two mornings a week as a chaplain. I offered to do spirituality groups, one-on-one spiritual counseling, and listen to Fifth Steps. White Oaks welcomed me because spirituality was so important to their patients. I didn't know it at the time, but God was "directing my path" in a new direction. While volunteering there the idea came to write a thirty-day spiritual journal that the patients could use. That's the journal I shared with you earlier.

After I'd been there for approximately six months, the director worked what I was doing into the budget, and they began paying me $7.50 per hour, in spite of the fact that the center was experiencing financial difficulties. Later that year White Oaks closed its doors. It was a sad time for many dedicated employees. One of the employees was hired at an Oregon Corrections alcohol/drug program called Cornerstone. I asked her if it might be possible for me to volunteer there as I had at White Oaks. She checked with the director, and a short time later I started doing some one-on-one counseling with the inmates. Cornerstone was an eighteen-month program that inmates completed prior to their release. It was an excellent program. I had volunteered there several months. One day when I arrived to volunteer, I was informed that I could no longer get in. Apparently I had not jumped through the right hoops to get in there, and when the chaplain found out, he shut the door. It was disappointing to me because I really liked sharing my experience, strength, and hope with the inmates.

One day I received a call from a former coworker at White Oaks. She was working at a relatively new treatment program called Springbrook Northwest in Newberg. She said that their census was increasing, and they were looking for a part-time spiritual care counselor. It would be a six- to eight-hour-a-week position. I contacted the man who was in charge of spiritual care and arranged an interview. We really hit it off. I was hired and began working the following week. After getting off at 7:00 AM at Hillcrest School, I drove to Newberg and worked three to four hours two days a week. The number of patients continued to grow, as did the hours they needed me. Within a year or so, I was working there twenty to twenty-four hours a week plus working full time at Hillcrest School. Working all of those hours began to take a toll on me. Something that I've struggled with through the years has been to know my limits.

About that time Springbrook said that they needed a full-time spiritual care counselor, and the position was mine if I wanted it. Rather than make a snap decision like I'd done when I started my business, I talked to Patsy, prayed to God about it, and sought counsel from people I trusted. I loved what I was doing at Springbrook, but at that time they didn't provide near the benefit package that the State of Oregon did. In fact, there would be no health insurance. We continued to ask God for direction. I would soon be fifty-five. Would it be wise to make a change? I then received a letter from the State of Oregon that said that I was eligible to retire when I turned fifty-five. I was approaching seven years at Hillcrest and wouldn't get a large retirement, but it was something. I had been leaning toward working full time at Springbrook, and the letter from the state was like a confirmation to us.

I turned fifty-five that November, retired on December 31, and began working full time at Springbrook on January 2, 1995. Eleven years after graduating from Bible college, I was finally working in full-time ministry. I thought I was ready for full-time ministry when I graduated, but God knew different. He was so right! Sometimes I don't always know what's best for me.

Twenty-Four Hours a Day:

Meditation for the Day

"Show us the way, O Lord, and let us walk in Thy paths." There seems to be a right way to live and a wrong way. You can make a practical test. When you live the right way, things seem to work out well for you. When you live the wrong way, things seem to work out badly for you. You seem to take out of life about what you put into it. If you disobey the laws of nature, the chances are that you will be unhealthy. If you disobey the spiritual and moral laws, the chances are that you will be unhappy. By following the laws of nature and the spiritual laws of honesty, purity, unselfishness, and love, you can expect to be reasonably healthy and happy.

Prayer for the Day

I pray that I may try to live the right way. I pray that I may follow the path that leads to a better life.[145]

Blessings,
Gary L.

12-18-08

Dear Matt,

I prayed for you this morning.

I received your letter yesterday and appreciate your response to questions I asked in a previous letter. Your examples of powerlessness and unmanageability were great. As far as determination and willpower are concerned I think I see it a little differently than you. My determination and willpower was never sufficient to get me sober. The recognition you have that you need God to help you is accurate, but the way I use my determination and willpower is to align it with God and recovery principles.

The Big Book on page 85 states: "Every day is a day when we must carry the vision of God's will into all of our activities. "How can I best serve Thee—Thy will (not mine) be done." These are thoughts which must go with us constantly. We can exercise our will power along this line all we wish. It is the proper use of the will.146

I loved my job at Springbrook Northwest. To see patients arrive beaten up by their addiction, watching their denial system begin to break down and then seeing the light come on in their eyes was so exciting to me. What a privilege to watch miracles of transformation unfold in front of me. I observed people begin treatment who were angry, bitter, and full of denial, change into people of faith, hope, and peace. Of course, that didn't happen for everyone, and that's the sad part. I've known many people who left treatment unchanged. Occasionally it would be reported back to us that a former patient had died from their disease. Addiction kills!

Big Book, page 58: "Those who do not recover are people who cannot or will not completely give themselves to this simple program, usually men and women who are constitutionally incapable of being honest with themselves. There are such unfortunates. They are not at fault; they seem to have been born that way." After the last night I drank I wondered if I fit that category. Hugh assured me that if I was incapable of being honest with myself, that I wouldn't wonder about it. That was helpful to me.

During the years I drank I developed an intricate denial system that became the fiber of who I was, because I could not imagine not having alcohol. Alcohol was my sleep aid, my courage, my confidence, my time-out from life, my social lubricant, and I felt more normal while under the influence. Thus, the denial system. Denial is shrouded in dishonest thinking, self-deception, and excuses. Denial has a voice and speaks messages such as, "It's not your fault," You don't drink as much as a lot of people," "One drink won't hurt you," "Alcohol is not your real problem," or "You didn't get drunk every time you drank." My denial system spoke other messages too, but I think you get the point. Denial distorted the reality in my life and convinced me that I was right and everyone else was wrong.

Three of denial's greatest weapons are rationalization, justification, and blaming. Denial blinded me from the truth. My denial system began to break down as I attended meetings and listened to others. I mirrored off their experiences and began to get honest with myself. Step Four was a huge piece of dealing with my denial. Hugh was instrumental, because he was willing to tell me the truth as he saw it. One of the biggest challenges in treatment centers is to help break down patients' denial systems. When that happens, miracles occur.

After I had been at Springbrook for approximately two years, I enrolled in a two-year course to become certified as a spiritual director. The course was offered at a retreat center in Mount Angel called the Shalom Prayer Center. Springbrook adjusted my work schedule so that I could attend. I was with a group of the same sixteen people for two years, except for one person who didn't attend the second year. It was a wonderful experience that not only helped my spiritual growth, but it also equipped me to better serve others.

As Bill Sees It, page 13:

The Shared Gift

A.A. is more than a set of principles; it is a society of alcoholics in action. We must carry the message, else we ourselves can wither and those who haven't been given the truth may die.

Faith is more than our greatest gift; its sharing with others is our greatest responsibility. May we of A.A. continually seek the wisdom and the willingness by which we may well fulfill that immense trust which the Giver of all perfect gifts has placed in our hands.[147]

Psalm 9:9–10: The Lord is a shelter for the oppressed, a refuge in the time of trouble. Those who know your name trust in you, for you, O Lord, have never abandoned anyone who searches for you.

Blessings,
Gary L.

12-19-08

Dear Matt,

I prayed for you this morning.

Big Book, page 59: Step Ten. "Continued to take personal inventory and when we were wrong promptly admitted it." If I had written Step Ten I probably would have left out the word *promptly.* Just kidding. It's perfect the way it's written. There are some who refer to Steps Ten through Twelve as daily maintenance steps. I certainly agree with that, although I haven't always practiced that. When I am diligent with Step Ten—keeping my side of the street clean—I can go to bed at night and have "sweet sleep." Proverbs 3:24 in the *New American Standard Bible* states: "When you lie down, you will not be afraid; when you lie down, your sleep will be sweet."

For many years, I was like a person going through life carrying a burlap bag over my shoulder. Each day I would throw rocks of resentment, anger, envy, dishonesty, unforgivingness, self-pity, etc. into the bag. Eventually the bag would become so heavy that I couldn't carry it. I was able to get relief from the load when I drank alcohol. Alcohol gave me a time-out from the weight. When I sobered up, the weight would return, and it was heavier. My alcoholism does not want me to apply Step Ten to my life, because if I don't I'm vulnerable to drink again.

Alcoholics Anonymous, page 84:

> This thought brings us to *Step Ten*, which suggests we continue to take personal inventory and continue to set right any new mistakes as we go along. We vigorously commenced this way of living as we cleaned up the past. We have entered the world of the Spirit. Our next function is to grow in understanding and effectiveness. This is not an overnight matter. It should continue for our lifetime. Continue to watch for selfishness, dishonesty, resentment, and fear. When these crop up, we ask God at once to remove them. We discuss them with someone immediately and make amends quickly if we have harmed anyone. Then we resolutely turn our thoughts to someone we can help. Love and tolerance of others is our code.[148]

Twenty-Four Hours a Day. August 28:

Meditation for the Day

Happiness cannot be sought directly; it is a by-product of love and service. Service is a law of our being. With love in your heart, there is always some service to other people. A life of power and joy and satisfaction is built on love and service. Persons who hate or are selfish are going against the law of their own being. They are cutting themselves off from God and other people. Little acts of love and encouragement, of service and help, erase the rough places of life and help to make the path smooth. If we do these things, we cannot help having our share of happiness.

Prayer for the Day

I pray that I may give my share of love and service. I pray that I may not grow weary in my attempts to do the right thing.[149]

What great principles of living the Twelve Steps give us!

Psalms 103:8: The Lord is merciful and gracious; he is slow to anger and full of unfailing love.

Blessings,
Gary L.

12-20-08

Dear Matt,

I prayed for you this morning.

In earlier letters I wrote about my relationship with Mom while growing up. My perception of those years is so different today than it was then. While working at Hillcrest School in 1989, I received a phone call from a cousin informing me that another cousin had died. She had been in a battle with cancer for a long time, and it finally took her. My cousin asked if I would call my side of the family and inform them. The first person I called was Mom. She was not surprised by the news. We talked for a while and then said our good-byes.

Approximately an hour later Dad called me, and he was frantic. Every day while working he would call Mom and check in. When he called that morning the line was busy, and after trying it several more times and still getting a busy signal, he had a feeling that something was wrong. When he arrived home he found Mom lying unconscious on the floor still holding the phone from our earlier conversation. After discovering her he called 911 and then made a frantic call to me. The ambulance arrived, and she was transported to a hospital in Vancouver. Dad called again and told us the location.

By the time we arrived at the hospital Mom was brain-dead from a massive stroke, and she died a short while later. I never shed a tear then or later at her funeral. When my grandma died when I was a child, I learned to not grieve. Crying was not okay. The message I received was that I should be happy because Grandma was in heaven. I learned how to stuff grief at that time and years later when Mom died I stuffed again. I could not work up within me any sense of sadness or loss. Then the feeling of guilt about that hit. I realized that I needed to do some serious work about loss.

It was about five years later that I finally did some work with the help of a spiritual director at the Shalom Prayer Center. I scheduled a three-day silent retreat at Shalom with the intention of finally doing the work regarding Mom. The only time I spoke during that time was when I met with the spiritual director. The first assignment she gave me was to write an angry letter to Mom, expressing the times when she made me feel so small. After processing the letter with my director, she gave me another assignment to write another letter and talk about the good times that we shared. Part of the second letter was to include my forgiveness to Mom. While processing the second letter, a flood of tears and emotion hit me, and I finally grieved. It was a powerful three days for me. Up to then, I had tried to get to forgiveness and acceptance without going through the anger and grief.

As I've continued to take personal inventory (Steps Four and Ten) areas continue to surface where some work is required. It took me more than twenty years in recovery before I finally did the work around Mom. I have to remember this is a lifelong journey, and there will always be things to work on. As painful as some of the work has been at times, the healing on the other side has been wonderful.

Psalm 27:14: "Wait patiently for the Lord. Be brave and courageous. Yes, wait patiently for the Lord."

Blessings,
Gary L.

12-21-08

Dear Matt,

I prayed for you this morning.

One place that I needed to inventory and get real honest with myself was my relationships with people. I wrote about this some in earlier letters, but need to touch on it again. As I reviewed relationships in the past, there were some things I discovered that I hadn't been aware of. Every broken relationship ended up with me resenting someone. I had to ask myself, "Why is that so?" The conclusion I came to was that I had clear expectations of how I believed people should treat me, and when they didn't meet my expectations I resented them. I had very little concern how I treated them. Bill W. really nailed me in his writing on page 176 from *As Bill Sees It*:

> **Domination and Demand**
>
> The primary fact that we fail to recognize is our total inability to form a true partnership with another human being. Our egomania digs two disastrous pitfalls. Either we insist upon dominating the people we know, or we depend upon them far too much.
>
> If we lean too heavily on people, they will sooner or later fail us, for they are human, too, and cannot possibly meet our incessant demands. In this way our insecurity grows and festers.
>
> When we habitually try to manipulate others to our own willful desires, they revolt, and resist us heavily. Then we develop hurt feelings, a sense of persecution, and a desire to retaliate.
>
> My dependency meant demand—a demand for the possession and control of the people and the conditions surrounding me.150

I think of the way I retaliated against my parents when they wouldn't come through for me. One time I asked Dad to use his car, and he refused. There was good reason for his refusal. From the time I received my driver's license until then, I had trashed three of his cars. He was fed up with me.

When he refused me, I stormed out of the house with the thought, "I'll show you."

I've since learned that anytime I follow through on that thought, I'm about ready to do something stupid. After drinking most of the night, I returned home early in the morning. A six-pack was in the refrigerator, and so I sat in the kitchen and emptied it. I was drunk but not so drunk that I was unable to go upstairs to my bedroom. But rather than go to bed, I lay down on the kitchen floor to sleep. I knew they would be horrified when they found me like that when they got up. Boy, I sure showed them, didn't I? What terrible games those are, but that's the kind of person I'd become. I remember a guy at an AA meeting talking about his mother when she refused to give him money. He said that his first thought was, "I'll show you. I'll kill me, and you're going to feel bad." I understand that kind of thinking.

Here's a great prayer from *Rooted in God's Love*:

> Lord, help me to build relationships that sustain honesty. Give me friends who will love me enough to tell me the truth. Help me to pay attention to correction. Give me the courage to see myself clearly. Keep me from shame and self-loathing. Give me the openness to correction that makes change possible. Amen.[151]

By the way, when is your release date? If at all possible I would love to see you baptized.

Mark 11:25: "But when you are praying, first forgive anyone you are holding a grudge against, so that your Father in heaven will forgive your sins, too."

Blessings,
Gary L.

12-22-08

Dear Matt,

I prayed for you this morning.

Big Book, page 59: Step Eleven. "Sought through prayer and meditation to improve our conscious contact with God as we understood Him, praying only for the knowledge of His will for us and the power to carry it out."

Step Eleven has been a step that has evolved for me. Early in recovery about the only prayer I could utter was, "God, help me not take a drink today." The book I used for meditation was *Twenty-Four Hours a Day*. My morning prayer and meditation took about three to five minutes. I didn't seek much guidance because what I wanted was for God to bless my plans. God understood where I was at the time and patiently began working in me. He also understood the long periods of time when I didn't pray or meditate at all. I certainly don't recommend that others follow my example. Then there were times when I was diligent and spent much time in prayer and meditation every morning without fail. So for me, there's been a real mix in my journey with Step Eleven. There have been times of prayer that I felt so enriched, and other times when I've prayed from a sense of duty or discipline.

In spite of my lack in this area, my conscious contact with God has improved, and my understanding of His will for me has grown. He has been a lot more faithful to me than I've been to Him. That is a lot of grace! Because of what God has done in me, today, Step Eleven has become an everyday step. Sometimes I go to a retreat center and have an Eleventh Step day. One of the key words in Step Eleven to me is improve. That tells me that no matter where I am in my relationship with God, or in my spiritual growth, there's always room for improvement.

Big Book, page 86:

> On awakening let us think about the twenty-four hours ahead. We consider our plans for the day. Before we begin, we ask God to direct our thinking, especially asking that it be divorced from self-pity, dishonest or self-seeking motives. Under these conditions we can employ our mental faculties with assurance, for after all God gave us brains to use. Our thought-life will be placed on a much higher plane when our thinking is cleared of wrong motives.

> In thinking about our day we may face indecision. We may not be able to determine which course to take. Here we ask God for inspiration, an intuitive thought or a decision. We relax and take it easy. We don't struggle. We are often surprised how the right answers come after we have tried this for a while. What used to be the hunch or the occasional inspiration gradually becomes a working part of the mind.[152]

There are many forms of meditation. I spend more time in reflection than meditation, but when I do meditate I use a simple method. I sit in a chair and have my open palms facing up. Open palms symbolize that I'm not holding on to something. Then I slowly, deeply, inhale through my nose what I need. Perhaps it's wisdom or forgiveness. Sometimes I breathe in understanding or guidance. But probably 90 to 95 percent of the time I breathe in wisdom. Not the wisdom of this world, but God's wisdom. When I exhale, I breathe out what I need to get rid of; perhaps it's anger, self-pity, resentment, selfishness, etc. You might give that method a try.

As I said earlier, Step Eleven has evolved through the years. For the last three years I've consistently spent one to two hours every morning in prayer, reflection, meditation, and study. Patsy and I began following the Bible reading guide in *Our Daily Bread* three years ago, and at the end of this month we will have read the entire Bible three years in a row. We plan on doing it again. That has been a most rewarding piece of my spiritual journey. None of that is about me—it's all about what God has done in me.

Luke 11:10: "For everyone who asks, receives. Everyone who seeks, finds, and the door is opened to everyone who knocks."

Blessings,
Gary L.

12-23-08

Dear Matt,

I prayed for you this morning.

I don't believe we have to be behind prison walls to be imprisoned. I was a prisoner to alcohol for sixteen years. As the Step Three prayer suggests, I was also in "bondage to self." Someone said that the worst kind of slavery is when we are enslaved to ourselves. Alcohol dictated to me a way of life that kept me in chains. It ruled me, as my life revolved around it. It dictated where I went, what I did, who I hung out with, and how I spent my money. The funny thing is, it robbed me but I was the one who ended up imprisoned. And then at age thirty–one, the people in the rooms of Alcoholics Anonymous gave me a message of hope. A message that said I could have freedom, I could be forgiven, and once I was on the path of freedom, I could pass the message of hope on to others. Big Book, page 60: Step Twelve. "Having had a spiritual awakening as the result of these steps, we tried to carry this message to alcoholics, and to practice these principles in all our affairs."

There are several parts to Step Twelve. The first part is, "Having had a spiritual awakening as the result of these steps." That tells me that if I've done the other eleven steps I will, if it hasn't already happened, have a spiritual awakening. Many of us have multiple spiritual awakenings as we journey with God, but the initial awakening was the one that got us going.

As Bill Sees It, page 85:

Life Is Not a Dead End

When a man or woman has a spiritual awakening, the most important meaning of it is that he has now become able to do, feel, and believe that which he could not do before on his unaided strength and resources alone. He has been granted a gift which amounts to a new state of consciousness and being.

He has been set on a path which tells him he is really going somewhere, that life is not a dead end, not something to be endured or mastered. In a very real sense he has been transformed, because he has laid hold of a source of strength which he had hitherto denied himself.[153]

Gary L.

Matt, you've told me that you are a Christian and that you want to be baptized. That is great! Would you share with me your spiritual awakening? How did that come about? What is new for you? I'd really like to hear that part of your story. I might have mentioned this before; there is a ministry called Prison Fellowship. If they have meetings there, you might check it out. How is your Bible course going? Does the chaplain help you with that? I hope I haven't asked too many questions.

Isaiah 61:1: "The Spirit of the sovereign Lord is upon me, because the Lord has appointed me to bring good news to the poor. He has sent me to comfort the brokenhearted and to announce that captives will be released and prisoners will be freed."

Blessings,
Gary L.

12-24-08

Dear Matt,

I prayed for you this morning.

The second part of Step Twelve is, "we tried to carry this message to alcoholics." A key word in that part is *tried*. Hugh explained to me one time that we carry the message, not the alcoholic. I wanted to sober people up, but Hugh pointed out that I didn't have the power to do that. He said that some people will be receptive to the message, and others won't.

While working at the South Coast Recovery Center, I would get so excited when someone accepted the message and would be really disappointed when the message was rejected. One day I realized that I was taking the credit for the successes, and blame for the failures. Hugh helped me to see that. The pieces of wisdom that he shared with me were so helpful.

Life Recovery Bible, page 867, commentary on Step Twelve:

> A life set free from all addictions by the Lord is a beautiful sight to behold. When we practice these principles and share our experiences, people will see the glory of God in our life and gain hope. We know from experience the depths of suffering, affliction, and brokenness. We know the pain of being enslaved to our passions and blinded by our denial. We have endured our seasons of grieving. We can relate to those who struggle to be free. We also know that there is more to life than bondage. In Christ are healing and freedom, clarity and mercy, beauty and joy.
>
> This mission has been passed on to us. Some people talk about "preaching the gospel" but may alienate those who need the Good News the most. We are in a unique position to share our experiences, our strengths, and our hope in a way that broken people can understand and receive it.[154]

Our mission and obligation is to pass on to others what we've received. Many times Hugh said to me, "If you want to keep it, you have to give it away." That's what keeps AA going.

As Bill Sees It, page 90:

> Life takes on new meaning in A.A. To watch people recover, to see them help others, to watch loneliness vanish, to see a fellowship grow up about you, to have a host of friends—this is an experience not to be missed.[155]

I'll finish up with Step Twelve in my next letter. I pray that God will comfort and encourage you through this holiday season while you're separated from family. That must be difficult.

Romans 8:38–39: "And I am convinced that nothing can ever separate us from his love. Death can't, and life can't, the angels can't and the demons can't. Our fears for today, our worries about tomorrow, and even the powers of hell can't keep God's love away. Whether we are high above the sky or in the deepest ocean, nothing in all creation will ever be able to separate us from the love of God that is revealed in Christ Jesus our Lord."

Blessings,
Gary L.

12-25-08

Dear Matt,

I prayed for you this morning.

The third part of Step Twelve is, "and to practice these principles in all our affairs." Well, let's take a look at some of the principles in the steps. In Step One is the principle of admitting powerlessness and unmanageability—a knowing that my way of doing life does not work and that I need help. There is also the recognition of insanity. How many of us are eager to do that? The principle within Step Two is about being restored. It is a recognition that I can't restore myself without help. It is a step of faith. To me, there are three major principles in Step Three: making a decision, surrender, and trusting.

Step Four's principle has to do with self-honesty—looking at my side of the street. The principle of Step Five is confession, not only to God, but to another person. It's an ego blaster, but it's also about healing and forgiveness. Steps Six and Seven continue the theme of surrendering to God and the understanding that I cannot change the inside of me, but God can as I open myself to Him. There is also the principle of humility that says that God will work in us His way and in his time.

Step Eight has to do with self-honesty—an honest look at the ways we've harmed others. The principle within Step Nine is restitution to those we've harmed—the principle of cleaning my side of the street. Step Ten is about self-honesty and confession when I'm wrong. Step Eleven is about seeking God's guidance and power. The principles in Step Twelve are about passing on what we've been given and practice, practice, practice of the other principles.

Big Book, page 60:

> Many of us exclaimed, "What an order! I can't go through with it." Do not be discouraged. No one among us has been able to maintain anything like perfect adherence to these principles. We are not saints. The point is, that we are willing to grow along spiritual lines. The principles we have set down are guides to progress. We claim spiritual progress rather than spiritual perfection.[156]

That paragraph has saved many of us who have perfectionist tendencies.
As I began journeying through the Twelve Steps, I believed that the steps ascended and that I needed to get to the top. Some years later I began to see them in a different way. Today, I believe the steps go down. When I first got sober my life was a wreck, but in spite of that, my huge ego (Easing God Out) was still intact. I was the supreme judge of everything in life. At the time, I didn't know that I was the one who wrecked the train. That revelation would come later. Step Twelve is not only about the spiritual awakening we experience, it's also about humility and service. When I see myself as being at the top, there is no room for humility.

As Bill Sees It, page 156:

Perception of Humility

An improved perception of humility starts a revolutionary change in our outlook. Our eyes begin to open to the immense values which have come straight out of painful ego-puncturing. Until now, our lives have been largely devoted to running from pain and problems. Escape via the bottle was always our solution.

Then, in A.A., we looked and listened. Everywhere we saw failure and misery transformed by humility into priceless assets.

To those who have made progress in A.A., humility amounts to a clear recognition of what and who we really are, followed by a sincere attempt to become what we could be.157

Psalm 27:14: "Wait patiently for the Lord. Be brave and courageous. Yes, wait patiently for the Lord."

Blessings,
Gary L.

12-26-08

Dear Matt,

I prayed for you this morning.

Proverbs 17:22: "A cheerful heart is good medicine, but a broken spirit saps a person's strength."

Life Recovery Bible, commentary, page 1,204:

> In recovery painful thoughts of a guilt-ridden past or an uncertain future often intrude and disrupt the present and sometimes cause us to feel depressed. Certainly these darker issues must be faced for us to break free from the patterns of the past. But Mary shows us how thoughts about God can lift our spirits and give us the courage to take the next step. She meditated on the things God was doing and wanted to do in her life. When we do the same, we take a step toward recovery and wholeness. Pondering the joy with the sorrow, the awesome with the awful, the gain with the pain will lead to emotional and spiritual healing.[158]

When I wrote about the principles found within the Twelve Steps, I did not give all of them. Perhaps, as you study the steps, you can find principles I did not list. If you discover some, please let me know. I'm sure you will agree we have a lot of practicing of the principles to do.

As Bill Sees It, page 94:

> **In All Our Affairs**
>
> The chief purpose of A.A. is sobriety. We all realize that without sobriety we have nothing.
>
> However, it is possible to expand this simple aim into a great deal of nonsense, so far as the individual member is concerned. Sometimes we hear him say, in effect, "Sobriety is my sole responsibility. After all, I'm a pretty fine chap, except for my drinking. Give me sobriety, and I've got it made!"

> As long as our friend clings to this comfortable alibi, he will make so little progress with his real life problems and responsibilities that he stands in a fair way to get drunk again. This is why A.A.'s Twelfth Step urges that we "practice these principles in all our affairs." We are not living just to be sober; we are living to learn, to serve, and to love.[159]

As Bill Sees It, page 192:

> The wonderful energy the Twelfth Step releases, by which it carries our message to the next suffering alcoholic (I'll add addict) and finally translates the Twelve Steps into action upon all our affairs, is the payoff, the magnificent reality of A.A.[160]

There is no greater joy for me than to see the light come on in someone's life as they accept the recovery message. The recovery journey is not about not using or drinking. That has to be in place, but it's a mere beginning to what God has in store for us. One of my constant prayers for you is that God will heal and equip you to carry the message of recovery to others. What would it be like for you if someone came to you after an NA or AA meeting and said, "Matt, I like to hear the things you say at meetings. Would you be my sponsor?" Think about it; someone sees such an example of recovery living that he wants to draw from you your experience, strength, and hope. The first time someone asked me to be his sponsor, it blew me away!

Blessings,
Gary L.

12-27-08

Dear Matt,

I prayed for you this morning.

John 14:27: "I am leaving you with a gift—peace of mind and heart. And the peace I give isn't like the peace the world gives. So don't be troubled or afraid."

I'm not sure if I ever had any real peace until I'd been sober some time. Even before I started drinking I was always in conflict. When I drank alcohol the first time at age fifteen, I experienced what I call counterfeit peace or serenity. It wasn't the real deal, but I settled for that during the sixteen years I drank alcohol.

It was at my first AA meeting that I heard the Serenity Prayer for the first time. I learned later that the prayer in its entirety was much longer than the four lines we open meetings with, and it was written by Reinhold Niebuhr.

As Bill Sees It, page 108:

Learn in Quiet

In 1941, a news clipping was called to our attention by a New York member. In an obituary notice from a local paper, there appeared these words: "God grant us the serenity to accept the things we cannot change, the courage to change the things we can, and the wisdom to know the difference."

Never had we seen so much A.A. in so few words. With amazing speed the Serenity Prayer came into general use.

In meditation, debate has no place. We rest quietly with the thoughts or prayers of spiritually centered people who understand, so that we may experience and learn. This is the state of being that so often discovers and deepens a conscious contact with God.[161]

Psalm 116:1–9:

I love the Lord because He hears and answers my prayers. Because He bends down and listens, I will pray as long as I have breath! Death had its hands around my throat; the terrors of the grave overtook me. I saw only trouble and sorrow. Then I called on the name of the Lord: "Please, Lord, save me!" How kind the Lord is! How good He is! So merciful, this God of ours! The Lord protects those of childlike faith; I was facing death, and then He saved me. Now I can rest again, for the Lord has been so good to me. He has saved me from death, my eyes from tears, my feet from stumbling. And so I walk in the Lord's presence as I live here on earth.

Life Recovery Bible commentary on above, page 735:

How wonderful that God hears and answers the prayers of those who turn to him in distress! When we were in the grip of our dependency or addiction, we may have been blind to the fact that we were in danger of losing our reputation, our friends, or even our life. But then we called out to the Lord, and he saved us. The natural response to this realization should be praise to God.[162]

All of that has been so true in my life.

I've enclosed a copy of the entire Serenity Prayer.

Blessings,
Gary L.

God grant me the Serenity
to accept the things I cannot change,
Courage to change the things I can,
and Wisdom to know the difference.
Living one day at a time;
Enjoying one moment at a time;
accepting hardships as the pathway to peace;
Taking, as He did, this sinful world
As it is, not as I would have it;
Trusting that He will make
All things right
If I surrender to His will;
That I may be reasonably happy in this Life
And supremely happy with Him forever in the next.
Amen

Reinhold Niebuhr

12-28-09

Dear Matt,

I prayed for you this morning.

I loved working at Springbrook Northwest and looked forward to going to work every day. I guess when a person looks forward to going to their place of employment, that it's not really work. The number of patients continued to grow, but the number of staff in the Spiritual Care Department didn't; a subtle transition began to happen that I didn't see until later. As time went on, I was unable to spend as much time with each patient because of the numbers. We were not allowed to work overtime, so the eight hours I worked was not enough to give the patients the quality care they deserved. Anyway, that was my perspective. Administration was extremely happy with the work our department was doing because of the positive feedback from patients during exit interviews. A huge mistake I made was that I didn't express to my supervisor that I was on the edge of burnout. I think I mentioned in a previous letter that I sometimes don't know my limits until I'm past them. My self-centered pride that comes up occasionally is such a block that stops me from asking for help.

One morning when I awoke, the first thought in my mind was, "I don't want to go to work today." That was a strong clue that something was wrong, not with Springbrook, but with me. I did go to work that day and finally talked to my supervisor about what I was experiencing. I requested an unpaid thirty-day leave of absence. My batteries really needed recharging. I decided that I would fly to Texas where my dad and sister lived, just to get away. When I bought my airline ticket, a thought went through my mind, "If the plane goes down, I'm really okay with that."

That moment I realized the depression I was in. After coming back from Texas, I made arrangements to go to a renewal center at a treatment center called Hazelden in Minnesota. I was there seven days, and it was a great experience. God began to do some healing in me. By the time I arrived home from Minnesota I was in pretty good shape. I went to many AA meetings with the remainder of my time and talked about what I was experiencing. By the time I returned to work I was looking forward to being there.

I liked the writing in the *Twenty-Four Hours a Day* book today:

A.A. Thought for the Day

A.A. may be human in its organization, but it is divine in its purpose. The purpose is to point me toward God and the good life. My feet have been set upon the right path. I feel it in the depths of my being. I am going in the right direction. The future can be safely left to God. Whatever the future holds, it cannot be too much for me to bear. I have the Divine Power with me to carry me through everything that may happen. *Am I pointed toward God and the good life?*

Meditation for the Day

Although unseen, the Lord is always near to those who believe in Him and trust Him and depend on Him for the strength to meet the challenges of life. Although veiled from mortal sight, the Higher Power is always available to us whenever we humbly ask for it. The feeling that God is with us should not depend on any passing mood of ours; we should try to be always conscious of His power and love in the background of our lives.

Prayer for the Day

I pray that I may feel that God is not too far away to depend on for help. I pray that I may feel confident of His readiness to give me the power that I need.[163]

1 Peter 5:6: "So humble yourselves under the mighty power of God, and in his good time he will honor you. Give all your worries and cares to God, for he cares about what happens to you."

God is so faithful to us.

Blessings,
Gary L.

12-29-08

Dear Matt,

I prayed for you this morning.

When I returned to Springbrook after my leave of absence, I was hopeful that another staffer would be hired to help in spiritual care, but that didn't happen. Several months went by, and I found myself not wanting to be at work again. I just couldn't seem to find the balance I needed.

For a number of years, Patsy and I had been attending a large church in Salem that had a program called Steps, which had to do with support and recovery. One day, I was speaking with the pastor in charge of Steps, and she said that I probably wasn't interested, but the church had authorized her to hire someone part time to assist her. I was extremely interested, and I told her so. It was a twenty-hour-per-week position, and it would mean a huge pay cut for me. Patsy and I talked about it and prayed about it, and we believed that I was supposed to make the change. I gave Springbrook a thirty-day notice, and when that time was up, I began my new job.

The Steps program addressed a myriad of life issues that included addiction, codependency, anger management, eating disorders, adult children of alcoholics, and divorce recovery. I was an assistant pastor of support and recovery for five years and then retired when I was sixty-four. One of the things that happened during the five years I was there was, as the program grew, so did my hours. By the time I retired it was almost a full-time job. After I retired, Patsy and I had a new home built in Sheridan, Oregon, where our youngest daughter lived with her husband and two children.

During the five years I worked at the church I had maintained my friendship with my supervisor at Springbrook. Not long after Patsy and I moved into our new home, I was having lunch with him, and he asked if I would like a part-time job. Springbrook had been bought by Hazelden, from Minnesota, and it was now called Hazelden Springbrook. Well, so much for retirement. I accepted his offer and worked for another two years. When I retired the last time they changed my status to on-call. Occasionally, I fill in for vacations.

Well, as you can see. I've moved around a lot. God has journeyed with Patsy and me the entire way. When I first got sober I would never have scripted all the wonderful things that have happened in recovery. The one constant in recovery has been God. His grace, mercy, guidance, love, and care have never wavered. I learned that God loves me just as much when I'm at my worst as when I'm at my best. That tells me that it's all about who He is. In spite of my inconsistency, He has always been consistent. We praise and thank him for all he's done and for what he will do in the future. I will end this letter with another meditation from *Rooted in God's Love*:

> God Walks With Me in the Valleys
>
> Sometimes the recovery journey takes us through the valley of the shadow of death. It is a frightening valley.
>
> What a difference it makes in times like this to hear God's promise to be with us. It's not that the fears vanish—they don't always. But we experience them differently when we are not alone. When we are alone our fears can become the focus of our thoughts and feelings—they can consume all of our emotional resources. But when our journey is a shared one, fear does not have the same power over us.
>
> God has made a very specific promise to us when we are going through the most difficult of life's struggles. God has promised to be with us. It is hard to say how God's presence will be made known. Our subjective experience of God's presence may vary widely. Sometimes when we least expect it, we may hear the still, small voice of God saying, "I am here." Sometimes God will use a friend, a sponsor, a counselor, or someone in a support group to speak to us in ways that help us to remember that we are not alone. Sometimes God will give us a peace that needs no words.
>
> The important reality is that God is with us. God does not come and go in the way our experience of God's presence comes and goes. God does not forsake us. God walks with us. Even through deep valleys.[164]

There have been many valleys in my journey, and God has been there with me. I'll write about some of the valleys in future letters and how God showed himself to me.

Psalm 71:20–21: "You have allowed me to suffer much hardship, but you will restore me to life again and lift me up from the depths of the earth. You will restore me to even greater honor and comfort me once again."

Blessings,
Gary L.

12-30-08

Dear Matt,

I prayed for you this morning.

Psalm 23:4: "Even when I walk through the dark valley of death, I will not be afraid, for you are close beside me. Your rod and your staff protect and comfort me."

I need to tell you about my stepdad. He raised me from the age of four, so he became Dad to me. Our relationship was contentious right from the beginning. In my mind, he was the reason my daddy was no longer around. I would not allow him into my world. Another reason for our contention was that he tried to hold me accountable for my behaviors. Anyone who did that was considered an enemy. I think there was also an element of fear about letting him in; he'll probably abandon me like my Daddy did.

My resentment and hate grew as the years went by. When I was a teenager I would think of ways to kill him but could never come up with a plan where I was 100 percent sure I wouldn't get caught. When I was in my 20s and still drinking, I received a call that he had been in an accident. He had been up an old logging road cutting firewood. My younger brother Jeff had followed him in his car and was helping. Driving back home with a fully loaded truck, the brakes went out. Dad's option was to go into a deep canyon or pull into the bank on the other side. When he pulled into the bank, an open container of chain saw gas that was in the cab of the pickup overturned and ignited. Dad came out of the truck on fire and headed for the canyon and the stream below. Jeff followed him and helped put the fire out with his hands. Dad ended up in the hospital with a burn tent over him in very serious condition. When I received the phone call about the accident and the details, my internal response was, "Yes! He's getting his." Oh, the hate inside me had become a terrible poison. I hid the hate from others, but it was still there.

The beginning of healing between us did not begin until years later when I got sober and began working the Twelve Steps. My initial attempt at making amends was met with a measure of coolness, and I understood that. I wanted him to trust me but understood why that was difficult.

Sometime during my second year while working at the South Coast Recovery Center, Mom called me. My brother Jeff and his wife and son had moved to Reno. He was in trouble with the law and in jail (alcohol and drug trouble). Mom asked if I would fly to Reno with her, bail him out of jail, and then take him to the treatment center. His wife was going to move back to Washington where her family was. We arrived in Reno and went to the jail.

After posting bail, Jeff was released and given permission to go to the South Coast Recovery Center. We drove to Oregon in his car. The trip reminded me so much of the time Mom and Dad had taken me from Reno to Oregon. Jeff seemed enthused about treatment, but after two weeks he decided to leave.

I was so disappointed, and so were Mom and Dad. This was in 1975. Jeff died in 1977. His cause of death was "died in a fire," but that's not the entire story. Jeff was separated from his wife at the time and was living in a travel trailer in a park. What we were able to piece together was that he had been out drinking and drugging. After returning to his trailer, he had put something on the stove to cook. Apparently he passed out, the trailer caught fire, and he died. What a tragedy. The record states that he died in a fire, but I know that he died from alcohol and drugs.

During the time of our family's grief, Dad and I leaned on each other for strength. What a miracle that was. Some more healing was happening between us.

What a deep valley that was to go through.

Blessings,
Gary L.

12-31-08

Dear Matt,

I prayed for you this morning.

My brother Jeff was twenty-seven when he died. He left a son, who was almost four, and a daughter, who was almost one. I said in my last letter that when Jeff died, Dad and I leaned on each other, and that was true, but I was also leaning on God. I had been sober over six years at the time, and there was never a thought of wanting to numb the pain with alcohol. What a miracle for an alcoholic.

When Mom died in 1989, Dad and I supported each other again. He was so broken by her death. She was his life. Dad lived in their home until 1991, when he decided to sell it and move to Texas where my sister Pat lived. He just couldn't stay in the house with all of its memories. Pat's husband, Gordon, and a friend of his flew to Oregon to help Dad move. After several days of packing, they were on their way. I was sad to see him leave because our relationship was growing closer.

Dad had been in Texas for a couple of years when he had a stroke. Therapy helped him to have about 90 percent recovery. One day he called me and asked if I would fly to Texas and hang out with him for a few days. He even offered to pay my air fare. I arranged some time off from work and flew to Texas. Dad and I had the best time. We were able to talk about the growing-up years, and the pain we caused each other. It was a time of amends from both of us. This time my amends to him were received. When I flew back to Oregon, I knew some deep healing had happened.

Early in 1996 Dad called and said that he wanted to move back to Oregon. He was going to have movers transport his belongings, and he wondered if I would travel with him in his car. Dad had a 1976 Lincoln Town Car that he'd bought when it was less than a year old. That car was his pride and joy. It was deep red with a white vinyl top. He also had a small Pontiac that we would tow. When I arrived in Texas, I discovered that Dad had had a few small strokes, and his lung disease had progressed so that he needed an oxygen bottle. He was unable to walk up a flight of steps without help. He was plugged into the VA system, and I tried to get him to go to the hospital to no avail. He said that if he wasn't better by the time we arrived in Oregon, he would go to the VA hospital in Portland.

We left Texas, and I was full of fear. "Would he make it?" I wondered. When we checked into a motel the first night, Dad's breathing was so labored that he was unable to lie down. Even with his oxygen bottle, he had to straddle a chair in order to get some rest. It took us five days to get to Oregon. My fear was overwhelming at times. I had rented a basement apartment for him, and when his belongings arrived, a friend helped me move them into the apartment. Dad was staying at our home while I was trying to get his place ready.

It became obvious after a few days that he needed to be taken to the VA hospital. He was eating nitroglycerine pills like they were candy. He finally agreed to go to the hospital. After the doctor checked him, he was immediately taken to ICU. After several days there, he was moved into a room. I drove to Portland almost every night to visit him. The recommendation was made after he was stabilized, to move him to a VA nursing home in Vancouver. He was there for a short while, had a setback, and was returned to ICU. After being stabilized again, he was transported back to the nursing home.

A week or so went by, and his doctor called and said that we needed to get the family together because there was nothing more that they could do for him. I made the calls to family members, and we all arrived at the nursing home at about the same time the following day. Dad knew he was dying. I don't know this for sure, but I believe Dad asked the doctor to let him die. He was so tired from the fight to stay alive.

One by one, Dad had a moment of closure with those who were there. I was standing over by the door. After Dad had spoken to the others, he motioned for me to come to the head of his bed. When I got there, he looked up at me, and, with a twinkle in his eye, he said, "Thanks." He closed his eyes and died later that evening. If someone had said to me when I first got sober that someday my stepdad would become my best friend, I would have laughed. But that's what happened. What a huge miracle that was. God was with us through that deep valley.

Psalm 136:1: "Give thanks to the Lord, for he is good! His faithful love endures forever."

Blessings,
Gary L.

1-1-09

Dear Matt,

I prayed for you this morning.

Proverbs 23:12: "Commit yourself to instruction; attune your ears to hear words of knowledge."

Well, my friend, we're beginning a new year. I always wonder what it will bring. My experience has been that God will be with us no matter what life gives us. I pray that God will bless you with truth, wisdom, strength, and power, and surround you with His love, compassion, and understanding. The Proverbs verse that is above tells me that I need to be able to take instruction. That really goes against the grain of self-centeredness. I also pray that God will give you an understanding of what true humility is. That is an area that we can all grow in.

As Bill Sees It, page 139:

Basis of All Humility

For just so long as we are convinced that we could live exclusively by our own individual strength and intelligence, for just that long was a working faith in a Higher Power impossible.

This was true even when we believed that God existed. We could actually have earnest religious beliefs which remained barren because we were still trying to play God ourselves. As long as we placed self-reliance first, a genuine reliance upon a Higher Power was out of the question.

That basic ingredient of all humility, a desire to seek and do God's will, was missing.[165]

There is so much wisdom in what Bill W. wrote.

Blessings,
Gary L.

1-2-09

Dear Matt,

I prayed for you this morning.

Proverbs 27:9: "The heartfelt counsel of a friend is as sweet as perfume and incense."

During early spring in 1984, I received a phone call from Marie. She was my biological father's second wife. I'm not sure how she found me. She said that my dad had become a Christian and wanted to meet with me. She then invited our family to have lunch with them on Easter Sunday. We agreed to have lunch with them. I had a lot of apprehension about seeing them. Marie had prepared a great lunch, and our conversation was mostly surface talk. They spoke of how important church had become to them. They then said that they would like to see us occasionally because they wanted to get to know us. We agreed to meet once a month for lunch after church.

A month later they came to our home in Salem for lunch. I kept expecting him to try to make amends for abandoning my sister and me, but he never did. He explained that since we had another dad in our lives, he didn't need to be a part of our lives. I recognized in him what I'd learned about myself—an incredible ability to justify poor behavior. We had great visits with them that continued until his death in 1985. I attended his funeral and was introduced as his son. Many people commented that they didn't know he had a son.

I realized after the funeral that I regretted that I never told him how much he had hurt me. I began to see how fear of his rejection and abandonment was still very much alive. Rather than confront, I stuffed those feelings. Sometime later with the help of a spiritual director, I was finally able to bring some closure to my relationship with him.

Rooted in God's Love:

> When we let go of the defenses that have protected us for so long, and we allow ourselves to be honest and vulnerable, it sometimes feels like we will "come apart." In these moments we can find courage in God's promise of protection. God's peace can guard our breaking hearts and our troubled minds.
>
> The peace of God is not a blessed-out euphoria that helps us minimize or ignore our problems. God's peace does not participate in denial. This peace is not another Novocain, another fix to alter our mood. It is the gentle guard that protects

> us so that we can face reality. It is the security that comes from knowing that God pays attention, that we are not forgotten, that God is with us, that we are loved.[166]

Well, Matt, I pretty much shared with you my life journey with all of its ups and downs. I won't be writing as often as I have, but it will be at least once a week. Keep me posted on how you're doing. I look forward to the day that we actually meet. Take care, friend.

Blessings,
Gary L.

1-3-09

Dear Matt,

I prayed for you this morning.

After writing yesterday many more thoughts have come to me. I've talked little about one of the most important parts of the recovery journey. It's the part about passing it on to those who come in behind us. I was in an AA meeting during my first month of sobriety, and a newcomer came in. After the meeting my sponsor Hugh approached me and told me to give the newcomer my phone number and tell him he could call me anytime night or day, seven days a week. I told Hugh that I was barely sober myself. Hugh said that the new guy would probably be able to identify with me more than himself with over ten years. Hugh said share with him what's going on with you—your fears, doubts, questions, and struggles. Hugh said to not try to pass on to him what you don't have. Hugh also said that if you want to keep what you have, you need to give it away. With great trepidation I approached the man and introduced myself. We discovered that where we worked was close to each other. We began meeting at a nearby bakery on our breaks. We really were the blind leading the blind. From that beginning a deep friendship blossomed, and neither of us has had a drink since.

As Bill Sees It, page 298:

> Even the newest of newcomers finds undreamed rewards as he tries to help his brother alcoholic, the one who is even blinder than he. This is indeed the kind of giving that actually demands nothing. He does not expect his brother sufferer to pay him, or even to love him.
>
> And then he discovers that through the divine paradox of this kind of giving he has found his own reward, whether or not his brother has yet received anything. His own character may still be gravely defective, but he somehow knows that God has enabled him to make a mighty beginning, and he senses that he stands at the edge of new mysteries, joys, and experiences of which he had never before dreamed.[167]

I looked through my *Twenty-Four Hours a Day* book and found the following on May 21.

A.A. Thought for the Day

One of the finest things about A.A. is the sharing. Sharing is a wonderful thing because the more you share the more you have. In our old drinking days, we didn't do much sharing. We used to keep things to ourselves, partly because we were ashamed, but mostly because we were selfish. And we were very lonely because we didn't share. When we came into A.A., the first thing we found was sharing. We heard other alcoholics frankly sharing their experiences with hospitals, jails, and all the usual mess that goes with drinking. *Am I sharing?*

Meditation for the Day

Character is developed by the daily discipline of duties done. Be obedient to the heavenly vision and take the straight way. Do not fall into the error of calling "Lord, Lord," and doing not the things that should be done. You need a life of prayer and meditation, but you must still do your work in the busy ways of life. The busy person is wise to rest and wait patiently for God's guidance. If you are obedient to the heavenly vision, you can be at peace.[168]

As Bill Sees It, page 29:

Gratitude should go forward, rather than backward.

In other words, if you carry the message to still others, you will be making the best possible repayment for the help given to you.

No satisfaction has been deeper and no joy greater than in a Twelfth Step job well done. To watch the eyes of men and women open with wonder as they move from darkness into light, to see their lives quickly fill with new purpose and meaning, and above all to watch them awaken to the presence of a loving God in their lives—these things are the substance of what we receive as we carry A.A.'s message.[169]

I really like the commentary in the *Life Recovery Bible* on page 674 regarding Psalms 34:1–7:

> When we experience deliverance through God's power, it should be natural for us to praise him and share the good news with others. If we care about other people who suffer as we did, we would be selfish not to tell how God has delivered us. Boasting about our God and the help he has given us is one kind of boasting that is good. This kind of Godly boasting will not only encourage others in the recovery process, but it will also strengthen our faith in God.[170]

As Bill Sees It, page 13:

> A.A. is more than a set of principles; it is a society of alcoholics in action. We must carry the message, else we ourselves can wither and those who haven't been given the truth may die.
>
> Faith is more than our greatest gift; its sharing with others is our greatest responsibility. May we of A.A. continually seek the wisdom and the willingness by which we may well fulfill that immense trust which the Giver of all perfect gifts has placed in our hands.[171]

Wow! That's a lot to consider isn't it? We have a tremendous responsibility to pass on what we've been given. There is no greater joy than to see the "light" come on in someone's eyes and then to see them begin to pass on that "light." So, my friend, I encourage you to begin passing on those great gifts you've received—your faith in Christ and your recovery.

Blessings,
Gary L.

1-4-09

Dear Matt,

I prayed for you this morning.

In the following letters I will share with you some of what has been so important to me in my journey. First of all, countless people have taught and encouraged me. Hugh W. was my first sponsor. At times he was relentless in reminding me that I had to get honest with myself. One day he said, "Gary, some people grow up; some people grow old. Which way do you want to do it?" His gaze pierced my soul as he said those words. He helped me to move from self-pity and being a victim, to gratitude and being responsible for my choices. For one who had gone through life blaming everyone else, that was huge. Many times I would become angry when he spoke truth into my life, but after mulling over what he said I would understand. I always knew he cared about me. One night I was unable to sleep and called Hugh around one thirty in the morning. He met me at an all-night restaurant and talked with me for several hours until it was time to go to work. Another AA member nicknamed Speed would encourage me when I wallowed in a morass of self-pity and despair. There was Ed L., who was the epitome of serenity. I often wondered if anything could "ruffle his feathers." What a calming influence he was during my tirades of how unfair life was to me. I'll never forget Glen S., who was an "in your face" kind of guy. Frank, who took me to my first meeting. Under his rough exterior I knew he loved me. All of the aforementioned completed their life journey sober. They carried a message of hope and healing to many. I know that Ed, Hugh, and Glen became Christ followers, and I suspect that Frank and Speed did as well. They all exhibited Christ's love to me when I hated myself. What a reunion we'll have some day!

Then there was Professor Bob, the man who listened to my first Fifth Step. He too, would tell me the truth, even when I didn't want to hear it. One day in his office, I was lamenting about the terrible husband and father that I was. I told him about some of my behaviors within the family and how disgusted I was with myself. He looked at me and said, "If you don't like those behaviors, then stop!" Wow! That never occurred to me. I always felt cared for and accepted by him.

I've just mentioned those who helped me early in the foundation of my recovery. Many, many more have spoken wisdom into my life, both in church and in AA. I would be remiss if I did not mention Pastor Grimes, who presented the gospel message of forgiveness in such a way that I was captured by it. Life has never been the same since that day.

I think of the many people in the Assembly of God church in Coquille, Oregon, who encouraged and financially supported us when we moved in order for me to attend Bible college. Every month we received a check from the church not knowing who had given.

I think of Rich and Mary, who prayerfully and financially helped us after my business failure when I'd been sober around fifteen years. They approached us and said that they believed that God wanted them to give us $600 to buy a car. We had taken the one we had back to the dealer because we couldn't make a payment. We ended up with a 1973 Plymouth Valiant that we drove for six years.

I couldn't begin to list all of the people in the recovery community and those we've known in the Christian community that have taught us by example how to live. Many pastors have unfolded the Word of God to us and taught us who we are in Christ.

One of the things I learned early in recovery that was kind of ego-puncturing is that I can't learn anything from me. All I know is what I know. That realization moved me to not only become involved with people who could teach me, but also to read books by people who could teach me. The most important book has been the Bible. In the Bible I learn about God, but I also learn about me. I'm the problem; God is the answer. Sometimes I don't want to remember that. Psalms 119:105: "Thy word is a lamp for my feet, and a light for my path."

I have read hundreds of books through the years that have been helpful .Following is a partial list of authors that I recommend: Henry Nouwin, Ethel Barrett, Joyce Landsdorf, Bruce Wilkinson, Chuck Colson, Phillip Yancey, Chuck Swindoll, Lee Strobel, Bruce Larson, Keith Miller, Robert McGee, Billy Graham, Brennan Manning, LaGard Smith, James Dobson, Lewis Smedes, Richard Foster, Max Lucado, A. W. Tozer, Andrew Murray, John Ortberg, Jeff VanVonderan, Dale Ryan, Juanita Ryan, Paul Tournier, Viktr Frankl, Andrew Murray, St. Therese of Lisieux, Thomas Aquinas, John Bradshaw, Charles Spurgeon, David Roper, Norman Vincent Peale, Charles Stanley, Ray Stedman, Ron Mehl, and Jack Hayford. There have been many more whose names don't come to mind right now. If you come across books by any of the above authors, I'd suggest that you check them out.

Now some final thoughts about Patsy. I could write volumes about the contribution she has made to my life. She is my angel, soul mate, lover, confessor, encourager, and life partner. She continued to love me when, in my opinion, I was not lovable. Patsy has never "rubbed my nose" in all of my mistakes of the yesterdays. I have often said that if every man was blessed with a wife like Patsy, the word divorce could be removed from the dictionary.

Words cannot begin to describe how much I love her. I am overwhelmed with gratitude as I write those words.

My story is about what got me into the rooms of AA. Since that time it's been His story. I can take no credit for the life He's given me.

1 Corinthians 1:27–31: "But God has chosen the foolish things of the world to shame the wise, and God has chosen the weak things of the world to shame the things that are strong, and the base things of the world and the despised, God has chosen, the things that are not, that He might nullify the things that are, that no man should boast before God. But by His doing you are in Christ Jesus, who became to us wisdom from God, and righteousness and sanctification, and redemption, that, just as it is written, *"Let him who boasts, boast in the Lord." New American Standard Bible* (emphasis mine).

Well my friend, I got little windy today. Sometimes I get on a roll because so many thoughts come into my mind. To God be the glory! Great things He has done!

Blessings,
Gary L.

Epilogue

After sharing my life story with Matt through letters, I decided to compile them in a book. Perhaps my story could be helpful to others. My story is just one of many about what God can do when we surrender our will and life to him. That is an ongoing daily process. I imagine that the night of my initial surrender God rolled up His sleeves and thought, "We sure have a lot of work to do."

Today, I believe I'm in a partnership with God. There are things He will do, and there is much that I have to do. In our partnership I need to remember who the senior partner is. He often reminds me of that as my self-will attempts to assert itself.

The spiritual journey has been about learning but also unlearning. I had many beliefs that were not serving me well. I needed to begin seeing myself as God sees me and live according to that. One of the biggest blocks to spiritual growth is, "I've always been this way." One of my beliefs today is that it's not important who I've been; what's important is who I'm becoming. In other words, don't be limited by who you've been. I cannot allow the yesterdays to be the director of my tomorrows.

After reading through all of the letters, I have some regrets. There are places I repeated myself, places that I could have gone into more detail, and places where I seemed to ramble. Another regret is that I wished I had saved letters from Matt and inserted them in the book. Through his letters, readers would be able to see the transformation that began in him. It was truly remarkable and definitely God's doing.

As I look back at changes that God has done in my life, I am overwhelmed with gratitude. I was thirty-one when God got me sober and would not have seen thirty-two without His intervention because of the state of mind I was in at the time. He has moved me from hopelessness to hope, from anger and bitterness to forgiveness, from being absorbed in myself to having compassion and understanding of others, from inner turmoil to peace of mind, from faithless to faith, and from many sleepless nights to sweet sleep.

There have been other changes as a result of those I mentioned above. I know there will be more changes as I continue my journey with Him. The journey has been exciting but also difficult at times. It seems to me that believing in God is a lot different than trusting Him, particularly when life goes sideways.

If a reader wants to have a relationship with the God who has changed my life and many others, accept the work that Jesus accomplished by going to the cross and paying the price for your sin. He died for you. Ask Him into your life, accept His sacrifice, and He will begin the work of transformation in your life that only He can do.

In conclusion, if you find anything in this book that might be helpful to someone else, please pass it on. I pray many blessings to those who have read my story. Thank you! Thank you! Thank You!

Isaiah 42:16: "I will lead the blind by a way they do not know, in paths they do not know I will guide them. I will make darkness into light before them and rugged places into plains. These are the things I will do, and I will not leave them undone. (NASB)

Notes

1. Bill W., *As Bill Sees It* (New York: Alcoholics Anonymous World Services , 1990), 97.
2. Dale Ryan and Juanita Ryan, Rooted in God's Love (Brea, CA: Christian Recovery International), 70.
3. Ryan and Ryan , 74.
4. Max Lucado, *Grace for the Moment* (Nashville, TN:, 2000), 190.
5. *Alcoholics Anonymous* (New York: Alcoholics Anonymous World Services, 1976), 58.
6. Ryan and Ryan, 123.
7. Ryan and Ryan, 135.
8. *Life Recovery Bible* (Wheaton, IL: Tyndale House, 1998), 685.
9. *Alcoholics Anonymous*, 56.
10. Anonymous, *Twenty-Four Hours a Day* (Center City, MN: Hazelden Foundation, 1996), 9/21.
11. Ryan and Ryan, 123.
12. *Alcoholics Anonymous*, 59.
13. Bill W., 174.
14. *Alcoholics Anonymous*, 58.
15. Anonymous, *Twenty-Four Hours a Day*, 6/23.
16. Ryan and Ryan, 133.
17. *Alcoholics Anonymous*, 60.
18. Ryan and Ryan, 132.
19. *Alcoholics Anonymous*, 64.
20. Ruth Myers and Warren Myers, *31 Days of Praise* (Sisters, OR: Multnomah, 1994), 134–35.
21. Anonymous, 6/27.
22. *Life Recovery Bible*, 735.
23. Ryan and Ryan, 127.
24. Anonymous, 7/1.
25. Bill W, 104.
26. Bill W., 234.
27. Ryan and Ryan, 32.
28. Anonymous, 10/6.
29. Anonymous, 10/8.
30. *Life Recovery Bible*, 1,434.
31. Bill W., 293.

32. Ryan and Ryan, 8–9.
33. Anonymous, 7/12.
34. Bill W., 8.
35. Lucado, 217.
36. Anonymous, 10/13.
37. *Alcoholics Anonymous*, 60.
38. *Twelve Steps and Twelve Traditions* (New York: Alcoholics Anonymous World Services, 1980), 76.
39. Ryan and Ryan, 123.
40. Anonymous, 7/19.
41. Ryan and Ryan, 6.
42. Bill W., 72.
43. Anonymous, 7/25.
44. Norman Vincent Peale, *The Power of Positive Thinking* (New York: Simon and Schuster, 2003), 160–62.
45. Bill W., 31.
46. Bill W., 82.
47. Anonymous, 10/25.
48. Lucado, 240.
49. Bill W., 58.
50. Bill W., 51.
51. *Alcoholics Anonymous*, 30.
52. *Alcoholics Anonymous*, 58.
53. Anonymous, 8/7.
54. *Alcoholics Anonymous*, 64.
55. Ryan and Ryan, 14.
56. *Alcoholics Anonymous*, 68.
57. Bill W., 238.
58. Bill W., 124.
59. Bill W., 152.
60. *Alcoholics Anonymous*, 58.
61. *Life Recovery Bible*, 313.
62. *Alcoholics Anonymous*, 59.
63. *Alcoholics Anonymous*, 44.
64. *Alcoholics Anonymous*, 84.
65. Lucado, 254.
66. *Alcoholics Anonymous*, 64.
67. *Alcoholics Anonymous*, 62.
68. *Alcoholics Anonymous*, 44.
69. *Life Recovery Bible*, 1,343.
70. *Alcoholics Anonymous*, 59.

71. *Alcoholics Anonymous*, 58.
72. *Life Recovery Bible*, 1,131.
73. *Life Recovery Bible*, 1,522.
74. *Life Recovery Bible*, 695.
75. Anonymous, 8/20.
76. Bill W., 196.
77. Anonymous, 11/15.
78. Lucado, 349.
79. Bill W., 33.
80. Anonymous, 11/21.
81. Ryan and Ryan, 120–21.
82. *Alcoholics Anonymous Comes of Age: A Brief History of AA*. (New York: Alcoholics Anonymous World Services, 1980), 63.
83. *Alcoholics Anonymous*, 64.
84. Ryan and Ryan, 18–19.
85. *Alcoholics Anonymous*, 63-64.
86. Bill W., 111.
87. Bill W., 261.
88. Bill W., 173.
89. *Life Recovery Bible*, 9.
90. *Life Recovery Bible*, 595.
91. *Life Recovery Bible*, 597.
92. *Life Recovery Bible*, 1,125.
93. *Life Recovery Bible*, 1,401.
94. *Life Recovery Bible*, 1,577.
95. *Alcoholics Anonymous*, 67–68.
96. Bill W., 270.
97. *Alcoholics Anonymous*, 72.
98. *Alcoholics Anonymous*, 73–74.
99. Bill W., 164.
100. Bill W., 248.
101. *Life Recovery Bible*, 57.
102. *Life Recovery Bible*, 1,035.
103. *Life Recovery Bible*, 1,345.
104. *Alcoholics Anonymous*, 75.
105. Bill W., 126.
106. Bill W., 318.
107. Bill W., 291.
108. *Alcoholics Anonymous*, 62.
109. *Alcoholics Anonymous*, 60.
110. Bill W., 294.

111. Lucado, 367.
112. Anonymous, 12/2.
113. *Life Recovery Bible*, 1,261.
114. *Life Recovery Bible*, 1,437.
115. *Life Recovery Bible*, 31.
116. *Life Recovery Bible*, 689.
117. *Life Recovery Bible*, 863.
118. *Life Recovery Bible*, 1,063.
119. *Alcoholics Anonymous*, 76.
120. *Alcoholics Anonymous*, 417.
121. Anonymous, 9/8.
122. Bill W., 8.
123. *Life Recovery Bible*, 313.
124. *Life Recovery Bible*, 455.
125. *Life Recovery Bible*, 1,183.
126. *Life Recovery Bible*, 1,395.
127. Anonymous, 12/9.
128. *Life Recovery Bible*, 780.
129. *Alcoholics Anonymous*, 127.
130. *Life Recovery Bible*, 1,512.
131. Bill W., 20.
132. Bill W., 145.
133. *Life Recovery Bible*, 147.
134. *Life Recovery Bible*, 47.
135. *Life Recovery Bible*, 1,119.
136. *Life Recovery Bible*, 1,239.
137. *Life Recovery Bible*, 1,525.
138. Bill W., 70.
139. *Alcoholics Anonymous*, 58.
140. *Alcoholics Anonymous*, 83–84.
141. *Alcoholics Anonymous*, 60.
142. Bill W., 259.
143. Bill W., 177.
144. Anonymous, 12/16.
145. Anonymous, 9/17.
146. *Alcoholics Anonymous*, 85.
147. Bill W., 13.
148. *Alcoholics Anonymous*, 84.
149. Anonymous, 8/28.
150. Bill W., 176.
151. Ryan and Ryan, 129.

152. *Alcoholics Anonymous*, 86.
153. Bill W., 85.
154. *Life Recovery Bible*, 867.
155. Bill W., 90.
156. *Alcoholics Anonymous*, 60.
157. Bill W., 156.
158. *Life Recovery Bible*, 1204.
159. Bill W., 94.
160. Bill W., 192.
161. Bill W., 108.
162. *Life Recovery Bible*, 735.
163. Anonymous, 12/28.
164. Ryan and Ryan, 82.
165. Bill W., 139.
166. Ryan and Ryan, 80.
167. Bill W., 298.
168. Anonymous, 5/21.
169. Bill W., 29.
170. *Life Recovery Bible*, 674.
171. Bill W., 13.

Bibliography

Alcoholics Anonymous. New York: Alcoholics Anonymous World Services, 1976.

Alcoholics Anonymous Comes of Age: A Brief History of AA. New York: Alcoholics Anonymous World Services, 1980.

Anonymous. *Twenty-Four Hours a Day.* Center City, MN: Hazelden Foundation, 1996.

Cavanaugh, Brian. *More Sower's Seeds.* Mahwah, NJ: Paulist Press, 1992.

Life Recovery Bible-New Living Translation. Wheaton, IL: Tyndale House, 1998.

Lucado, Max. *Grace for the Moment.* Nashville, TN: Thomas Nelson, 2000.

Myers, Ruth, and Warren Myers. *31 Days of Praise.* Sisters, OR: Multnomah, 1994.

New American Standard Bible. Anaheim, CA: Lockman Foundation, 1995.

Peale, Norman Vincent. *The Power of Positive Thinking.* New York: Simon and Schuster, 2003.

Ryan, Dale, and Juanita Ryan. *Rooted in God's Love*: Brea, CA: Christian Recovery International, 2007.

Twelve Steps and Twelve Traditions. New York: Alcoholics Anonymous World Services, 1980.

W., Bill. *As Bill Sees It.* New York: Alcoholics Anonymous World Services, 1990.